Culinary Shakespeare

T0384081

Medieval & Renaissance Literary Studies

General Editor

Rebecca Totaro

Editorial Board

Judith H. Anderson
Diana Treviño Benet
William C. Carroll
Donald Cheney
Ann Baynes Coiro
Mary T. Crane
Stephen B. Dobranski
Wendy Furman-Adams
A. C. Hamilton
Hannibal Hamlin
Margaret P. Hannay

Jonathan Gil Harris
Margaret Healy
Ken Hiltner
Arthur F. Kinney
David Loewenstein
Robert W. Maslen
Thomas P. Roche Jr.
Mary Beth Rose
Mihoko Suzuki
Humphrey Tonkin
Susanne Woods

Originally titled the *Duquesne Studies: Philological Series* (and later renamed the *Language & Literature Series*), the **Medieval & Renaissance Literary Studies Series** has been published by Duquesne University Press since 1960. This publishing endeavor seeks to promote the study of late medieval, Renaissance, and seventeenth century English literature by presenting scholarly and critical monographs, collections of essays, editions, and compilations. The series encourages a broad range of interpretation, including the relationship of literature and its cultural contexts, close textual analysis, and the use of contemporary critical methodologies.

Foster Provost
EDITOR, 1960–1984

Albert C. Labriola
EDITOR, 1985–2009

Richard J. DuRocher
EDITOR, 2010

Culinary Shakespeare

Staging Food and Drink in Early Modern England

Edited by

DAVID B. GOLDSTEIN AND AMY L. TIGNER

DUQUESNE UNIVERSITY PRESS
Pittsburgh, Pennsylvania

Copyright © 2016 Duquesne University Press
All rights reserved

Published in the United States of America by
DUQUESNE UNIVERSITY PRESS
600 Forbes Avenue
Pittsburgh, Pennsylvania 15282

No part of this book may be used or reproduced,
in any manner or form whatsoever,
without written permission from the publisher,
except in the case of short quotations
in critical articles or reviews.

Library of Congress Cataloging-in-Publication Data

Names: Goldstein, David B., 1972– editor. | Tigner, Amy L., editor.
Title: Culinary Shakespeare : staging food and drink in early modern England /
edited by David B. Goldstein and Amy L. Tigner.
Description: Pittsburgh, Pennsylvania : Duquesne University Press, 2016. |
    Series: Medieval and Renaissance literary studies | Includes
    bibliographical references and index.
Identifiers: LCCN 2016005243 | ISBN 978-0-271-09212-6 (pbk : acid-free paper)
Subjects: LCSH: Shakespeare, William, 1564–1616—Knowledge—Manners and
    customs. | Food in literature. | Food habits in literature. | Drinking
    customs in literature. | Cooking in literature. | Food
    habits—England—History—16th century. | Food
    habits—England—History—17th century. | BISAC: LITERARY CRITICISM /
    Shakespeare. | LITERARY CRITICISM / Renaissance. | COOKING / History.
Classification: LCC PR3069.F64 C85 2016 | DDC 822.3/3—dc23
LC record available at http://lccn.loc.gov/2016005243

∞ Printed on acid-free paper.

Contents

Introduction

DAVID B. GOLDSTEIN, AMY L. TIGNER, AND
WENDY WALL

Smack in the middle of *The Tempest*, in one of the strangest episodes of an already strange play, Ariel performs an elaborate culinary happening: *"Enter several strange Shapes, bringing in a banquet; and dance around it with gentle actions of salutations."*[1] These shapes magically conjure a feast for the hungry nobles recently shipwrecked on the island. In the brief time that the lavish food appears before them, Gonzalo, Alonso, and the other characters marvel at the perplexing nature of the gentle islanders who have produced such bounty. Since these supernatural beings strike their viewers as having materialized out of fictional travelers' tales, the spectacle begins to blur the line between fact and fiction, knowledge and fantasy, being and seeming. After the characters debate whether to give way to their sharp appetites (their growling "stomachs") or to be prudently suspicious, the banquet vanishes and Ariel reprimands the men for past sins. In this scene, food's appearance prompts a discussion of epistemology and imagination, and ultimately becomes the fantastical starting point for generating self-recognition and catalyzing a new political structure. The need for material food, coupled with the desire raised by its spectacular, cognitive, and imaginative dimensions, produces an opening into possibility.

This culinary Shakespearean moment, by crystalizing questions about knowledge, power, ethics, colonialism, labor, and desire, introduces us to the grave importance of food in the early modern period and to the dangers of ignoring eating as an ontological and epistemological phenomenon. Since Plato, philosophers and other thinkers have longed to leave the dining table, with its pleasures and burdens, behind. The preoccupations of cuisine—all that pushing and shoving

1

around of food and drink—remove us from the life of the mind, driving us inexorably into our bodies. Plato dreamed of a life unsullied by physical appetites. His Socrates was indifferent to food and drink, and his ideal drinking party was one in which conversation would form the only necessary sustenance. "Do you think that it is right," he asks rhetorically in the *Phaedo,* "for a philosopher to concern himself with the so-called pleasures connected with food and drink?" Simmias provides the right answer: "Certainly not."[2] Influenced by Platonic philosophy, Western society has often treated cuisine as a less than serious focus for discussion. We may enjoy it, we may acknowledge its necessity for our survival and happiness, but we shouldn't spend too much time talking about it lest we be marked as unthinking and intemperate gluttons, practitioners of what Michel de Montaigne satirically termed *la science de gueule*—the "science of the gullet."[3]

If philosophy has tended to denigrate food, literature has always actively engaged with it as a central aspect of human experience. Shakespeare, while well aware of negative philosophical attitudes toward food and drink, was equally attuned to a strong countermovement throughout intellectual history. This countermovement addresses itself to cuisine for precisely the reasons that Plato wanted to distance himself from it. In studying and discussing food and drink, we confront human beings in all their embodied fleshiness—their messy desires, appetites, and excretions. Shakespeare and his contemporaries, in their avid fascination with what makes humans human—and indeed more or less than human—turned to cuisine to illustrate and explore the fundamentals of experience. Food is not only a bodily phenomenon, but by necessity also a phenomenon of the body as situated within its relationships, within the mesh of the human world. Cuisine lies at the center of culture. For this reason, although the volume's title refers to a culinary Shakespeare, our understanding of the term is broad.

In the social sciences, a productive distinction has been made between the "culinary" and the "commensal," with the former describing the "what" of eating—ingredients, food, the biology and labor that create them, etc.—and the latter referring to the "how" of eating, including the rituals of the table and interactions among humans and groups.[4] This book implicitly adopts a commensal as well as a culinary outlook on culture. Our contributors are as interested in modes of gathering and interacting as in foodstuffs. In fact, all contributors would agree with the adage of the great philosopher of cuisine, Emmanuel Levinas: "Food is not the fuel necessary to the human machine. Food is a meal."[5] Food and drink, in Shakespeare as in all other literature, always occurs in and is inflected through social context. While the culinary and the commensal describe different aspects of a continuum, we mean for the term "culinary" to stand here for all points on that continuum. A cuisine is not just a set of edibles; it is an integral element of social and intellectual life. And a culinary Shakespeare is a Shakespeare of and in culture, a writer attuned to the pleasures and perils of the table around which we all, in one way or another, must gather.

For all its importance in Shakespeare and in literary writing more generally, food in Shakespeare studies has only just begun to garner its share of critical attention. Recent cross-disciplinary research reveals myriad ways in which food helps to define us and our relationships.[6] By exploring the ways food and writing interact, literary scholars are starting to recognize the centrality of eating to forms of meaning-making.[7] Shakespeare studies has emerged at the forefront of this research, demonstrating that food, eating, drinking, and its attendant processes (cooking, digesting, purging, excreting) perform crucial work, as both material and metaphorical phenomena, in all of Shakespeare's writings.[8] This volume emerged out of the need to articulate the centrality of food, eating, and drinking for Shakespeare, and to illustrate the diversity of approaches that have the potential to reshape our understanding of culinary culture both within literature and beyond it. The scholars represented here, taken together, show that cuisine in Shakespeare functions as a system of representation with material causes and effects. This system gives structure to relationships among individuals, groups, nation-states, and nonhumans; it also provides more metaphysical links between being and nonbeing, between the material world and its ineffable yet immanent counterparts. Finally, the relationship between eating and theater is explored in every Shakespeare play, to one or another degree, with each acting as a metaphor and even a scaffold for the other. For Shakespeare, the culinary is primary.

Amid abundant references to individual food and drink in the Shakespearean corpus are few everyday scenes of cooking and eating. While Shakespeare does not, as commentators astutely note, present conventional cooking scenes onstage, he does revel in *fantastic* kitchens and dining rooms—from brutal cannibalistic scenes of revenge in *Titus Andronicus* where pasty pies secret baked children, to Macbeth's nightmarish dinner party haunted by Banquo's ghost, to the idyllic sheep-shearing feast glimpsed as a grocery list in *The Winter's Tale*. This culinary phantasmagoria is, nevertheless, at the heart of what early modern food culture meant in its most capacious sense. *The Tempest's* banquet, for instance, smacks of the surprisingly complicated intellectual issues that surface even in mundane domestic labors and moments of food consumption, issues that we glimpse in the archival record of early modern recipes as well as descriptions of household life in writing and in performance. What is at stake across these domains is the productive tension between victuals as strikingly material and yet ever so ephemeral. Even banal operations of eating, we are reminded, stage a vanishing act, since food carries the capacity to ripen, rot, and be recycled through the human body. Prospero plays off food's inherently vexed substantiality and insubstantiality when he authorizes a piece of ethically charged and politically motivated revenge theater for the noble Italians who ousted him. The outlandishness of the meal takes meaning from magical acts threading throughout the play. It echoes, for instance, Ariel's famous sea change song to Ferdinand:

> Full fathom five thy father lies;
> Of his bones are coral made;
> Those are pearls that were his eyes;
> Nothing of him that doth fade
> But doth suffer a sea change
> Into something rich and strange.   (1.2.396–401)

The image of a sea corpse crystalizing into valuable exotic jewelry trades off the expected transformation that the song attempts to hold at bay: the human body degenerating into fish food, an image that Hamlet calls forth vividly: a "king may go a progress through the guts of a beggar."[9]

Shakespeare was fascinated by how the meanings of food and drink change according to different contexts, and his fantastical uses of food always bring us back to lived experience. His plays—with their frequent mentions of particular comestibles; the physical and emotional changes that food effects in the body; the rituals and bonds created or broken by cultures of the table; and the metaphors that food activates in religious, sexual, theatrical, and intellectual experience—explore the tremendous power of food and drink in all manner of cultural phenomena. Cuisine helps to structure moments of joy and reconciliation (as in the al fresco forest meal of *As You Like It* or the promised banquet to end the hijinks of *The Comedy of Errors*) of tragedy and horror (as in the "funeral baked meats" turned too soon to wedding pies in *Hamlet*, or the violent culinary imagery of *The Merchant of Venice*), or, more often, an ambiguous mixture of the two (think of the discomfiting banquet that closes *The Taming of the Shrew*, or the cannibal language of *Pericles*). Perhaps because of the close connections between cuisine and theater, food and drink feature less prominently in Shakespeare's poems than in the plays. Thus, the current collection focuses exclusively on the plays, though analysis of foodways in the poems is a potentially rich vein of inquiry awaiting future scholars.[10]

Many of the authors in this volume attend to issues of cuisine in historical perspective. But these inquiries also point us toward the present. If our attitudes about how Shakespeare and his contemporaries viewed food and drink in their historical context have changed and broadened, so too has our interest in the subject changed to accommodate current concerns and modes of thinking. The most pressing matters involving food in our own time—especially the ecological ramifications of agriculture and consumerism upon the environment, food security, the health of our food supply, trade relationships, and the ethics of the table—appear here under various guises. Each of the volume's contributors, explicitly or implicitly, addresses the challenges raised by food, eating, and drinking in the early twenty-first century as well as the late sixteenth.

The scholars gathered around the table of this text have been selected both for their breadth of approaches and subjects, and for the depth of their sustained commitments to particular questions and plays. The plays discussed include a thorough sampling of comedies

(*The Merry Wives of Windsor, Much Ado About Nothing, Twelfth Night, The Comedy of Errors*, and *The Taming of the Shrew*), histories (*1* and *2 Henry IV, Richard III*), tragedies (*Romeo and Juliet, Hamlet, Coriolanus, Macbeth, Timon of Athens*), and romances (*The Tempest, The Winter's Tale*). At the same time, however, the contributions of four scholars—Peter Parolin, Barbara Sebek, Karen Raber, and Rebecca Lemon—converge upon (or perhaps diverge from) the body of Falstaff, whose importance to issues of Shakespearean eating and drinking is surely unrivaled. These issues include the place of drink in discussions of eating, the place of consumption in Shakespeare's understanding and staging of history, and the role of trade in building and challenging models of national identity. Raber and Lemon indeed launch out from the very same speech—Falstaff's rousing defense of sack in *2 Henry IV*—but their analyses lead them in very different directions. It is our hope that this simultaneously synchronic and diachronic approach will both provide a strong foundation for scholars wishing to study Shakespearean eating and will give a sense of the ramifying potential that a single facet of such a study can entail.

One of the unique features of this book lies in its consideration of eating and drinking as complementary meaning-making phenomena. At first glance, it may seem bizarre ever to have separated the two, for the simple reason that most meals involve both. But drinking as part of a meal is often considered simply as an extension of eating, while drinking on its own—which in Tudor England most often took the form of imbibing alcohol in one or another social context—is usually analyzed in relation to that social context.[11] Adam Smyth, for example, identifies three issues pertinent to early modern drinking in his groundbreaking collection on the topic: its "cultural ambiguity," its relation to sociability and conviviality, and its "changing political resonances."[12] These concerns also feature prominently in writing about food and dining during the period.[13] A consideration of the connections between eating and drinking is not only fruitful but necessary for understanding how culinary culture works as a synthetic whole in Renaissance England. To approach eating and drinking as aspects of the same literary formations, as we do here, is to identify productive similarities and tensions. Drinking is an integrated aspect of the culinary and commensal world and needs to be treated as such.

Another aspect of our approach that deserves mention is that we have attempted to reproduce, as much as possible, the experience of table talk within the abstracted and immaterial bounds of the text. The idea for this book emerged at several conferences over actual meals and face-to-face discussions; we have continued a semblance of these interactions by encouraging all contributors to read and respond to one another's essays within the body of their own work. Rather than imagining the volume as a collection of individual essays, we imagine it as a more collaborative endeavor.[14] Thus, most of the essays here mention other essays in the volume, and in many cases the details and arguments of each essay have been productively shaped by these readings.

Culinary Shakespeare bears witness to the admirable range of ways that scholars imagine early modern audiences to have conceptualized food: as commodity, gift, tool, national emblem, personal foible, and love. We also begin to understand how culinary meanings were generated and processed, with food starring as metaphor, metonym, symbol, and figurative device. We hope that the reader's harvest of this book will include recognizing the dynamic ways that the Shakespearean text can be mobilized so as to appreciate structural connections between kitchen and theater, *poiesis* and manual making. The art of the kitchen involves the transformation and conversion of the natural world into goods and other cultural products that then recycle back into the body. As such, dramatic allusions to food and food practices make visible the meditations prompted by culinary life offstage, the philosophical quandaries of baking and brewing that force practitioners to contemplate the line between nature and culture, the conundrums of seasonality and temporality, the bewildering nature of matter, and the power struggles enacted in and through culinary arts and rituals.

As *Culinary Shakespeare* unfolds the complexities of early modern culinary production and consumption, it demands additionally that we assess methods by which scholars interpret food acts and meanings. When, for instance, do master stories unwittingly haunt our accounts? When does our writing partake of the food "fall" from Eden narrative (where commensality gives way to capitalism)? or the mystification narrative (where eating always masks exploitive labor)? or the nostalgia narrative (food recovering lost desires)? When is our scholarly task a *recovery* of historical meanings embedded in a food commodity that may or may not be taken up in dramatic representation? And when are we seeking to identify the representational strategies by which food meanings are shaped? Many arguments in this book rest on analogical thinking, founded as they are on both an early modern love for "likening" and our own scholarly tendency to construct associative chains of meaning—the theater as *like* an alehouse, courses of meals as *like* theatrical scene changes, cooking as *like* rhetoric, the history of beer as *like* a character's trajectory, conserves as *like* memory banks. We doggedly follow the metonymic associative logic that imaginative works construct.

The limits and tradeoffs of our literary strategies emerge in these essays as well. Scholarly attraction to methods of interpretation based on "likenings" has the salutary benefit of showing how food can be a mode of thinking everything. Food can represent national desires but also national threats, morally charged generosities, and, simultaneously, exploitative ideological power plays; it can reveal memory and forgetfulness, the instantiation of class-based taste and its most severe critique. Our desire to repeat—and sometimes impose—logical contradictions stemming from similitude on symbolic culinary networks makes it difficult to *limit* our claims in meaningful ways (especially as judged by those outside our discipline). Argument by analogy stymies attempts to identify the specific food politics at play in a given cultural moment or even to imagine the evidentiary standards that might guide counterclaims to our arguments. This methodological quandary is not peculiar to the study of culinary Shakespeares or early modern literary criticism. It is, however, a problem productively on display in this volume as the very richness of the analyses sometimes precludes a means for determining between interpretative options. The characteristic that encapsulates the strength of food discourse and food scholarship—food's exciting *mobility*—generates an almost endlessly proliferating significatory system that can sometimes thwart definitive argumentation. This is one of the major theoretical challenges that this volume seeks to introduce and solve by constructing and announcing delimiting frameworks of analysis. The stakes for and the means by which to reign in food's associative ubiquity emerge in these pages.

PART 1: GLOBAL AND LOCAL

The essays in *Culinary Shakespeare* generally—and in part 1 specifically—vivify, identify, and historicize characteristics that make the culinary world fascinating. Keeping in mind the topical pressures of current debates about locavorism and the trade in global food commodities, this section considers Shakespearean food and drink as starting points for mapping locales of food production, consumption, and spectacle. These "locales" constitute interrelated symbolic and material networks crossing time and space—networks through which the social, hermeneutical, intellectual, economic, and ethical meanings of food and drink develop. In the first section, the writers consider the multivalent possibilities of food and drink origins and how they affect national and personal identity. How food is categorized—as local (grown in the native soil, produced by fellow compatriots, and then consumed as a token of character) or as global (foreign in origin, suspect as rare and exotic commodity and a sign of prestige)—shifts meanings in these plays. Locally produced food and drink, valued for both freshness and familiarity, were often culturally and politically marked as "English." At the same time, new (or newly revitalized) trade routes to the east and New World discoveries to the west brought novel foods to English shores and increased the prevalence of those already being imported, and these commodities in time become normalized, naturalized, and finally accepted as English. From the Americas came, among many other products, turkeys, potatoes (often called "Virginia potatoes" in this period), and, most importantly, cane sugar, which, during Shakespeare's lifetime, began to emerge as a major colonial product.[15] From the Netherlands in the late Middle Ages came beer, which, as Peter Parolin notes here, replaced the unhopped English ale as the national drink during the Renaissance. From Iberian trade routes came fortified and sugared wines, as Barbara Sebek details in depth in her essay. The Mediterranean provided exotic fruits such as oranges, which English botanists began to grow in earnest, and which, argues Peter Kanelos, play a significant role in *Much Ado about Nothing*.

In his essay, "The poor creature small beer: Princely Autonomy and Subjection in *2 Henry IV*," Peter Parolin locates the somewhat indeterminate meaning of "small beer" firmly within the Henriad's negotiation of monarchical authorization. Prince Hal, as Parolin suggests, must accommodate social lowness because he has a desire that he cannot control: his "appetite," Hal confesses, "was not princely got" (33). Providing a history of small beer, the cheapest and least alcoholic of brews, Parolin demonstrates that this drink both changed and reflected class economies, gender dynamics, and national identity in early modern England. Such a history, Parolin deftly shows, plays out in the Henriad with Hal "emerg[ing] at the end of *2 Henry IV...* deeply shaped by the social forces represented by small beer" (24). If Falstaff's reliance upon sack sacrifices human connection for chemical addiction, Henry's inexplicable fondness for small beer keeps him anchored to precisely the lower social class he might otherwise forget as king: "desiring small beer," writes Parolin, "can be a constitutive element of his rule" (39). Today the desire for an unfashionably oaky chardonnay belies a lack of refined taste; for Hal, small beer unearths the trauma of a hybrid national dynasty.

As Parolin examines the multivalent meanings of beer and ale, Barbara Sebek uncovers the complexities associated with wine, specifically sack, in early modern England. In "'Wine and sugar of the best and the fairest': Canary, the Canaries, and the Global in Windsor," Sebek globalizes *The Merry Wives of Windsor*, moving the play beyond its domestic context by tracing the broader arc of the Anglo-Spanish wine trade. Sebek reminds us that wine, which features so prominently in this provincial play, was a foreign commodity, and London a port town that was intimately involved in seafaring and global trade. Sebek shows how sack and other Spanish wines formed part of a larger network of a trade that "involved widespread participation of unregulated, non-Company traders, the city's domestic tradespeople and ship captains" (43). For Sebek, Falstaff's beloved sack stands as the commodity that links the native and the foreign. Sebek discusses the significance of the Spanish importing sugar cane production to the Canary Islands, which began to arrive in quantity in northern Europe in the mid-sixteenth century. To turn people into global commodities through the slave trade is also to transform the global ecology imbricated in such moral and economic horrors. Sebek thus unfolds the anxieties about and desires for foreign trade that saturate *Merry Wives'* production of Englishness.

Early modern culinary representations often seem anxious that a basic human physical need must be served by a substance with a problematic nonfoundational status; food is transient, subject to decay, and sometimes rendered frivolous when made into elaborate cuisine. As Peter Kanelos observes in "So Many Strange Dishes: Food, Love, and Politics in *Much Ado about Nothing*," food choices are a particularly fraught domain of life because "eating lies at the conjunction of desire and necessity" (61). Kanelos carefully anatomizes the ways in which food imagery guides the play, arguing that its seemingly arbitrary discussion of Seville oranges (or "civil oranges") "opens into a greater discourse on food, love, and politics" (58). Kanelos's essay, like the others in this section, articulates how particular foodstuffs that populate Shakespearean plays—beer, ale, sack, sugar, oranges—map social, economic, and international relations. As Kanelos notes, to take a bite of an orange was to experience the end point of a long journey inhabited by numerous collectives that had engaged in struggles for power. To serve a particular orange in England was to reference unwittingly one's evolving national and cultural identity as shaped by ever-changing political, social and economic boundaries.

PART 2: BODY AND STATE

Culinary phenomena unfold not only through place and geography, but also through power relations that are no less influential for being less graspable. A major theme of the early modern food experience is the role of the state and religion in ideologies of eating. How someone eats and even whether someone eats has everything to do with the biopolitical and theological structures and convolutions in which the eater is immersed. To enjoy a bite of an orange or a drink of sherry was, then as it is now, to court not just economic and national border-crossings, but also heated moral and governmental debates with clear ideological stakes. The scholars in this section all concern themselves with the ideological and doctrinal frameworks surrounding food in the period, detailing how Shakespeare makes use of food to expose and question these frameworks.

In "Fluid Mechanics: Shakespeare's Subversive Liquors," Karen Raber examines how wine might be a metonym for Englishness but also its potential contaminant. Providing a companion piece to Sebek's exploration of viniferous trade routes and Parolin's identification of small beer with English identity, Raber addresses the moral topography of nationhood. For Raber, alcohol in Shakespeare's plays always activates notions of England as a national body—a body with foreign trade in its veins. "Shakespeare's literary references to sack, malmsey, canary wine, sherry and other wines," she writes, "saturate his plays with allusions to philosophical, medical, ideological and mercantile discourses that can only be fully distilled if we consider the broader individual, national, and international dimensions of wine consumption" (76). Whether discussing Falstaff's addiction to sack, or the drowning of poor Clarence in a butt of malmsey in *Richard III*, or Caliban's drunken shenanigans in *The Tempest*, Raber argues that Shakespeare views alcohol as a problematic commodity enmeshed in international bonds of trade and politics. Her argument leads to questions surrounding the role of theology in early modern cuisine, demonstrating that *The Tempest* directly addresses the tension between metaphorical and literal ways of eating and drinking eucharistically. Caliban's susceptibility to the lure of wine is not just a sign of his sensual nature legible within a colonialist logic, Raber argues, but also a Protestant-inflected denunciation of corruption by false sacrament.

The state's management of food commodities has a direct impact on who eats and who starves. Ernst Gerhardt's contribution to the volume, "Feeding on the Body Politic: Consumption, Hunger, and Taste in *Coriolanus*," investigates ways that digestion in the individual body maps political struggles. During Shakespeare's lifetime, England and Europe experienced tremendous food insecurity punctuated by waves of dearth and famine. In England, enclosures of public land to create private hunting grounds (which create the backdrop for the shepherd Corin's struggles in *As You Like It*) as well as bad harvests in 1594–97 and 1607–08 (which are mentioned in *Romeo and Juliet* and *Coriolanus*, respectively) raised food prices and lowered living standards.[16] As Gerhardt argues, *Coriolanus* responds directly to this environmental unrest. Although the tale comes from Plutarch's *Lives*, Shakespeare changes the plebeian uprising from a protest against usury to one against dearth. *Coriolanus* interrogates who gets to eat and who does not—who hungers and who hoards. For Gerhardt, the play stages a contest between those who would erase the origins of food in production and agriculture and those who would make it appear "ready made, a product readily available for the body politic's consumption" (100). The politics of cuisine are never far from the mind of Shakespeare and his contemporaries.

When do socially and governmentally valued acts of hospitality and conviviality conflict with individual matters of ingestion? When do these conflicts enter the terrain of the ethical? These are the questions posed by Rebecca Lemon's essay, "Sacking Falstaff." While it may seem perverse in a volume about Shakespearean food not to discuss Falstaff's gluttony—arguably the most famous culinary crux in Shakespeare, at least for the lay reader—Lemon's essay on Falstaff's drinking opens a prospect largely neglected by critical focus on his appetite for food. "Falstaff's gluttony has attracted a degree of critical attention," writes Lemon, "yet it is his drinking rather than eating that proves oppositional as the plays develop" (114). Starting from the same point as Raber's contribution—Falstaff's famous paean to sack—Lemon travels in the opposite direction, from national identity to individual ingestion. While Falstaff's appetite proves a touchstone both for his role as a festive, carnivalesque figure and his threat to English agricultural resources, his drinking reveals a subtly different tension—between conviviality and isolation. Lemon argues that, contrary to appearances, Falstaff's drinking fails to achieve the social bonding that he claims as the primary property of sack. Instead, Falstaff's addiction—a concept that emerges in early modernity, as Lemon carefully attests—weakens and ultimately destroys the convivial relationships that drink purports to found. The *Henry IV* plays thus become an object lesson in eating and drinking in interpersonal as well as political terms. To drink without surcease is to risk the dissolution of the very bonds that make food sharing and convivial drinking both enjoyable and mutual, whether at the level of the tavern or the nation.

PART 3: THEATER AND COMMUNITY

Lemon's essay provides a transition to the question of how community is generated, shaped, and destroyed by culinary practices and theories. In Shakespeare, this question is routinely imbricated in theatricality, since the theater also forms a chief locale for the generation, shaping, and (occasional) destruction of community. Performative and transformative, food was inherently theatrical in Shakespeare's world, and food also permeated the spaces of theater. More broadly, eating in company was, then as now, an act of theater, a set of performances played out around the stage of the dining table. In describing various scenarios of host and guest, Ken Albala writes of the Renaissance banquet, "the meal re-stages, if you like, a central human drive to dominate, to woo, to challenge. Each is also a kind of play."[17] The idea of the table as a kind of stage resonated with humanist philosophy, which took the meal as a kind of staging ground for the practice of good citizenship. The dining scenes of Rabelais, More's *Utopia*, and Erasmus's *Colloquies* all strive to teach a close relationship among theater, properly regulated subjecthood, and obligation toward others, a nexus that forms a cornerstone of humanist political theory. What happens to this theory over the course of the century is the subject of Douglas Lanier's essay on what he terms "the broken banquet" in *Macbeth* and *Timon of Athens* and forms a backdrop for the other essays of this section, both of which consider the deep lineaments of community as created and exposed through culinary processes.

In "Cynical Dining in *Timon of Athens*," Douglas M. Lanier identifies what he calls "banqueting ideology," which constitutes the "ethical and socio-political ideals" of humanism and is bound up with Renaissance banqueting practices of the sixteenth century English royal court. In Shakespeare's theater, the humanist ideals of harmonious commensality are tested and shattered in play after play. Throughout his career, especially in *The Taming of the Shrew*, *Titus Andronicus*, *Macbeth*, and *Timon of Athens*, Shakespeare sets up a banquet only to trump it by means of theater itself. Our opening example of Ariel's illusory banquet in *The Tempest* provides perhaps the sine qua non of this technique, in which Shakespeare takes the great feast—food at its most performative—as an icon to be both amplified and destroyed. Lanier reads this scene as a displacement of traditional moral debates carried out at classical symposia, for edification becomes a phenomenological experience in which the temptation and withholding of food erode the authority of the shipwrecked nobles.

The mere presence of a staged banquet raises the uber-civilizing mission endowed upon it in Western humanist writing—an ideal, Lanier argues, that was increasingly treated with suspicion and cynicism in the early modern period. Shakespeare often only exposes this ideal in its corrupted form, with its moral edification depicted as a sham or ideological pretense. Even when the failed banquet is shown to be a toxic site of disorder, however, it triggers speculation about how and whether "bestial" appetitive desires can be regulated. In this sense, the extraordinary banquet of *The Tempest* points to ethical quandaries that crop up in everyday eating.

Food in the theater works experientially and sensually: the physical and metaphorical presence of food on the stage and the audience's sensual experience of comestibles are mutually reinforcing. This co-interaction lends itself to explorations of eucharistic eating, in which the line between the physical and metaphorical is a matter of urgency. Tobias Döring explores this phenomenon in "Feasting and Forgetting: Sir Toby's Pickle Herring and the Lure of Lethe," arguing, "spectators of [*Twelfth Night*] find themselves included in the community of drinkers they are watching.... Under Sir Toby's prompting, spectators turn into fellow feasters" (164). For Döring, food in *Twelfth Night* brings together communities; that is, the theatrical/food connection in the play is commensal, as if the characters and the audience were sharing a meal together. Döring reads Sir Toby—the play's "Lord of Misrule"—as the lynchpin that creates a community of audience and actor through what Döring calls the "work of feasting" (165). Yet Sir Toby also represents a figure of forgetting, "physically countering the culture of commemoration" (173). In this paradox lies the complexity of how cuisine operates in the play. Drinking, argues Döring, enacts a kind of addiction to oblivion and forgetting, much like the work of cultural erasure that English Protestantism undertook against its Catholic past.

Julian Yates's essay for the volume, "Shakespeare's Messmates," radically expands the community of eaters to include the nonhuman world, in the process showing us how Shakespeare both acknowledges and challenges the supposed anthropocentricity of culinary relationships. Yates applies the figure of Donna Haraway's "messmate" to reevaluate what it means to share the table with nonhumans: as companions, as those we eat, and as those who eat us. For Yates, *Hamlet* is most interested in the latter category: that "certain convocation of politic worms" that consumes priests as readily as beggars, making of either a vermicular meal. Yates reads this moment, with its eucharistic overtones, as "the successive transformations of flesh (back) into soil that describes an unreduced or general ecology" (183). *The Comedy of Errors* provides another example of the human body being "kitchened," or rendered into cuisine. Although the play stages no eating, Yates argues, there is "no need to put the kitchen on stage, as the theater is already an analogous space of transformations and try-outs, a space of rehearsal and practice" (192). Messmates of human and nonhuman forms take on another meaning in *The Tempest*, as shipwrecked victims, exiles, captive sprites, and native creatures find themselves at table. Yates sees the whole island as Prospero's kitchen, wherein various messmates are invited to dine and then are disappointed by vanishing feasts. In each of these three plays, the normative anthropocentric hierarchy of the kitchen and table is overturned to the advantage of the nonhuman messmates.

The strangeness of *The Tempest*'s supernatural food seems, at first glance, far removed from the basic tasks of baking, slicing, and serving in the domestic sphere. In fact, as many commentators in this volume note, the spirit-produced banquet seems more akin to theater than the *domus* in its deep structural ability to query taxonomies of being and rearrange modes of thought. Yet, as Yates notes, the scene's articulation of a "near-kitchen experience" brings to light the cognitive puzzles and theoretical issues involved in mundane household acts. Performing an "ecology of the kitchen," the banquet serves as a microcosm of Prospero's artistic power and, as such, underscores the critical affinity between mental and manual labors. Prospero's illusions may seem to leave not a wrack behind as they fade, but in their wake lie reordered social and cosmological worlds—as well as much food for thought. In the movement from desert island to dessert, Julia Reinhard Lupton wittily observes in chapter 10, we see that commensality carries its own potential deprivations.

Lupton's contribution, "Room for Dessert: Sugared Shakespeare and the Dramaturgy of Dwelling," illuminates how the architecture of sweet dishes creates the mise-en-scene of a meal and, in turn, how the clearing away of dishes to ready the table for the sweet course—making "room for dessert"—reverberates theatrically in *The Taming of the Shrew, Romeo and Juliet, The Tempest,* and *The Winter's Tale.* Lupton demonstrates that early modern dessert was conceived as the only course of the meal that involved a full clearing of the table instead of the collating of new dishes with half-eaten ones. Because this voiding or clearing initiated an intellectual pause button in the rhythms of eating, it prompted rumination on the experience of dining; it fused the life of the mind with the creaturely needs of the stomach. The early modern banquet, or void, produced a self-conscious moment of substitution and interruption. Dessert both gives shape to the meal and is itself shaped into fabulous confections, in what Lupton calls "a kind of culinary landscape architecture." As such, the dessert creates a self-referential ecology, in which the ingredients create a kind of pastoralism drawn from the very ingredients of the orchard, dairy, and garden. The built culinary environment imitates theatrically the landscape from which it emerges. Dessert thus recognizes an ecology that is not only physical but also temporal—a pause in which the table is reset, in which theater, with its cruelties and reconciliations, gives itself the space to work magic in and through time.

Lupton's meditation on the philosophical implications of clearing the table (of contents) concocts for you, the reader, the very meaning of concluding edibles and textual finales. They can be appreciated as occasions for cycling back to other courses and times so as to reimagine, perhaps even to rezone, reconsider, and renew, their meanings. "To clear the table completely is to reset the evening, to allow for a new beginning" (213), Lupton writes. And after clearing the table, we move on to other courses.

Part 1

LOCAL AND GLOBAL

"The poor creature small beer": Princely Autonomy and Subjection in *2 Henry IV*

PETER PAROLIN

Scholars of *2 Henry IV* have always had to confront, as I will here, the play's relationship to its more popular and more performed predecessor, *1 Henry IV*. Introducing the play in *The Norton Shakespeare*, for example, Jean Howard raises the fundamental question of "why Shakespeare wrote two plays dealing with the reign of Henry IV"; one of her suggestions is that he intended "to undertake two quite different explorations of the prodigal narrative by which the wild Prince becomes first a chivalric hero and eventually the King of England."[1] As distinct interrogations of the same narrative, the plays have independent integrity; however, this essay reads them together as a single story in which Prince Hal achieves the greatness of kingship by first articulating and then revising his relationship to *lowness*, to the common people, common things, and common desires that undergird royal sovereignty but stand apart from its official articulation.

In *1 Henry IV*, the prince's relation to lowness is a crisis for others but not for himself. The king frets to "See riot and dishonor stain the brow / Of my young Harry" and regrets that his son cannot exchange identities with the conventionally chivalric Hotspur.[2] By contrast, the prince understands his lowness as being essential to his planned trajectory for becoming king. Consorting with plebeians in the tavern, he promises a future day in which he will repudiate his socially degrading friends: "I know you all, and will a while uphold / The unyoked humour of your idleness" (*1H4*, 1.2.173–74). When the "while" of playtime comes to an end, the prince will "imitate the sun" (175), and "please again to be himself" (178), "By breaking through the foul and ugly mists that did seem to strangle him" (181). In this telling, the prince's temporary immersion in a socially low environment is nothing more than a necessary prelude to his future reformation: "I'll so offend to make offence a skill, / Redeeming time when men think least I will" (1.2.194–95). This bold plan leaves no room for self-doubt: Hal is using his tavern friends to lower the political expectations that he will spectacularly exceed as king. Far from questioning his ties to the socially low, the self-congratulatory prince depends on them, smugly anticipating his future dominance over the drawers of London, who promise him that "when I am King of England I shall command all the good lads in Eastcheap" (2.5.10, 12–13). *1 Henry IV* presents a prince fully in control of his lowly social environment: understanding it in ways it does not understand itself, he dominates it, planning, at the appropriate future moment, to repudiate it in the service of his own uncontaminated greatness.

2 Henry IV might seem to enact Prince Hal's promised separation from his low companions: he spends much less time in the tavern in *Part 2* than in *Part 1*, he embraces the elite world of royal power by making peace with his father and submitting to the authority of the lord chief justice, and he utterly rejects the tavern's claims on him by rejecting Falstaff: "I know thee not, old man."[3] Yet in this play, ostensibly about the prince's dissociation from common ties, Hal is much more troubled than he was in *Part 1* by his links to commonness. The confidence he displayed in *Part 1* is replaced by a sense of internal crisis in *Part 2*, a crisis that is especially well articulated in the prince's desire for small beer, a weak brew that sustained the poor in early modern England. At the very moment Hal should be breaking his ties with common things, he reveals that the socially low has entered his desires, potentially contaminating him and ruining his plan to become England's ideal king. Hal's predilection for this common drink in *2 Henry IV* powerfully represents the prince's wide-ranging fears about what has happened to him through his immersion in the tavern world.

A history of small beer in early modern England will demonstrate that low desires end up being a constitutive element of elite identity: the prince's task in 2 *Henry IV* is not to *expel* social lowness but to *accommodate* it. This process of accommodation turns out to be as shifty and paradoxical as the history of small beer itself, a history that profoundly changed crucial aspects of national identity, economic practice, and gender relations even as it occluded its enforcement of preexisting hierarchies and identity positions. Marked indelibly by his desire for small beer, Prince Hal becomes a king who embraces aspects of the socially low in order to attain greatness and who paradoxically accepts that, in order to dominate the external world, he must allow himself to be acted upon by it. But perhaps the paradox is not really so: new models of Englishness, in the realms of both drink and kingship, depend on complex histories even when they hide them. Small beer obscures the complex domestic and international relations that attended its rise as an unambiguously English drink; so, too, Henry V occludes the unchanging social privilege and the relentless exploitation of low desires that undergird his self-presentation as a quintessentially English ruler.[4]

Small beer enters 2 *Henry IV* at the same time the prince does, in act 2, scene 2, a scene of crisis in Hal's relationship to his social identity. The prince announces, "Before God, I am exceeding weary"; and when Poins replies, "I had thought weariness durst not have attached one of so high blood," Hal assures him that "it does me, though it discolours the complexion of my greatness to acknowledge it." He continues, "Doth it not show vildly in me to desire small beer?" (2H4, 2.2.1–6). The issue is the extent to which Hal's elite identity has been contaminated by inappropriate common elements—he fears that his desire for small beer degrades his status. To Poins's cautious rejoinder that, "A prince should not be so loosely studied as to remember so weak a composition," Hal responds, "Belike then my appetite was not princely got, for by my troth, I do now remember the poor creature small beer" (2.2.6–10).[5] Citing his low desires, the prince astonishingly questions his very legitimacy. The desire for small beer raises questions about the prince and suggests aspects of himself that he does not understand, much less control. This moment in *Part 2* strikingly counters the prince's self-assessment in *Part 1*, where he proudly reveled in his low associations, never seeming to fear that they threat-ened his capacity for self-determination. In *Part 1*, there was no shame, only a will to power, when Hal identified his tavern friends as pawns in a game that he fully controlled. So why, in *Part 2*, is the prince so troubled by his affection for small beer?

The prince's crisis of confidence in 2 *Henry IV* may occur because he is possessed by—subject to—a desire that he does not understand. For a prince who plans to dominate the external world, the desire for small beer indicates a reversal in which the world works on him rather than the other way around.[6] The prince's desire for small beer signals a significant fissure in his identity, marking the space where the social realm stops being merely object to the prince's subject and instead pushes back, exerting its own defining pressure. Indeed, the fact that Prince Hal refers to small beer as a "creature" is significant because it suggests that beer possesses a vital social agency enabling it to affect its drinkers. The *OED* defines "creature" as "A created thing or being; a product of creative action; a creation" (def. 1a),[7] which places it in the object world that the prince aspires to dominate while also stressing the object as the product of complex human labor and relationships.[8] More startlingly, the prince's term "creature" may also suggest that small beer possesses subjective qualities, in keep-ing with the *OED*'s definitions of "creature" as "a human being; a person, an individual" (def. 2) and a "fellow-creature" (def. 2b). After all, the yeast that was crucial to beer's fermentation was literally alive, changing the drink's characteristics. Frequently brewed in the home, beer would have revealed its vital changes firsthand to early moderns, who might in turn have understood it as a living entity. The prince certainly has a keen sense of beer's vitality when he calls it "the poor creature"; however, his apparent empathy obscures the ways in which small beer was not merely abject, a social victim, but a social agent with the capacity to alter even the Prince of Wales.[9]

The king who emerges at the end of 2 *Henry IV* is deeply shaped by the social forces represented by small beer. Through small beer, the social realm makes its claim on Henry V; it makes him a *creature* by shaping his desires and undercutting his assumption of control over the world around him. When he becomes king, Henry V acknowledges his proper subjection to the external world, specifically to the legal and cultural norms of English society. Small beer looms large in Henry's shift away from the self-flattering fantasy of an autonomous ruler and toward the position of a socially constrained monarch; the analysis of small beer in the play shows how patterns of desire and consumption shape and reveal aspects of elite identity, including the constitutive links between high and low.

So what is small beer, where does it come from, and how does it signify in early modern England? One of the weakest brews available in early modern London, small beer has powerful implications: it points to changes in economic processes, gender relations, and ideas about what it means to be English. Linked to social change, small beer shares affinities with wine, which both Karen Raber (chapter 4) and Barbara Sebek (chapter 2) argue in this volume figures in shifting economic relations and a concomitantly shifting sense of Englishness. The circumstances surrounding the production and consumption of beer—its social ubiquity, its success in the marketplace—mark it as a common object of public desire. The fact that a prince is drawn to small beer, albeit in ways that he finds problematic, makes it clear that low desires feature integrally in the formation of his elite identity, and not necessarily only through negation. In 2 *Henry IV*, small beer has multiple valences: it is a product that satisfies physical desire, it is a source of pleasure, it is a source of shame, it has a changing history, and it is a form of knowledge. It is an apt figure not only for the wastrel prince who becomes a heroic king but also for the shifting ingredients that construct identity.

One of the first things to notice about beer in 2 *Henry IV* is that it is an anachronism. Although beer was introduced to England in the fourteenth century, it was not until the late fifteenth century that the beer brewers of London formed their own guild and not until the early sixteenth century that beer rivaled ale in popularity as the national drink.[10] The historical Prince Harry would have drunk ale, not beer; the Shakespearean prince's desire for small beer marks him as a sixteenth century figure, activating other histories beyond his ostensible period.[11] The prince's crisis is a sixteenth century crisis of identity and desire that intersects with beer's supplanting ale as the predominant beverage in England. This supplanting indicates that innovations in drink link to, and to some extent manage, changes in the social order, presiding over new identity formations.

Thinking about beer in *2 Henry IV* thus requires a consideration of historical transition. Before beer, the most common English brew was ale, prepared in a multistep process in which the brewer or brewster would grind malt, mix it with boiled water, and pour it into a mash tun. The brewer would steep the mixture, draw off the resulting liquid (the wort), and add yeast and herbs to enable fermentation and enhance flavor. After a day or so, the ale would be ready to drink.[12] Ale was brewed locally and in relatively small quantities, both because it spoiled quickly and because it deteriorated easily when transported.[13] The advent of beer profoundly changed the economy of drink in England. The major difference between ale and beer is the addition of hops to the latter drink; Peter Clark notes that "the introduction of hops (in place of spices) produced a more stable, palatable, and long-lived liquor."[14] Hopped beer originated in the Low Countries; indeed, the first brewers of beer in England seem to have been Flemish and Dutch. Only through a gradual process over the sixteenth century did beer become the dominant English drink, especially popular in London.[15]

Initially, beer faced the challenge of being seen as an upstart foreign drink. As Andrew Boorde states in his *Dyetary of Helth* (1542), "Ale for an englysshe man is a natural drynke," while "Bere...is a natural drynke for a dutche man."[16] Throughout the century, however, beer was increasingly naturalized; not only did English brewers brew beer domestically but they also cultivated the central ingredient, hops, in their own gardens. In *A Perfite platforme of a Hoppe Garden* (1574), Reginald Scot explicitly characterizes expertise in hops-growing as a new national virtue that protects the English economy from Flemish competition: "I see the Flemmings envie our practise herein, who altogither tende their owne profite, seeking to impownde us in the ignoraunce of our commodities, to cramme us with the wares and fruites of their Countrie...dazeling us with the discommendation of our soyle."[17] For Scot, local conditions—in this case, the English soil—guaranteed the excellence of English beer. Praising beer allowed English brewers, and writers, to assert the value of specifically English natural resources and English commodities, resisting foreign misrepresentations. The advent of beer, then, came to be tied up with English economic self-promotion.

Casting England as a natural home to beer, Scot praises it at the expense of ale; clearly, by the end of the sixteenth century beer was engaged in an intense competition with ale that played out in terms of husbandry, economics, taste, social custom, and national values. Scot writes, for example, that a bushel of malt produces over twice as much beer as ale, adding that the hops in beer not only extends the drink's lifespan but also enhances its taste: "What grace it yeeldeth to the taste, all men maye judge that have sense in their mouths, and if the controversie be betwixte Beere and Ale, which of them two shall have ye place of preheminence: it sufficeth for the glorie and commendation of the Beere, that here in our owne countrie, Ale giveth place unto it, and that most part of our Countrymen doe abhore and abandon Ale, as a loathsome drincke, whereas in other nations Beere is of great estimation, and of straungers entertained as their most choyce and delicate drinke."[18] For Scot, beer is not only a more plausible national drink for the English than ale, but it allows the English to define themselves as a race of people who truly have "sense in their mouths." If drinkers prove their "mouth sense" by recognizing beer's superiority to ale, then the English, who "abandon" ale for beer, pass the test.

The domestication of beer is apparent, too, in *The Description of England* (1577), where William Harrison champions English brewing methods. He praises the "industry of our brewers" and describes English brewing in detail in order to correct the mistakes of "foreign writers," who "have attempted to describe…the making of our beer, wherein they have shot so far wide as the quantity of ground was between themselves and their mark."[19] In Harrison's handling, beer becomes not only an English drink but also essentially a mode of English knowledge that must be defended against foreign misrepresentations. Fynes Moryson furthers this notion of specific English excellence in beer brewing by stressing that even Flemish brewers strive, unsuccessfully, to reproduce English beer: "They say that there be 300 brewers at Delph, and there they imitate the English Beere, and call that kind Delphs English. But with no cost could they ever make it as good as the English is."[20] By the time of the pamphlet *Wine, Beer, Ale, and Tobacco: Contending for Superiority* (1629), English Beer is so confident in its own national status as to attack Wine for its foreign origins. Beer asks, "Whence come you pray?" Wine responds, "From France, from Spaine, from Greece." Beer: "Thou art a mad Greeke indeed."[21] In this exchange, Beer speaks from a position of secure, if implicit, Englishness; the fact that it speaks at all literalizes its social life, enabling it to assert an array of English attitudes, including the easy ability to put strangers in their (subordinate) place.[22]

The naturalization of beer occurred alongside changes in the economic practices and social relations that had characterized the brewing industry when ale was the dominant product. As Judith Bennett explains, beer brewing offered several commercial advantages that ale brewing did not share: "beer lasted longer, traveled better, and cost less to produce." Bennett adds that these qualities in beer allowed brewers to exploit expanding markets in a way that ale brewers could not. Beer brewing required more standing equipment and supplies than ale brewing did, and its more complex processes required more laborers. As an industry, then, beer brewing was a larger, more heavily capitalized enterprise. Bennett concludes, "the story of [beer's] slow acceptance by English brewers and drinkers is a story of urbanization, immigration, capitalization, and professionalization."[23] Beer thus rises as an English drink by participating in profound economic changes; after its ascendance, it comes to symbolize the new order that brought it into being.

Crucially, this new order included the masculinization of the field. Where women brewed most of the ale in fourteenth century England, the gender dynamics changed over the next 200 years. Bennett points out, "As the actual production of ale and beer—that is, brewing per se—became so much more profitable and prestigious, it passed into male hands."[24] Women certainly continued to brew, often alongside husbands. William Harrison cites his wife, Marion, who came from a Flemish immigrant family, as his authority on brewing methods; in *The Merry Wives of Windsor*, Mistress Quickly includes brewing in the catalogue of household jobs she performs for Doctor Caius (1.4.83–85).[25] Thus, while women's role was reduced in the beer industry, they continued to be involved in the production of what was becoming the national drink. The industry's social and legal constraints increasingly privileged men; this process of masculinization occluded women's ongoing work.[26] While beer may have been naturalized as an English drink, the processes that shaped it were anything but natural, if "natural" is taken to mean freedom from implication in cultural categories like gender. The beer-brewing economy hindered women from profiting in a lucrative industry, and it simultaneously occluded women's continuing involvement, largely domestic, in brewing.

In addition to the masculinization of brewing, the production and consumption of beer had clear social and class valences. Brewing produced different categories of beer, each of which was associated with different tastes, drinking habits, and classes. The strongest brew, made with extra hops, was March beer, favored at festivals and times of special hospitality.[27] Gervase Markham defines the next grade of beer as "ordinary beer, which is that wherewith either the nobleman, gentleman, yeoman, or husbandman shall maintain his family the whole year."[28] Beer, in all its hierarchical gradations, saw the English through both the ritual year and daily life, becoming thereby an English means of experiencing time.

At the bottom of the brewing hierarchy comes the small beer of Prince Hal's desire. Not only was it the weakest category of beer, brewed when a second, smaller yield of wort was drawn from the grains and boiled with the hops, but it was the socially lowest category. Comparing March beer, household beer, and small beer, Markham notes that, "the first is for strangers, the second for the Master, Mistress and better sort of the family, and the last is for ploughmen or hind servants."[29] Peter Clark confirms Markham's classification, calling small beer "the daily liquor of the lower classes" and citing "the wife of an Essex victualler," who brewed "small beer to sell to a great number of the very poor people who could not otherwise know how to be maintained."[30] With beer increasingly becoming the drink of England's urban population, small beer, the weakest and cheapest brew, was associated with the bottom strata of society; it was the water substitute that sustained the poor. In a world where different types of drink reflected status, small beer indicated the neediness and disempowerment of its drinkers.

With the gradations of beer mapped onto distinctions in social status, it is potentially all the more puzzling that "the poor creature small beer" is the prince's object of desire in *2 Henry IV*. Prince Hal could easily have access to other, more elite drinks, but his desire directs him toward small beer. In contrast to the prince's presence in the tavern in *1 Henry IV*, his desire for small beer in *2 Henry IV* does not integrate easily into an overarching vision of his identity; indeed, small beer provokes a crisis in the prince's conception of self and quickly prompts further troubling questions about what has happened to him through his immersion in a socially low milieu: why does he, a prince, even remember Poins's name, for example; why does he have so much information about Poins's laundry, including the number and color of his pairs of silk stockings; what does it mean that he refers to the debilitating costs of the brothels, bantering with Poins about how his "low countries" eat up his "his holland"; and what is the impact of the speculation that he is to marry Poins's sister Nell? In all these cases, the questions raise the issue of material contagion, the possibility that Hal's experience in the tavern has fatally compromised his social nobility. Hal blushes when he admits this possibility ("it discolours the complexion of my greatness"); the blush is a visible physiological sign that eludes the prince's control and that puts him in a vulnerable position in relation to the political power he will soon be called on to wield. In a variety of ways, then, the tavern world threatens the prince's ability to control his own identity. Small beer may merely be the most prominent of these ways because it is the one thing the prince explicitly admits has insinuated itself into his desires.

The most obvious answer to the puzzle of small beer is that it stands in for the common companions the prince must renounce in order to assume his greatness. Yet the prince's own uneasiness about small beer calls this obvious answer into question. In *1 Henry IV*, the prince is untroubled about rejecting his low companions. So why, in *Part 2*, should small beer perplex him so much, if it represents those same expendable companions, unless it has wormed its way into his desires, working on him and changing him rather than merely gratifying him temporarily before he renounces it and moves on? Small beer becomes a more complex phenomenon when we consider that rather than standing in for the prince's companions, it might stand in for the prince himself. Indeed, many of the qualities of English beer—its hybrid national identity, the fact that it was originally underestimated by foreigners, its production efficiency, its increasing masculinization—have been taken as hallmarks of the reformed prince who as king would thwart expectation to win a war in France and found his own nationally hybrid dynasty. Rebecca Bach writes that Shakespeare's histories ask "what kind of a man the king should be"; *2 Henry IV* probes this issue by asking what kind of beer the king should drink and what his beer says about the king and his model of rule.[31]

By the end of the play, Hal becomes a king who, like small beer, is implicated in the world around him. Far from an automaton who dominates others unfeelingly, he displays empathy, struggles internally, and accepts that his identity depends on his being in relation to the external world, abandoning a simple model in which the subject overmasters the object. At the same time, this empathetic, interrelational monarch performs the very exclusions he promised in *Part 1*, dismissing Falstaff and dazzling the English court with his reformation. Small beer ensures that the new king can pull off this balancing act: the unfeeling model of autonomous rule outlined in *Part 1* gives way in *Part 2* to a properly English model in which sovereignty, though powerful, is still constrained and in which the king's dominance is achieved through acknowledging shared characteristics with his subjects rather than asserting his radical difference.

If Prince Hal's desire for small beer points to the kind of king he will become, then it also contrasts significantly with the drinking habits of others, specifically Falstaff, who prefers strong and costly imported wines such as sack, sherry, and bordeaux. In their contributions to this volume, Sebek and Raber investigate the impact of foreign wines on the English scene. In the play, Doll Tearsheet claims that "there's a whole merchant's venture of Bordeaux stuff" in Falstaff (*2H4*, 2.4.50–51). Doll herself makes her first entrance sick from having drunk "too much canaries," which Mistress Quickly calls a "marvelous searching wine" (2.4.21). In his encomium on sack, Falstaff links wine to masculinity, specifically in terms of hot blood, good soldiership, and nimble wit: "Hereof comes it that Prince Harry is valiant, for the cold blood he did naturally inherit of his father he hath, like lean, sterile and bare land, manured, husbanded and tilled, with excellent endeavor of drinking good and good store of fertile sherries, that he is become very hot and valiant" (4.1.464–69). Describing the prince drinking sherry, Falstaff sounds like English writers describing the anglicization of beer: local land, tended well, yields an excellent product. Like small beer, Prince Hal is indeed being cultivated, only not in the way Falstaff imagines. The knight errs when he ascribes his own love of sack to the prince. Falstaff prefers a sherry-drinking Hal to his brother John because the "young sober-blooded [John]... drinks no wine." Falstaff concludes, "There's never none of these demure boys come to any proof, for thin drink doth so overcool their blood... that they fall into a kind of male greensickness, and then when they marry they get wenches" (4.1.438–40, 441–42). The irony here is that, like John, Prince Hal does favor thin drink, which, *pace* Falstaff, the play codes as English and opposes to the dangerous excess associated with foreign wines.[32] Far from effeminizing Hal, small beer may in fact be seen as the foundation of the prince's future rule through its evolution as a particularly English product in which native masculinity supplants and occludes foreignness and femininity.

Small beer embodies the social nature of the world that defines the prince. It embeds him deeply in external experiences and moves him from the fantasized autonomous figure of *Part 1* to a king who depends more openly on the world around him in *Part 2*. Christine Hoffman notes that Shakespeare's kings assume that their political survival depends on their disconnection from the world around them; she cites *1 Henry IV* where the king upbraids his son for having "lost thy princely privilege / With vile participation" (*1H4*, 3.2.86–87).[33] Hal echoes his father's language when he worries that his desire for small beer "shows vildly," in the sense of defining him as both morally despicable and socially low.[34] Yet there was nothing morally despicable about small beer by the time *1 Henry IV* was first published in 1598, although its social lowness did entail vile participation. Over the course of *2 Henry IV*, social participation emerges as an essential component of kingly rule, one that can benefit the prince and that scholars note is required of kings across Shakespeare's history plays. Bach, for example, shows the interrelationality of masculinity in these plays, stressing that successful masculine rule depends upon accepting one's place in networks of reciprocal relationships.[35]

Applying Bach's insight, we could say that Hal's power in *2 Henry IV* comes not simply from princely begetting but from accepting that he is subject to networks of relationships larger than himself. His fondness for small beer exemplifies his subjection, despite the fact that he repeatedly depicts himself as separate from the vile world around him. Indeed, his persistent efforts to gain the upper hand over his companions suggest a need to assert boundaries in constant danger of collapse. For example, delighting in his plots against Falstaff in *Part 2*, the prince establishes a categorical opposition: "How might we see Falstaff bestow himself tonight in his true colors, and not ourselves be seen?" (*2H4*, 2.2.131–32). Seen versus not seen, known versus not known: Hal's question recalls his assertion of superiority in *Part 1*: "I know you all." Articulating his power, the prince insists that he knows and is superior to his companions, that he knows himself while remaining unknown to others. The desire for small beer complicates the prince's supposed mastery because it suggests that Hal does not know himself as fully as he should, that he is operated on by a force (his desire) that he neither controls nor understands, and that his desire makes him legible to others, subject to their knowledge, in a way that undermines his autonomy. In effect, the poor creature small beer acts upon the prince much as Julian Yates in chapter 9 of this volume argues that the messmates, licensed by death, transform the human subject into object. In *2 Henry IV*, Hal is deeply unsettled by his recognition of this ontological transition.

The prince asserts his autonomous desire in the early moments of *1 Henry IV*, presenting himself as the intellect that acts on the world. What is perhaps unexpected about *Part 2* is that it casts Hal's desire as a force that he himself does not control, a force specifically shaped by the historical and social context of small beer. The prince's fondness for small beer prompts him to speculate that "my appetite was not princely got." But if Hal dismisses princely begetting as the source of his desires, it begs the question of where, in fact, his desires originate. In this context, it is worth applying Pierre Bourdieu's insight about taste in artistic matters to taste in drink.[36] Arguing that there is nothing essential about taste, Bourdieu notes that "cultural needs are the product of upbringing and education: surveys establish that all cultural practices...are closely linked to educational level...and secondarily to social origin."[37] For Bourdieu, taste emerges from one's training and one's habits in the world. Hal may be "princely got," but his appetite and his identity are shaped more by his social milieu than by any act of royal procreation. A world of elite opportunities is open to Hal as Prince of Wales, but his extended time in the tavern predicts that his tastes will be those of the tavern. The shock for Prince Hal in *2 Henry IV* is that, despite his intention of using the tavern to further his own political aspirations, the tavern has used him back and shaped him, too. The tavern leaves its traces on the prince, especially in the form of the deep desires that he articulates in a longing for small beer.

Desiring small beer may be troubling for the prince precisely because it indicates his subjection to social systems that he does not control. Bourdieu argues that "taste classifies, and it classifies the classifier"; in this way, Hal, who prefers to classify and dominate others, instead becomes the princely object of their systems of classification.[38] For example, if he should claim that "my heart bleeds inwardly that my father is so sick," Poins assures him he would immediately be branded "a most princely hypocrite" (*2H4*, 2.2.36, 41). It makes sense, therefore, that Hal would be uncomfortable revealing his desires, since they not only threaten his position as the autonomous judge of others (the sun "breaking through the foul and ugly mists" [*1H4*, 1.2.180]) but also reveal an affinity with the low members of society, which is not merely a performance on Hal's part but a constitutive element of who he has become.

Because taste reveals the social forces that shape subjectivity, the prince's predilection for small beer reveals a specific network of social considerations that constrain him and that in turn indicate something about the kind of king he will become. Small beer, and beer more generally, not only links Hal to the tavern but also shares features with him. For example, beer faced challenges in gaining widespread acceptance; broadly stated, this is Hal's predicament, too. Beer was initially seen as an upstart foreign drink that had to earn its supremacy in the English marketplace. Similarly, Hal is the unruly scion of an upstart dynasty that needs to earn its right to rule.[39] Just as beer had risen to preeminence through success in the commercial marketplace, so the prince establishes his political preeminence through success in the marketplace of tavern and theater, edging out all competitors until he has the sole political and characterological claim to rule. As much as the prince questions his desire for small beer, his kinship with the weak English brew helps to position him sympathetically as he prepares to rule. It reinforces his bond with Poins, even as he expresses uneasiness about that bond, and later it permits the commoners in *Henry V* to idolize the king even as he decimates their community: "The King is a good king," says Nim after Henry breaks Falstaff's heart, "but it must be as it may."[40]

The political disposition coalescing around Prince Hal can also be seen in the masculinization of brewing in the age of beer. The changing economy of brewing marginalized the women who had historically dominated the trade. *2 Henry IV* establishes an increasingly masculine political community, exemplifying the wider tendency in Shakespeare's second tetralogy to shift women to the margins of the historical stage that they had occupied much more centrally in the *Henry VI* plays.[41] Not only are Nell Quickly and Doll Tearsheet degraded to the point of being dragged off stage by the beadle in their final appearance in the play, but Falstaff, the male figure of feminine fecundity, is decisively rejected by the new King Henry V. The prince's rise to kingship seems to require the collapse of the feminine, literally and metaphorically, a process consistent with Harry's desire for small beer, because even though beer is associated with the feminized space of the tavern and is brewed domestically by women, it comes to national prominence through processes that downgrade and downplay women's role, ending up as a predominantly masculine drink produced by a masculine industry.

To a prince who initially imagines himself as the sun, the desire for small beer is problematic. It embeds him in histories and social processes that he does not control. Tellingly, immediately after Hal confesses his proclivity for small beer, he compares himself to Jove, possibly using the powerful god to reassert a model of identity in which the autonomous subject dominates the object. But by *2 Henry IV*, the model of autonomous kingly power has become deeply fraught, more a residual fantasy than a viable option; even conjuring the mightiest of the classical gods returns Hal to the dilemma of interimplication. When the Prince and Poins hatch their plan to spy on Falstaff by disguising themselves as drawers, Hal waxes philosophical: "From a god to a bull? A heavy descension! It was Jove's case. From a prince to a prentice? A low transformation that shall be mine" (*2H4*, 2.2.135–36). The prince alludes to Ovid's account of the rape of Europa, in which

Jove transforms himself into a bull and entices Europa to ride on his back. Once she mounts him, Jove swims out to sea, landing on the isle of Crete where, in Golding's translation of *The Metamorphoses*, "he laide aside his borrowed shape of Bull" and raped her.[42] Hal's allusion to Jove points to the sovereign will of a god untrammeled by physical limitations.[43] But if the prince alludes to Jove to inoculate himself from the impact of his low desires, he fails. Like the prince himself in relation to small beer, Jove does not stand above desire but is subject to it. Caressed and dressed by Europa, Jove the bull momentarily shifts from being the subject of his own desire to the object of hers: "he offred eft his brest / To stroke and coy, and eft his hornes with flowers to be drest." Moving out to sea, Jove is ridden by Europa, and while he is in control of the overall arc of the scene, for the moment he is subordinate, even degraded, the ridden beast. As Ovid comments through Golding, "Betweene the state of Maiestie and love is set such oddes / As that they can not dwell in one."[44]

Yet majesty and love patently *do* coexist in Jove, with love representing subjection to bodily desires and needs, which stands in stark contrast to disembodied, autonomous majesty. So Jove, too, returns Hal to the problem of relationality. Like Jove, the prince is humbled by his "low transformation" and is subject to his desires. Wanting to see Falstaff woo the diseased prostitute Doll, the prince is assisted in his endeavor not by another god, as Jove had been by Mercury, but by the tavern denizen, Poins. Enacting his desires, especially in the company of Poins, the prince is immersed in the reciprocal processes of identity formation. The prince may think he can don and doff a drawer's costume while still protecting his sovereign identity, but *2 Henry IV* suggests that the tavern milieu literally changes him. Dressed as a servant, he risks becoming a servant: Falstaff tells Doll that the prince "would have made a good pantler, a would ha' chipped bread well" (*2H4*, 2.4.193–94). Far from a god shining through his disguise, the prince is here a lowly carver of bread; his elite identity risks collapsing into the status of the servant whose costume he wears.[45] When Hal reveals himself, he specifically redresses the class insult, upbraiding Falstaff for calling him "pantler and bread-chipper and I know not what" (2.4.255–56). For the prince, it is one thing to choose to disguise himself as a drawer and quite another to be associated by others with the habits and inclinations of servitude. In *Henry V*, the king continues to experiment with disguise, donning the cloak of a commoner to hide his identity and to sound out his subjects on the eve of the Battle of Agincourt. The Agincourt scene, however, presents a Henry whose disguise confirms rather than undermines his identity. When he reveals himself to Williams after the battle, the English soldier who had promised to fight Harry *le roi* instead abases himself before his acknowledged king. It is a far cry from the moment of revelation in *2 Henry IV* where Hal, the drawer-*cum*-Prince of Wales, has to fight to establish his credentials in an uncertain skirmish of wit with the unrepentant Falstaff and where Falstaff's first words upon recognizing the prince are "Ha? A bastard son of the king's?" (2.4.231).

Desiring small beer and donning the drawer's garb, the prince inhabits a milieu that increasingly seems capable of transforming him. He craves small beer, which, like the pantler's bread, is a basic staple of the poor. As one pamphleteer put it, "we shall not heare the cry of the poor complaining of want, so long as for a small matter they can send for so much good bread and beere as will suffice their whole families."[46] It is not so surprising that a prince who hankers for small beer should be linked to the servant who looks after bread: both associations raise the question, explicitly posed by Hal himself, of whether his appetite was "princely got." Appetite, desire, and the claims of the material world are precisely what is at stake for Prince Hal. Idealizing himself as an autonomous ruler in *1 Henry IV*, he confronts in *Part 2* the ways in which his environment shapes his base bodily desires.

The prince who emerges as king in *2 Henry IV* has one final chance to imagine himself as the all-powerful Jove. At Henry V's coronation, Falstaff addresses the new monarch as "My king, my Jove, ... my heart" (*2H4*, 5.5.42). For Falstaff, to imagine "King Hal" (5.5.36) as Jove is to imagine him as an autonomous figure, unconstrained by allegiance to anything but his own (and Falstaff's) desires. As Falstaff says when he hears of Hal's accession to the throne, "Let us take any man's horses, the laws of England are at my commandment" (5.3.111– 12). But Falstaff is mistaken. As king, Henry V imagines himself far differently from an autonomous god with the right to do whatever he pleases. Instead, King Henry articulates a modest sense of himself. Having admitted his desire for small beer, he recognizes that networks of external relationships define his identity. These networks are literally embodied in the king in the form of his desires. In this sense, far from undermining him, the new king's taste for small beer strengthens his position, assuring his subjects that he will recognize their claims on him. In other words, Henry recognizes himself not just as king but also as subject.

The king acknowledges his limitations in speeches to two sets of elites. First, he assures his brothers that as an English king he will subordinate his personal impulses to an English system of law and custom: "This is the English, not the Turkish court: / Not Amurath an Amurath succeeds, / But Harry Harry" (*2H4*, 5.2.47–49). Henry then solidifies his guarantee of English civility by submitting himself to the counsel of the lord chief justice, who represents the laws of the land: "My voice shall sound as you do prompt mine ear, / And I will stoop and humble my intents / To your well-practised wise directions" (5.2.118–20). Even the images of the voice sounding and the body stooping indicate a king who recognizes that his own body must encode the social relationships that constrain him. The king who articulates these images of himself acknowledges that he is properly limited by his membership in a community larger than himself.

The acknowledgment of political limitations complements — even perhaps fulfills — the prince's earlier desire for small beer. As king, Henry may end up living sumptuously and performing theatrically (his public rejection of Falstaff is a spectacular kingly *coup de théâtre*). But his desire for small beer suggests that even kingship involves variations on the same subjection that constrains all the admirable men in Shakespeare's history plays. Certainly, in his final speech, the king distances himself from his earlier identity and so might seem to be distancing himself from small beer and the world of subjection and enmeshment that it entails: "Presume not that I am the thing I was, / For God doth know — so shall the world perceive — / That I have turned away my former self" (*2H4*, 5.5.52–54). But once again an assertion of transcendence reveals subjection — the speech to Falstaff is, in effect, his first act of submission to the laws and customs of England that he vowed to respect.

Thus, the rejected "former self" might be less the roguish royal loved by Falstaff and more the naïve prince of *Part 1* who thought to exist independently of those around him. In the end, then, rather than discrediting the king, small beer draws on English history and the life of the tavern to establish him as a complex English sovereign who prefers humble authenticity but manipulates spectacular theatricality and who accepts his subjection to law even though he rules aggressively. The plebeian drink by no means answers all the questions surrounding the enigmatic figure of Prince Hal, but it does complicate the idea that his success depends on repudiating habits and desires deemed socially low. On the contrary, he succeeds by acknowledging, however reluctantly, that low habits and desires are important elements of his identity and that desiring small beer can be a constitutive element of his rule.

Chapter 2

"Wine and sugar of the best and the fairest": Canary, the Canaries, and the Global in Windsor

BARBARA SEBEK

After an unexpected plunge in a body of cold water, the chilled Falstaff downs a quart of sack with a piece of toast, then calls for another "pottle" (two quarts) to be brewed and served straight up, without eggs: he'll have no "pullet-sperms in [his] brewage."[1] Thwarted in his first "voyage" (2.1.160) to the English housewives whom he figures as a "region in Guiana" (1.3.59) and "my East and West Indies" (1.3.61), Falstaff consoles, warms, and restores himself with wine that was produced in the sixteenth and seventeenth centuries in the Spanish-controlled Canaries or in Xeres or Malaga in mainland Spain. Although the trade was officially prohibited when this play was first written, performed, and printed,[2] wines imported from Spain and the Canaries persisted in popularity and, when the trade was once again legal, came to saturate English culinary experiences and literary culture alike. This chapter situates *The Merry Wives of Windsor* in the context of these phenomena and asks questions akin to those posed by Sebastian and Alonso in *The Tempest* when they reunite with their drunken servants: "where had [they] wine? ... where should they find

41

this grand liquor?" (5.1.281–83). Although Falstaff is Shakespeare's most renowned drinker of sack, I discern a larger pattern of references to these wines and their purveyors in Mistress Quickly's language and elsewhere in the play, along with images of nautical conflict and uneasy alliances that were a feature of Anglo-Spanish and other international encounters entailed in the Anglo-Spanish wine trade. In thus discerning pointed, and pointedly anachronistic, references to these sixteenth century wines in the vaguely fifteenth century world of the play, I will globalize or "un-English" *Merry Wives*, thereby suggesting the broader importance of trade history for scholars of food and drink.

Informed by the premise that the local, the domestic, and the everyday are crucially impacted by the global, especially in a port town during a period of commercial expansion, I describe transglobal trade networks that impinge on this most "English" and "domestic" of Shakespeare's comedies. The play conveys a heightened sense of the interrelatedness of sexual and financial desires and anxieties, a characteristic feature of the city comedies of Shakespeare's contemporaries such as Middleton and Jonson. It is my contention here that this heightened sense stems at least in part from the muted but discernible awareness of the risks entailed in transglobal trade—particularly though not only the Anglo-Spanish wine trade—and of the shifting bases of wealth and power ushered in by it. The promises and perils of overseas ventures inform the play's interest in domestic surveillance and regulation, and underlie its depiction of antagonisms of class and nationality in the English town.

Critics frequently remark on the distinctiveness of *Merry Wives* among Shakespeare's dramatic works, noting its interest in the everyday, its atypical topicality or locatedness, as well as its focus on the middling sort and a domestic realm controlled by women. Among Shakespeare's comedies, critics view the play as singular in its "Englishness," however they construe the latter notion.[3] Many feminist critics foreground a feature of the play that once relegated it to the critical margins: its focus on domestic spaces ruled by women.[4] Although many of these critics consider how wider or overlapping spheres and scales of action—neighborhood, nation, and so on—shape how the play interprets the domestic realm,[5] there is nonetheless virtual consensus on its status as "Shakespeare's most domestic play," as Wendy Wall puts it, "thoroughly immersed in the world of pots and pans."[6] I don't dispute that the play offers this emphasis, but a study of the Anglo-Spanish wine trade attends to the material and conceptual interplay between local and global, domestic and foreign. By foregrounding where these wines originate and how they are procured and purveyed, I disrupt a too often assumed binary between native and foreign, and between the local or domestic and the wider world. When critics mention the play's engagement with international or global matters, they usually do so only in passing,[7] often by targeting Falstaff's metaphor for his scheme to profit from the wives: they are "my East and West Indies, and I will trade to them both" (*Wiv.*, 1.3.61–62). Walter Cohen cites the line and comments that Falstaff here imagines his potential profit "figured as the fruits of mercantile imperialism." Ania Loomba also notes this line in passing as part of a discussion of how "the formation of English nationhood is intricately interwoven with that of overseas trade and empire." Jonathan Gil Harris uses this line as the epigraph to his chapter on postcolonial theory. In presenting the wives' successful resistance to Falstaff's figurative conquest, Harris argues, the play offers an "imaginative space in which not only the (metaphorical) conquest of the Indies is doomed to fail but also its inhabitants volubly resist the man who would be their conqueror"—a resistance that is a central theme of postcoloniality.[8] In these instances, critics note the play's attention to English participation in activities and discourses of trade, travel, and conquest but do not analyze it in a sustained way or explore the trajectories of specific imported commodities or the practices of the merchants and factors who procure them. *Culinary Shakespeare* allows us to offer such an analysis, as we consider the status of wine as an imported commodity and the obvious yet pertinent and often overlooked fact that London is a port town, where seafaring and global trade were emphatically local, everyday, and topical matters.[9]

The awareness in Shakespeare's day of how sack and other Spanish wines were complexly implicated in larger networks of trade becomes quite apparent if we consider, as Robert Brenner does, that until 1625 the Spanish trade—in contrast to all of England's other overseas trades—involved widespread participation of unregulated, non-Company traders, the city's domestic tradespeople and ship captains.

These London-based victuallers and retailers, including shopkeepers, vintners, and ordinary mariners, could be at odds with the so-called "mere merchants," the overseas traders who were members of the intermittently operative chartered Spanish Company.[10] In considering the various occupational groups whose livelihoods were crucially affected by the importing of Spanish wines, we need not restrict ourselves to London, nor to its domestic tradesmen. The Berkshire Record Office indexes include a wine tavern license granted to Richard and Joan Washington in Windsor on February 21, 1592/93, a tantalizing glimpse of a husband-wife team that might have earned their keep by capitalizing on the popularity of these contraband wines.[11] Viewed from the perspective of tavern keepers like the Washingtons, imported wines presented a potential means of income, not an abstract threat of foreign contamination.

In London, members of these occupational groups and consumers of the wines they purveyed would be among the play's first viewers. For them, Falstaff's figuration of Mistress Page as "a region in Guiana" and both wives as "my East and West Indies" to whom he will "trade" would trigger awareness of various networks of trade that traversed the Canary Islands and other Spanish dominions. Many European voyagers stopped for provisions in the islands before setting sail for points farther west, and as I have discussed elsewhere, many English merchants and factors traded directly or even lived there for extended periods, making the Atlantic islands their adopted home.[12] In late sixteenth and seventeenth century English literature, sacks and canaries from the archipelago and other Spanish regions often signaled concerns about rival groups *within* English trade and retail organizations; at the same time, these wines raised questions about England's position in an expanding world economy, as well as a variety of responses to England's exclusion from profitable trade in Iberian-owned regions.[13] In reading how *Merry Wives* engages these concerns, my work here complements that of Karen Raber in chapter 4 of this volume, which studies how Shakespeare views imported wines in a range of plays as both an instrument for creating national wealth and a signal of England's dangerous foreign entanglements, both an impetus for overseas ventures and a potential agent of contamination of national identity. Departing from Raber's emphasis on the sense of threat, however,

I argue for the interpenetration of native and foreign, as sack is thoroughly integrated in the world of Shakespeare's Windsor even as its Spanish origins are jestingly invoked and riffed on.[14] Dynamics of class, nationality, and gender in the play further disrupt the binary between domestic and foreign.

Trade between Castile and England was already well established by the thirteenth century, with both Castilian and English ships bringing southern foods, including wine, into Bristol. Even the active trade in wine from Gascony, the region in modern southwestern France centered on Bordeaux, crucially involved Spanish shippers who carried most of the wine that came into England. As William D. Phillips Jr. points out, Gascon wine constituted "a large proportion of the ordinary table wine for English tables. But that wine was not carried in English ships. Instead Gascon and Spanish shippers shared the trade, with the Spaniards carrying the bulk of the wine."[15] While French wines continued to dominate the wine trade overall in the early modern period, Spanish wine and oil became staple imports of the flourishing Anglo-Spanish commerce starting in the early sixteenth century, and wine was always the most vital component of that commerce. Describing the whole range of imports and exports between England and Spain, Pauline Croft notes, "wine was extensively purchased, above all sack," which was often the single most popular item. After the vintage—the time of the harvest when growers gathered grapes and undertook other preliminary processes of wine-making—"ships carrying nothing but tuns of sack were unloaded in London and Bristol."[16] As Croft details, and as L. Alberti and A. B. Wallis Chapman discuss in their introduction to printed excerpts from the archive of the Inquisition in the Canaries, English trade in the mid-sixteenth century to Spain, Portugal, and the Atlantic islands under Spanish and Portuguese dominion proved an increasingly valuable alternative to the faltering markets of the Low Countries.[17]

When Elizabeth's difficulties with the Habsburgs led to embargos in the 1560s, trade nonetheless continued, with English ships carrying English goods and selling them off in Spanish ports, a practice to which local officials turned a blind eye. When the embargo was lifted in 1573, Anglo-Iberian trade witnessed a decade of great prosperity. After Philip closed Spanish ports to English merchants again in May 1585, the pattern of 1569–73 soon repeated. "Even as hostilities between England and Spain escalated, trade began tentatively to resume," Croft points out, and "undercover voyages soon began."[18] Because illicit commerce persisted during the war years, the open trade returned rapidly with the Treaty of London in 1604, so that from a longer perspective, the war years were merely a temporary halt in a vigorous, long-established trade: "The embargo of May 1585 temporarily silenced the voice of the merchant community, but the network of illicit trade which operated during the war years kept alive the contacts and expertise that allowed the rapid re-opening of the trade in 1604."[19]

On mainland Spain and in the Canaries during the war years, English traders resorted to feigning nationalities other than their own, especially Irish or Scottish, in order to circumvent official crown prohibitions. Such practices are amply evidenced throughout the period 1585–1604 in the Canary Islands, where English merchants and factors faced not only the prohibition from Seville but also the challenges of inquisitorial informers and interrogators in the islands, and prolonged prison sentences even when ultimately cleared of charges of heresy.[20] Delicately juggling competing central directives and local authorities, English traders maintained an active presence in the Canaries from the early sixteenth century until Cromwell's war with Spain sent them home at last in the 1650s. If the English factor Thomas Nichols is correct, the English might have even settled in the islands earlier after assisting the Spanish conquest of them in the late fifteenth century,[21] an established community that further complicates a simple notion of the Spanish as "the enemy" and disrupts a simple binary between English and non-English. From the perspective of these English wine merchants in Tenerife and other Canarian locales, and even others involved in the trade back in England, aggressive English policies against Spain—including Sir Francis Drake's plunder of Spanish shipping in general and his unsuccessful raids on the Canaries in the 1580s and 1595 in particular—were disastrous in their disruption of the regular trade. We thus could consider their more aggressively anti-Spanish compatriots as the greater enemy of English merchants than the Spanish.[22] *The Merry Wives of Windsor*—with its images of nautical conflict and its depiction of various antagonisms among the residents of Windsor, signaled and effected by the consumption of Spanish wine—registers these intersecting international and intra-English conflicts.

Officially banned, entailing considerable risks, but steady and even flourishing, the Anglo-Spanish trade to the Atlantic islands and peninsular Spain during the time that *Merry Wives* was produced and first printed ensured that the increasingly popular and profitable sacks and canaries continued to be carried into English ports and towns. The illicit trickle became a full-on flow once the official ban on Anglo-Spanish trade was lifted in 1604. Spain's willingness to consider a pact was in part a consequence of a sense of its own weakness after the raid of Cadiz in 1596 and the Dutch raid and occupation of Gran Canaria (one of the seven isles comprising the Canaries) in 1599.[23] Brokered and ratified at Somerset House in August 1604, the Treaty of London ushered in fundamental changes in the organization of and participation in the trade. Shortly after the ratification of the treaty, the Spanish Company charter was renewed.[24] The renewal of the charter was met with an immediate outcry from non-Company retailers, artisans, shopkeepers, sea captains, and ordinary mariners who wanted a continued role in the lucrative trade. Despite the resistance of the London-based retailers, a new charter restricting anyone other than Company members was issued in 1605, only to be suspended by parliament the next year. As Brenner notes, this suspension of the new charter meant that "literally hundreds of non-Company, non-merchant traders invaded Spanish commerce."[25] With the "invasion" of this broader group of purveyors of Spanish imports, sacks came to be an even more familiar offering in English taverns and households.

Attesting to this familiarity, Gervase Markham in his chapter on wines in *The English Housewife* (1615) asserts, "your best sacks are of Seres in Spain" and "your strong sacks are of the islands of the Canaries and of Malago."[26] Markham's familiarity with the distinctions between different sacks and his laudatory view of Canary sack—as well as the impression he offers of widespread English consumption of these wines in a text that is otherwise notable for its preference for local foods—is likewise conveyed in a 1634 letter in which the epistolarian, traveler, and trader James Howell describes the wines imported from Grand Canary as the "richest," "most firm," "best bodied," "lastingest," and the "most desiccated from all earthly grossness of any other whatsoever." Sounding rather like the Falstaff of *2 Henry IV*, who characterizes sack as the source of all warmth, wit, and valor (*2H4*, 4.2.79–111), Howell claims, "this is the wine that digests, and doth not only breed good blood, but it nutrifieth also," as opposed to French wines which merely "pickle meat in the stomach." Howell describes the English rage for sack amusingly, saying that this wine more than any other

> verifie[s] that merry induction, that good wine makes good blood, good blood causeth good humours, good humours cause good thoughts, good thoughts bring forth good works, good works carry a man to heaven; ergo, good wine carrieth a man to heaven. If this be true, surely more English go to heaven this way than any other, for I think there is more canary brought into England than to all the world besides.... When sacks and canaries were brought in first among us they were used to be drunk in aqua-vitae measures... but now they go down every one's throat, both young and old, like milk.[27]

Here Howell, as is usual throughout this period, uses "sacks" and "canaries" together to refer to this category of superior wines, jestingly invoking both contentious reformation debates about the path to salvation and the guzzling propensities of his compatriots.[28]

Hyperbolic as they might seem, Howell's vivid claims are corroborated by figures for customs charged at London's ports: 284,382 gallons of Canary wine were taxed in 1606, just two years after the embargo was lifted, and 744,282 gallons in 1633, the year before Howell's letter.[29] Domestic advice addressed to English housewives and custom figures alike reveal that the body and tavern receipts of Falstaff are not the only things that are replete with a great deal of sack. Acquainted as we Shakespeareans are with the Falstaff of the Henriad—"sack-and-sugar Jack" (*1H4*, 1.2.100), the "globe of sinful continents" (*2H4*, 2.4.258) who consumes this "intolerable deal of sack" (*1H4*, 2.5.243)—it is perhaps too easy to overlook the presence of sacks and canaries in *Merry Wives*, not to mention England's collective intake of these wines in Shakespeare's period and the larger trade networks of which sack was merely a part. In chapter 6 of this volume, Rebecca Lemon reads sack in the two Henry IV plays, discerning a movement from the carnivalesque festivity of the tavern subculture to Falstaff's degenerate status as a lone drinker. Lemon argues that the "lexicon of conviviality" comes to signal disease and destructive, rebellious forces, as sack drinking ultimately "drains rather than sustains" the tavern community. Because of the ways that *The Merry Wives of Windsor* invokes multilateral, global, commercial engagements—as well as a range of intra-English tensions—this "English" comedy instead allows for a view of sack that departs from the pattern that Lemon discerns in the history plays.

To complicate a sense of bilateral Anglo-Spanish trade arrangements and to contextualize the frequently uttered "sack and sugar" and "wine and sugar" epithets (including Mistress Quickly's phrase in the title of this essay), I would like to offer one more brief foray to the Canaries and the wider world before turning to the play-text. Before the Spanish introduced viticulture to the Canaries in the sixteenth century, they brought sugarcane production as part of the process of colonizing the islands.[30] The primary crop and export of the archipelago, Canarian sugar began to arrive "in quantity" in northern Europe, including Bristol, by midcentury. The flourishing of sugar production on the islands is signaled by how, at some points, sugar was so plentiful in the islands and specie in such short supply that sugar, or "white gold," was used as a medium of exchange.[31] In elucidating the great changes in the world of food of early modern England, Joan Thirsk notes that "very large quantities" of sugar were increasingly imported into London, and that even occasional visitors to London started buying more sugar than ever before.[32] Once transatlantic sugar production and shipping undermined the Canaries' sugar economy, which fell to competition from Brazil and the West Indies, grapes became the sole crop and wine the sole export. At first the export markets for Canary wines were several, but by the early seventeenth century they had narrowed to one market exclusively: England. Even then, Canary wines were part of sprawling transatlantic and Mediterranean systems of exchange, often accompanied by sugar from the West Indies. Spanning several continents and the Atlantic and Mediterranean worlds, the enterprises of later seventeenth century Portuguese trader Diogo Fernandes Branco exemplify the global exchange networks in which

wine and sugar imports were implicated. Branco exported Canary and
Madeira wine to Angola in exchange for slaves that he sold in Brazil
for tobacco and sugar. Many Madeiran women made conserves out
of the Brazilian sugar that were then shipped to northern European
ports, including Hamburg, Bordeaux, and London, and that ultimately
appeared on English dining tables. Thus, social and economic developments on the islands were directly related to the demands of the
European Atlantic world, a system of exchange that reflected a network of intertwined bourgeois and aristocratic interests in all locales
bound up in this economy.[33] Though they postdate our play, I describe
the business interests of Branco because they illustrate compellingly
how English households were increasingly and complexly implicated
in global trade systems.[34]

So too are the households and the financial, social, and sexual transactions of our Windsor. When Falstaff initiates his plan to "trade to
them both," the letter of entrée that he writes to the wives emphasizes sack: "you love sack, and so do I. Would you desire better sympathy?" (*Wiv.*, 2.1.8). Mistress Quickly promises Rugby a treat of an
evening "posset" (1.4.7–8)—warm milk curdled with ale or sack—if
he performs the task with which she has charged him: watching for
her master Doctor Caius so that he does not discover that she has
invited his rival suitor's servant into his house. At play's end, after
Herne-scam, Mr. Page offers the same treat to the chastened Falstaff,
inviting him to his house to share a laugh at Mistress Page (5.5.158).
Mr. Ford uses sack to initiate his Brooke plot, offering a "pottle of
burnt sack" (2.1.187) to the Host if he allows him access to Falstaff and
holds up his guise as Brooke.[35] Ultimately, Ford thinks this guise will
allow him to oversee and punish what Page calls Falstaff's "voyage" to
his wife (2.1.160–61). Sack continues to be used to grease the wheels
of Brooke-scam when Bardolph announces the arrival of "Brooke" to
Falstaff with "a morning's draught of sack" (2.2.132). The Host of the
Garter Inn calls for sack to convince Welsh Evans and French Caius
to sheathe their swords, so that in a twist on traditions of conviviality
and hospitality, this import commodity—produced in the dominions
of England's "official" enemy, carried by merchants who ran the risk
of extended imprisonment or worse while overseas, and who came to
be at odds with non-Company retailers back in England—is to serve
as the palliative of the antagonisms between the foreign would-be

duelers. The Host enjoins, "Your hearts are mighty, your skins are whole, and let burnt sack be the issue" (3.1.91–92). In this play, gestures toward conviviality and pacifism verge on their opposite—verbal violence and physical threats—evoking the dangers of the actual Canary trade in the minds of voyage financiers, whether of middling or aristocratic status, and in the minds of those who returned from voyages as factors or sailors on their ships.

In the scene immediately following his gesture of cross-national peacekeeping after the nonduel in act 3, scene 1, the Host ignores the invitation that Mr. Ford extends to the group of men to enjoy "good cheer at home" (3.2.43–44), opting instead to go to the "honest knight Falstaff, and drink canary with him" (3.2.73–74) at the Garter Inn.[36] Thus, Spanish wines play a variety of roles in forming and negotiating various antagonisms or alliances of class, rank, wealth, gender, and nationality. In the case of the episode with which I began this essay—and consistent with what scholars have recently noted in dietary writing and culinary practices—sack plays a medicinal role: Falstaff repeatedly calls for it to warm him after being dunked in the Thames, illustrating the notion that wine is a heating agent and thus can adjust humoral imbalance: "Come, let me pour in some sack to the Thames' water, for my belly's as cold as if I had swallowed snowballs for pills to cool the reins" (3.5.17–19). We find ample evidence of this medicinal use of sack in recipe books that include such concoctions. For example, Mrs. Corlyon's receipt book calls for "a quart of Sacke" to be boiled with pennyroyal and other herbs. The steam from this concoction, "as hot as you can suffer it," taken into the ears twice a day, was to cure singing in the ears.[37] Put to a wide range of uses in the period and in this play—medium of exchange, strategy of seduction, means of entrée, mechanism of reconciliation, medicinal aid—sack crops up repeatedly and shows the seepage of the wider world into homely Windsor. Mr. Ford's throwaway remark that Falstaff cannot hide in his "pepperbox" (3.5.126) after he discovers that Falstaff had infiltrated his household and plans to do so again suggests the casual familiarity of the presence of luxury imports in the Windsor household. Although Mistress Page claims that the communally orchestrated Herne-the-hunter ruse will "mock [Falstaff] home to Windsor" (4.4.63), literally and imaginatively Windsor is always already infused with the wider world.

Just as the would-be "trader" to the wives assumes that the shared love of sack will woo them, Mistress Quickly creates a wine-laced scenario in which Falstaff surpasses the lavish but unsuccessful efforts of previous courtly wooers to seduce Mistress Ford. Conveying the first message from the counterplotting, revenge-seeking wives after they have received Falstaff's letters, Mistress Quickly arrives at the Garter Inn to initiate the ruse that Mistress Ford has succumbed to Falstaff's charms:

> You have brought her into such a canaries as 'tis wonderful. The best courtier of them all, when the court lay at Windsor, could never have brought her to such a canary. Yet there has been knights, and lords, and gentlemen, with their coaches; I warrant you, coach after coach, letter after letter, gift after gift, smelling so sweetly, all musk; and so rustling, I warrant you, in silk and gold, and in such aligant terms, and in such wine and sugar of the best and the fairest, that would have won any woman's heart; and, I warrant you, they could never get an eye-wink of her....And, I warrant you, they could never get her so much as sip on a cup with the proudest of them all. (*Wiv.*, 2.2.57–70)

Usually glossed as a blunder for "quandaries" and "quandary" (Norton, Folger, Pelican), meant to indicate Mistress Ford's state of "extremes" (Arden) or "excitement" (Bevington, Riverside),[38] Mistress Quickly's "canaries" and "canary" work together to suggest the intoxication of the Spanish wine, the energy of the lively dance, and the continual seepage of the wider world into the homely life of Windsor. In addition to upholding the bourgeois wife's imperviousness to courtly assays—illustrating the tensions in the play between town and court, bourgeois and aristocrat[39]—Mistress Quickly unwittingly calls up the very commodities—"wine and sugar of the best and the fairest"—for which the actual Canaries were widely known and whose circulation constituted the source of English mercantile treasure or ruin, not to mention the potential profit of many a tavern host or Company merchant who competed over access to the trade—a trade that was itself characterized by a blurring of the lines between legitimate trade and "piracy."[40] Patricia Parker's discussion of how the verbal texture of *Merry Wives* yokes transport and theft, and her explication of the mercantile puns at work in Falstaff's address of Mistress Quickly as "she-Mercury" (2.2.73), extends this line of thought.[41] What Quickly describes as the previous courtiers' "aligant terms" contrast what I see as Falstaff's rugged, simpler, and quite inept appeal to the shared taste for sack in his letters: "you love sack and so do I. Would you desire better sympathy?" Usually glossed as a blunder for "elegant" or "eloquent" (or a conflation of them), Mistress Quickly's use of "aligant" more aptly evokes alicant, a Spanish white wine, as editors Melchiori (Arden) and McDonald (Pelican) note. In fact, in the 1634 letter cited above, James Howell uses the very spelling that Quickly's speech does ("Aligant") in a list of Spanish wines that English merchants import,[42] indicating that there is a cheeky and perhaps scandalously pointed set of Spanish wine references at work in the Quickly passage.[43]

In addition to its wine-saturated verbal play, the fun of this passage lies in Quickly's ability to flatter gullible Falstaff into thinking that he outstrips courtly rivals, even as the play so insistently presents him as a desperate figure who embodies the Stonean "crisis of the aristocracy," pilfering deer from Shallow's estate and breaking into his keeper's lodge (*Wiv.*, 1.1.93–97), hiring out Bardolph to the Host to defray expenses (1.3.3–11), and later "hiding [his] honour in [his] necessity" and being forced "to shuffle, to hedge, and to lurch" (2.2.22–23), primarily by preying so ineffectually on Windsor wives. As already noted, he figures this scheme as trading to a "region in Guiana" and "my East and West Indies" (1.3.59–62). In this way, and as Mary Ellen Lamb convincingly shows, Falstaff becomes a "walking social contradiction"[44]—both a schemer of the sort associated with the London criminal underworld and a venturer who grandiosely imagines his exploits in global terms.

The transglobal resonances of the scene in which Quickly delivers her "canaries" speech continue as Pistol utters an aggressive verse aside, delivered immediately after she exits: "This punk is one of Cupid's carriers. / Clap on more sails! Pursue! Up with your fights! / Give fire! She is my prize, or ocean whelm them all!" (2.2.122–24).[45] At first glance, Pistol's references to ships' fighting screens, naval battle cries, and shipwreck seem odd or disjointed, but in fact they are part of a persistent pattern of association between sexual and nautical activities, and they accord perfectly with the Canarian echoes in Quickly's "wine and sugar" speech.[46] The wives themselves offer a comparable jest on ships and naval conflict when they liken receiving Falstaff's letter to being "boarded" by him:

> MISTRESS PAGE. I'll entertain myself like one that I am not acquainted withal; for, sure, unless he know some strain in me that I know not myself, he would never have boarded me in this fury.
> MISTRESS FORD. "Boarding" call you it? I'll be sure to keep him above deck.
> MISTRESS PAGE. So will I. If he come under my hatches, I'll never to sea again.   (2.1.75–82)

The wives figure themselves as seafaring vessels, not as traded goods, nor as the rich trade destinations to which Falstaff had likened them ("my East and West Indies"). The wives wrestle with this imagery that analogizes rich foreign territory and the female body when they playfully figure themselves as ships. In so doing, they, like Mistress Quickly in the passage above, position themselves as resistant transactors. The wives wittily grant themselves active roles in determining their worth, even as they accept chastity as the primary guarantor of it. Interestingly, for Mistress Page, the mere fact that Falstaff sent the letter to her indicates that he has already "boarded" her in a "fury."

Natasha Korda offers fruitful analysis of the self-alienation and internalized surveillance at work in Mistress Page's concern that she is not entirely visible to herself—a set of concerns that Korda ties to a repeated trope of wifely vigilance in overseeing the household. In my reading, the "chastity panic" at issue here is both registered and jestingly dispelled by the nautical and piracy imagery—similar to the multiple functions of Spanish wines at other points in the play.[47] Questions of financial solvency and of property in the self and in the wife conjoin markedly when overseas ventures are in view. Given the promises of those ventures to generate actual wealth for individual traders and victuallers, both abroad and at home, Falstaff is mocked as not only an ineffectual "trader," but as a sedentary one—his transglobal venturing is figurative only. The sack that he sees as central to his (failed) scheme was carried in by actual traders and financiers. Even as the residents of Shakespeare's Windsor thoroughly shame Falstaff for presuming that he has access to the wives—a presumption based in part on the shared love of sack—sack drinking functions to ease intra-English antagonisms: husbands versus wives, middling citizens' wives versus predatory courtiers and knights, overseas merchants versus local victuallers, and so on. These antagonisms comprise an English locality that has already begun to assimilate the wider world.

Many critics of *Merry Wives* have queried the degree to which the town and citizens of Windsor maintain independence from or defer to upper-class, external institutions and forms of power and have analyzed how these dynamics of rank, location, and class are inflected by ideologies of gender. Studying wines procured through long-distance trade further complicates the play's engagement with these cultural preoccupations. At the opening of the play, Justice Shallow, fed up with the predations of Falstaff, threatens to appeal to the Star Chamber: "Sir Hugh, persuade me not. I will make a Star Chamber matter of it" (*Wiv.*, 1.1.1–2). Just as Mistress Page's threat to "exhibit a bill in the Parliament" (2.1.25) in response to Falstaff's initial letter never materializes—thanks to the Windsor community's use of Spanish wine-saturated plots and ruses—Shallow's threats are dodged. When Anne Page appears on stage with wine to offer the quarreling group, Page enjoins, "Nay, daughter, carry the wine in; we'll drink within" (1.1.157), extending the invitation to include dinner: "Wife, bid these gentlemen welcome. Come, we have a hot venison pasty to dinner. Come, gentlemen, I hope we shall drink down all unkindness" (1.1.162–64). As occurs often in the play and in early modern culture, conviviality and hospitality serve to dispel conflict, if only temporarily. Interestingly, the easing of conflict in this episode consists of pairing a decidedly local foodstuff (venison) and an imported beverage, suggesting how the play helps to enact a vision of the culinary that moves easily across the divide between local and global.

We have viewed *The Merry Wives of Windsor* and English wine consumption through the lens of various multilateral trade networks and intra-English antagonisms entailed in the Spanish wine trade. Doing so has complicated seemingly straightforward oppositions between local and global, native and foreign, and has attuned us to Mistress Quickly's "aligant terms," which register the complex interpenetration of these categories. The local and the global meet in Page's dinner, shattering a stable binary between English and foreign and inviting scrutiny of the category of "Englishness" itself. Page's dinner, like other depictions of sack-drinking in this play and in Shakespeare's culture, provides at least a temporary resolution of conflict, an opening into an "English" hospitality that is, in fact, a global one, predicated upon taking in not just strangers but also foreign comestibles, even in English inns, homes, cellars, mouths, and bellies.

Chapter 3

So Many Strange Dishes:
Food, Love, and Politics in *Much Ado about Nothing*

PETER KANELOS

There is a dish prepared in Sicily by the name of *cicirelli all'arancia*, small fish simmered with oranges. Oranges, not native to the island, were believed to have been brought to Sicily by the Spaniards, whose cuisine since the Middle Ages utilized citrus to flavor such delicacies as *pez espada a la naranja* (swordfish with orange sauce).[1] And it is in this spirit that Shakespeare colors, so to speak, the Messina of *Much Ado about Nothing*, which chronicles, albeit obliquely, the arrival in Sicily of Spanish rule.[2] Shakespeare's Don Pedro, the presiding authority in the world of this play, is a recasting of the historic Piero of Aragon, who in 1282, as Shakespeare read in Novella 22 of *La prima parte de le novelle de Bandello* (1554), seized the opportunity to take control of the island after the native population rose against their Angevin overlords: "King Piero of Arragon hearing of this came quickly thither with his army, and made himself lord of the Island."[3] As the Spanish established their authority, they brought with them, for Shakespeare's purposes, similes ready-made.

Much Ado about Nothing, like all of Shakespeare's comedies, is a prism through which the phenomenon of love is examined. With perfect pitch, Beatrice quips that Claudio, sulking because he believes that Don Pedro has filched his beloved, Hero, is "a civil count—civil

57

as an orange."[4] Her jibe depends upon her audience (both on stage and off) hearing the pun on "Seville orange," Seville being the Spanish city renowned for its bitter oranges, *bigerades*.[5] Claudio is bitter, like a Seville orange, but also made bitter by one who has come, like oranges, from Spain. It is also possible that underpinning Beatrice's remark is an even subtler critique, that the "civil count" is one of them, a "Seville" count, an ally of the new civil order, and, perhaps, like the Aragonese *arrivistes*, arrived to stake his own claim in Messina. With great economy, Shakespeare creates atmosphere and provides commentary by importing the oranges of Spain to Messina. Yet we might be inclined to leave this bit of wordplay behind were it not for a second appearance of "orange," this time at one of *Much Ado's* emotional cruxes. Claudio, convinced once again that his love has been undermined, this time by his beloved, throws her back to her father before the wedding altar: "Give not this rotten orange to your friend" (4.1.27). Shakespeare mentions oranges on only two other occasions in his dramatic works, and each time in a rather occluded manner.[6] The second appearance of the word in this play is, therefore, conspicuous and invites attention. The journey from bitter orange to rotten orange, I would like to suggest, provides poles between which the perils of love might be charted. Moreover, it opens into a greater discourse on food, love, and politics that runs throughout *Much Ado about Nothing*.

It cannot be without irony that in a play entitled *Much Ado about Nothing* abundance is so strikingly evident. The feast is seemingly perpetual: "I will not fail him at supper; for indeed he hath made great preparation" (1.1.208–09); "I know we shall have reveling tonight" (248); "I came yonder from a great supper" (1.3.32); "Let us to the great supper" (63); "Come, let us to the banquet" (2.1.134); "Dinner is ready" (2.3.170); "Against my will I am sent to bid you come in to dinner" (2.3.199), and so forth. Shakespeare takes his cue from Bandello: "While [Piero] was holding Court most royally there...all was joy because of his victory, joustings and balls being held daily."[7] A celebratory feast is generally the endpoint of Shakespeare's festive comedies. In *Much Ado*, however, we find consumption conspicuously ever-present; it is as if we have found the Land of Cockaigne, or Cocagna, as the Sicilians would have it, where the banquet is unending. And this, it seems, may be the problem. The early modern conception of Sicily was of an island of plenty, likely inspired by its position at the crossroads of commerce and by its reputation as the breadbasket of the Mediterranean.[8] Yet plenty can be attended by peril. The island's most famous monarch, Frederick II (son of King Piero), a renowned hunter and gastronome, although admired greatly by the Florentine, was placed by Dante in the sixth circle of hell for his overindulgence in pleasure and feasting.[9] In a similar vein, *Much Ado about Nothing* presents a Messina of sumptuous balls, perfumers and perfumed gloves, exquisite gowns; it is a play that both represents what is luxurious and queries its worth.

By interlacing the language of courtship and romance with metaphors tied to consumption and, specifically, eating, Shakespeare exposes a sort of chthonic selfishness that underlies human relationships, confusing, distorting, and impeding the course of love. Feasting is pervasive in *Much Ado*, but it fails to generate the "festive" spirit associated with Shakespeare's comedies of this period. C. L. Barber only glancingly includes *Much Ado* in his discussion of Shakespeare's festive comedies. What Barber seems to intuit is that the festive environment is present in Messina, but not the pattern that is found in the festive comedies. In comedies such as *A Midsummer Night's Dream, As You Like It,* and *Twelfth Night,* a swerving from routine and hierarchy provides the occasion for saturnalian release, mirroring English social custom: "'Merry England,'" Barber writes, "was merry chiefly by virtue of its community observances of periodic sports and feast days."[10] The abuse represented in the main plot of *Much Ado* undermines the celebratory moments of the play; it disrupts, most brazenly, the central festive event — the marriage of Hero and Claudio. "In the Claudio-Hero business in *Much Ado*," Barber contends, "the borrowed plot involved negative behavior on the basis of romantic absolutes which was not changed to carry the festive feeling."[11] Beatrice and Benedick, who seem to be playing out the flyting motif, find in their sportive roles not liberty but constraint; they are released, achieving clarification, as Barber would put it, not through their "merry war" but in the crucible of a painful epiphany generated by Claudio's mistreatment of Hero. Moreover, the festivities in Messina are not organic — they do not represent the periodic sports and feast days that Barber identifies as constitutive of local culture and identity but, rather, are imposed by the presence of a foreign sovereign, one who has come to secure

Sicily as his own: "There is a provincial overtone in the strain felt by Leonato on receiving Don Pedro and his party," notes Sheldon Zitner, "The formality is excessive and observed to be so. Leonato is unused to such exalted guests or to such entertaining. Public rooms, evidently not often open, must be perfumed by specially hired staff; for music Leonato must depend on the Prince's man Balthasar. This is hardly the upscale Messina of banquets."[12] The feasting in *Much Ado* is imposed upon the participants, who are compelled to play roles that generate more discomfort than pleasure. Beatrice's ginger rejection of Don Pedro at the masked ball reveals her pragmatic sensibility: to his offer to take him as husband, she replies, "No, my lord, unless I might have another for working days: your Grace is too costly to wear every day" (2.1.255–56). This formal-dress version of life is not sustainable, and in Beatrice's cautious warding off of a "lord," who had earlier identified himself as Jove visiting the humble cottage of Baucis and Philemon, we sense the precarious position in which mortals find themselves when hosting the gods, and, more urgently, the danger that attends upon those who attract the amorous glances of the high-born.

There is something foreboding about the celebrations in *Much Ado;* we might turn to another midcentury critic to sort out why. In "The Argument of Comedy," Northrop Frye contends that comedy works toward social reconciliation: "In the last scene, when the dramatist usually tries to get all his characters on stage at once, the audience witnesses a renewed sense of social integration. In comedy as in life the regular expression of this is a festival, whether a marriage, dance, or a feast."[13] Yet by the time we reach the finale of *Much Ado about Nothing,* we have already been through a marriage, a dance, and several feasts—each of which, counter to the customary comic pattern, has led us further from resolution and toward greater confusion and disorder. The presence of a melancholic malcontent throughout the play, who wants to disrupt the feast because he is not inclined to participate, explains part of the problem. Melancholiacs, like Don John, are, according to Galen, "covetous, self-lovers, cowards...fearful, careful, solitary...stubborn, ambitious, envious"; it is in their interest to refrain from excessive eating and drinking because of their faulty digestion.[14] Don John, who will only eat when he "has stomach," declares that Claudio's interest in Hero will "prove food for [his] displeasure" (*Ado*, 1.3.11, 48). But it has always been clear that the blame for the play's near tragic turn lies well beyond Don John and that he is simply a catalyst for events beyond his immediate control (Shakespeare even divests Don John of what motivated him in the sources he used for the play—jealousy over the impending marriage; thus, the "villain" appears less dimensional than the other characters and more bound to his humoral temperament). Shakespeare uses Don John's misguided appetite as a glass through which one might scrutinize the appetites of men in general and thereby examine the effect of the appetitive male on the prospect and progress of romantic relationships.[15]

Eating lies at the conjunction of desire and necessity, which is why oranges, as we will see, provide the perfect metonym for the romantic relationships in *Much Ado*. Food is never a neutral matter. As Joan Fitzpatrick writes in her study, *Food in Shakespeare*, "Early modern dietaries make clear the view that food and drink are not mere necessities but also indices of one's position in relation to complex ideas about rank, nationality, and spiritual well-being; careful consumption might correct moral as well as physical shortcomings."[16] The latter part of this claim—that moderating diet might improve immoderate behavior—is comically applicable to Don John. But Shakespeare leaves behind the rather flat assumption that eating well leads to living well to explore something much more complex: the question of how and why human desires often contravene human necessities. Toward this end, food and consumption are released by Shakespeare from their narrow humoral commerce, and beliefs about, associations with, and assumptions concerning food and eating are employed in a web of metaphorical and symbolic affiliations.

The early modern English believed that certain foods were salutary, others harmful. Fitzpatrick writes, "Some odd beliefs emerge, in particular that vegetables and especially fruit should be treated with caution (regarded as an indulgence as it were) and that animal flesh (they tend to use the term 'meat' to signify food in general) was especially good for the body."[17] But what was good for the body was not necessarily salutary for the mind; thus, Sir Andrew Aguecheek in *Twelfth Night* complains, "I am a great eater of beef, and I believe that does harm to my wit."[18] As might be expected, assumptions about food were informed by other prejudices. Citrus in particular was suspect;

because the vast majority of citrus was imported, it was not considered "English." And because fruits such as oranges and lemons were imported from Mediterranean climes, the characteristics that were attributed to Mediterranean peoples were obtained in their foodstuffs as well. Thus, oranges were associated with intemperance and volatility.

Yet oranges were also considered desirable luxury items, in spite of (and perhaps also because of) their correlation with the exotic and passionate. As early as 1568, 40,000 oranges were recorded as arriving in London from Spain on a single ship.[19] As luxury items, they began to be cultivated, like other temperamental fruits, by the aristocracy: "A chronology of the court's preferences would show that around 1600 infinite care was taken to protect exotic fruit trees in winter using glass screens, coverts, and heated walls. In fact, the fruit-growing ambitions of the wealthy knew no bounds at this time."[20] The vogue for orangeries began in the late sixteenth century. The first known orangery in England was built around 1580 by Sir Francis Carew at his estate in Surrey, and by 1587, as William Harrison notes in his *Description of England*, the wealthy were cultivating a wide variety of nonnative species: "So haue we no lesse store of strange fruit, as abricotes, almonds, peaches, figges, cornetrees in noble mens orchards. I haue seene capers, orenges, and lemmons, and heard of wild oliues growing here, beside other strange trees, brought from far, whose names I know not."[21] By 1631, Gervase Markham would recommend sheltering vulnerable fruit trees — "Orange, Lemon, Pomegranate, Cynamon, Olive, Almond" — in "some low vaulted gallerie adjoining upon the Garden."[22] As the term "orangery" suggests, it was oranges in particular that commanded the attention and dedication of aristocrats. Oranges were the most fashionable of exotic fruits; the capacity to cultivate them was, therefore, a marker of status.

The capacity to cultivate oranges could also have political implications. "When James I and his queen," writes the agricultural historian Joan Thirsk, "celebrated the making of peace between England and Spain at a banquet in Whitehall in 1604, James handed to his principal guest, the Constable of Castile, a melon and six oranges still hanging on a green branch. These were the fruit of Spain, he said, now transplanted into England."[23] The "fruit of Spain" was almost certainly grown on Sir Francis Carew's estate, and his opportunity to provide it, fresh on the branch, for this occasion, he hoped, would enhance his status at court (earlier, when Elizabeth had paid a visit to his estate at Beddington, Carew had managed, by carefully delaying their ripening, to provide for the queen fresh cherries on her arrival). The treaty being celebrated by James was drawing to a close the 19-year Anglo-Spanish War, the most salient episode of which was the attempted invasion of England by the Spanish Armada in 1588. The Spanish had failed in their bid to possess England. Spanish fruit, James was making manifestly clear, was now grown on English soil on English terms.

The range available to Shakespeare and his audience of possible associations with oranges included, but was not limited to, that which was Spanish, fashionable, exotic, passionate, rare, desirable, delicate, and deceitful. These affiliations would all be linked to one another within *Much Ado*, directly or indirectly, in a network of significations. All of these associations are present in the play and amplify one another through their proximity and interchange. Yet there were further, unsettling connotations that ran side-by-side those that led an ambitious aristocrat like Carew to cultivate oranges at great expense and present them to his monarch. Oranges represented the darker side of intemperance and desire as well: as the Arden Shakespeare volume asserts, "Oranges were associated with prostitutes (perhaps because pocked skin was an effect of venereal disease); they are also a symbol of deception, as one cannot tell from their covering what taste lies within."[24] Thus, what was on the one hand fashionable, a luxury item enjoyed by the discerning few, was, on the other hand, an object associated with what was base, diseased, and shared in common. Historically, this correlation holds as well: the connection between orange-sellers and prostitutes was so firmly established in later centuries that Claudio's "this rotten orange" reference "was considered unsavory enough to be bowdlerized from most productions from Garrick (1748) to the first decade of the twentieth century, replaced by 'blemished Brilliant.'"[25] Mary Meggs earned the nickname "Orange Moll" when she was licensed to "vend, utter and sell oranges, lemons, fruit, sweetmeats and all manner of fruiterers and confectioners wares" within the theater; among her "orange-girls," who would offer their wares, both licit and illicit, to playgoers, was the young Nell Gwyn.[26] The remarkable rapidity of the "fall" of the orange, as it declined from the aristocratic orangery to the dissolute "Orange Moll," is charted in *Much Ado*. But what the play is most interested in is the uncomfortable overlap between the two. By interrogating the ways that men, under the guise of love and honor, transform an unequivocally virtuous woman from object of desire to object of derision, *Much Ado about Nothing* opens up a larger discourse on the relationship between desire and the effects of desire, between what is salutary and what is harmful, that manifests itself within the play in a variety of ways: in the customs of marriage, in Spanish authorities converging on Sicily, in frayed bonds of brotherhood and friendship, and beyond. In the end, we are compelled to admit that Leonato's offering of Hero to Claudio, Carew's offering of his oranges to his sovereign, and Orange Moll's offer of her wares to all takers have quite a bit in common.

"I pray you, how many hath he killed and eaten in these wars? But how many hath he killed? For indeed I promised to eat all of his killing" (*Ado*, 1.1.31–33). Beatrice's early salvo in the skirmish of wit is rather arresting. On the surface, she is making fun of a braggart soldier just returned from combat (Cf. *Henry V*: "I think he will eat all he kills" [3.7.92]).[27] Yet Beatrice conflates love and combat so immediately, so instinctively, that the timbre of her remark passes beyond irony toward something revelatory. Beatrice's first words spoken are, "I pray you, is Signor Mountanto returned from the wars or no?" (*Ado*, 1.1.24). "Mountanto," from *montanto* or *montant*, is a term from fencing indicating an upward thrust of the foil, but it can also refer to a sexual opportunist.[28] Beatrice elides Benedick's supposed combat prowess and his sexual prowess to comic, deflationary effect. She continues, "He set up his bills here in Messina and challenged Cupid at the flight; and my uncle's fool, reading the challenge, subscribed for Cupid and challenged him at the bird-bolt" (29–31). This rather enigmatic line indicts Benedick for his attitude toward love: he treats it as a competition, or, more damningly, a zero-sum game, in which one party's gain is another party's loss; as Harry Berger Jr. argues, "Love *of* contention gives way to love *as* contention."[29] Beatrice may be indicting herself as well, if we are to read her as her "uncle's fool," for engaging

Benedick on his terms. In Beatrice's questions, "how many hath he killed and eaten in these wars," the recent martial action, Benedick's bird-bolt challenge, and the "merry war" all collapse together.

The Messenger, unaware of the "merry war" betwixt Beatrice and Benedick, attempts to defend Benedick's soldierly reputation: "He hath done good service, lady, in these wars" (*Ado*, 1.1.36). Beatrice continues the badinage: "You had musty victual, and he hath holp to eat it. He is a very valiant trencherman; he hath excellent stomach" (37–38). In these wars, the victors not only conquer but also consume the vanquished. Benedick is a "trencherman," a glutton, distinguished by his appetite. The Messenger continues to play the straight man: "And a good soldier too, lady" (39). Beatrice retorts, "And a good soldier to a lady" (40). Benedick handles women as a soldier rather than a suitor; for him love is an agon, a contest of will and appetite. His treatment of others in general is high-handed and selfish; he runs through friends cavalierly as well, having "every month a new sworn brother" (53–54). As Beatrice makes clear, however, it is reprehensible to treat emotional attachment as a game. When one lets loose the arrows of love recklessly, collateral damage is inevitable. Even worse, when one hunts with purpose and resolve, intending simply to salve one's ego, the object of love becomes an object of prey. Beatrice indicates her contempt for such conduct by pushing metaphor to its limits: what is preyed upon is preyed upon to be eaten. Lady Disdain turns the tables back upon the trencherman: "Is it possible Disdain should die, while she hath such meet food to feed it as Signor Benedick?" (90–91). The "merry war" is not light-hearted repartee between two free and equal opponents; it is, rather, a war of attrition imposed upon Beatrice by Benedick, in which she is compelled against her will and judgment to feed as openly as he, and she scorns him for it, even as she is incapable of desisting.

In the character of Don John, Shakespeare affiliates unalloyed malignity with a self-serving appetite. Don John insists that he will "eat when [he has] stomach" (*Ado*, 1.3.11). While others feast, he broods. His ability to restrain his appetite is a mark of his autonomy, allowing him to act, or so he believes, as a free radical engaged in "mortifying mischief" (9–10). Don John seems at first the inverse of the gregarious Benedick, whose "excellent stomach" is a sign of his conviviality.

Yet the two are not so far apart from one another in their dealings with others. When Borachio enters—"I came from yon great supper" (32)—with news of the intended marriage, Don John declaims, "This may prove food to my displeasure" (58). Feasting and the promise of marriage are the hallmarks of comedy, signifying that community, often frayed over the course of the narrative, has been reaffirmed. Don John intends on this festive occasion to foster disarray. He will join the feast to serve his own appetite at the expense of others. He assumes that those who were his enemies on the field of battle remain antagonistic toward him in this time of peace—"Let us to the great supper; their cheer is the greater that I am subdued" (53–54)—and thus goes not to feed *with* others, but to feed *upon* others. "Cheer," as George Lyman Kittredge notes, indicates, "festivity—especially in the way of good things to eat."[30] Don John adds menacingly, "Would the cook were o'my mind" (67–8). Don John's poisonous desire would turn the comic feast toward tragic denouement, striking a cannibalistic note, by making the feast not simply an occasion for revenge but the means by which vengeance is attained. To subvert the impending marriage, Don John will alter appetite, making Claudio's love for Hero, to borrow from Orsino in *Twelfth Night*, "not so sweet now as it was before" (*TN*, 1.1.8). Beatrice remarks upon the unsettling, acidic nature of Don John, "How tartly that gentleman looks! I never can see him but I am heart-burned an hour after" (*Ado*, 2.1.3–4). Don John's tartness, a quality of the bittersweet *bigerade*, makes him disagreeable and indigestible. He will convince Claudio that Hero is of like flavor.

Claudio's dreamy valuation of Hero, "Can the world buy such a jewel?" (1.1.135), is unmitigated objectification, so much so that Benedick cannot help but undercut it: "Yea, and a case to put it into" (136). "Being a professed tyrant to their sex" (125), Benedick is querulous, "Do you play the flouting Jack, to tell us Cupid is a good harefinder?" (136–37). He associates Cupid with the hunt, with spotting prey to be tracked down and killed (his joke, of course, being that Cupid is blind). Jibing aside, this is the nature, as pointed out by Beatrice, of Benedick's tyranny. Yet Claudio insists that Hero is "the sweetest lady" (140)—a refrain he repeatedly applies to his beloved. She is an exquisite object, an inimitable confection. The metaphor implicit in "sweet" is soon converted by Benedick explicitly into food.

When Claudio is convinced that he has lost Hero to Don Pedro, and his mood sours even toward his friends, Benedick teases him, "'Twas the boy that stole your meat, and you'll beat the post" (2.1.158–59). Meat, as noted above, was a general term for food; in this case, stolen from a boy, it likely suggests sweetmeats. Yet the corporality and carnality implicit in considering women as fleshy meat, fit for consumption only for a brief while, is also nested within Benedick's remark. When Beatrice arrives later, Benedick announces, "O God, sir, here's a dish I love not!" (213–14). And in describing Claudio's revived love for Hero, Benedick remarks derisively, "his words are a very fantastical banquet—just so many strange dishes" (2.3.20–21). Love, it appears to Benedick, in turning a "soldier" to "orthography," makes the beloved palatable in ways that are beyond his own imagining. Benedick declaims, "I will not be sworn but love may transform me into an oyster; but I'll take my oath on it, till he have made an oyster of me he shall never make me such a fool" (19–22). Foolishness and fancy wind together again, and we are given, through Benedick's metaphor of an oyster, a glimpse into what for him is irrational about love. He fears that if he leaves himself open to love, he will be consumed. As Claire McEachern notes, "An oyster represents a man made vulnerable to perfidious female appetite."[31] The image of oyster and crab is rather distressing. We find ourselves in a sort of Hobbesian world of atomic individuality, of kill or be killed—or one even more savage, of eat or be eaten.

To transform Benedick, his friends believe that he must be converted of his own accord from one who preys to an object of prey. Claudio rallies his co-conspirators as they prepare to ensnare the scorner of love: "O, ay! Stalk on, stalk on: the fowl sits." (2.3.82). Like a bird in the bush, Benedick is circled and trapped. And when he is caught, he describes his own conversion from a derider of love to one *in* love in terms of ingestion: "But doth not the appetite alter? A man loves the meat in his youth he cannot endure in his age" (191–92). "Meat" represents the seemingly intractable habit he is now rejecting— his preying and feeding upon women. We witness such a sudden, radical emotional metamorphosis (not yet maturation), that the simple truth of love in Shakespearean comedies is evident—at the root of love is surrender, when the individuated will willingly dispossesses itself of its singularity so that it might join with another. And as is generally the case in Shakespearean comedy, the accession to love is followed by feasting, a sign of communion. When Beatrice arrives, she invites him to the feast: "Against my will I am sent to bid you come in to dinner" (199). Benedick accepts the invitation to feast gladly, even ecstatically, because it is conveyed by his beloved. Rather than feasting *on* women, he is now eager to feast *with* this particular woman. "'Against my will I am sent to bid you come in to dinner'—there's a double meaning in that" (206–07): the meaning is double or, at least, represents two perspectives that are not yet aligned. Even as Benedick is willing to surrender his willfulness to Beatrice, she is not yet prepared to do so for him.

The same net is then cast for Beatrice. Hero and Ursula employ the metaphor of fishing to describe their charge:

> The pleasant'st angling is to see the fish
> Cut with her golden oars the silver stream
> And greedily devour the treacherous bait.
> So angle we for Beatrice.   (3.1.26–29)

They lay "false sweet bait" (33) to entice Beatrice. The image, implicit in angling, is of one who would catch being caught themselves, of the hunter becoming the prey, of one who, attempting to consume what appears edible, ends up on the plate herself. Hero appropriates language used earlier in the play by Beatrice ("I promise to eat all of his killing" [1.1.33]) to describe their success: "Some Cupid kills with arrows, some with traps" (106). Ironically, Hero herself will soon be "killed" by a trap set by one whom she supposes to be in love with her. As one romantic arc is moving toward resolution, the other moves into darker territory.

Even as Benedick resolves to change his ways, Claudio turns in the opposite direction: the scorner of love is transformed into its advocate, the resolute lover into one who scorns his beloved. The language of consumption charts this shift as well. Don Pedro declares to Claudio, "I do but stay till your marriage be consummate, and then go I toward Aragon" (3.2.1–2). Nested within "consummate" is the insinuation that Claudio will consume Hero; that is, that she is for him a sweet-meat, an exotic treat, a luxury item. This is the attitude of Don Pedro, of the Spanish possessors of this island, of men of "honor" in this play, who bandy about an ideal of brotherhood that feeds off the qualities of women. Shakespeare suppresses the ruthlessness and acquisitiveness of Bandello's Don Piero, but it still lies beneath the surface of *Much Ado*. Borachio (whose name indicates a loss of appetitive control) connives to convince Claudio that Hero is a "contaminated stale" (2.2.19). The phrase indicates a prostitute, but also that which is "stale," food that has lost its flavor, that is no longer fresh and therefore no longer desirable. It is no longer desirable to Claudio because what had been singular, rare, is now common. Originally, Hero had been to Claudio "the sweetest lady." Benedick's trajectory is opposite: he now eats his meat without grudging; he embraces his organic human appetites. Yet Claudio throws back "this rotten orange" (4.1.27). Having been in a "luxurious bed" (36), Hero is now, as Borachio had intended, seen as contaminated. Don Pedro, too, has fallen into the perfidious trap that women set for men: "I stand dishonor'd that have gone about / To link my dear friend to a common stale" (59–60). Hero is no longer a sweetmeat but given over to "savage sensuality" (56); she is a piece of meat, the staleness of which, according to even her father, the sea has "salt too little which season may give / To her foul tainted flesh" (137–38). She cannot be preserved. The friar follows the train of this metaphor obliquely: "If this sweet lady lie not guiltless here / Under some biting error" (164–65). The error is, in fact, "biting" in more ways than one. Claudio is soon after referred to derisively as "Count Comfect": he has gone from *bigerade* to sweetmeat while Hero has been transmuted from sweet to rotten; this chiastic pattern is at the heart of the play's disorder.

Claudio, by tossing back the "rotten orange," enacts an alternative history, one in which Adam rejects the fruit of transgression offered to him by Eve, thus avoiding the slide into lurid sexuality. In Tyndale's translation, consumption and desire are clearly conjoined: "So the woman (seeing that the tree was good for meat, and that it was pleasant to the eyes, and a tree to be desired to get knowledge) took of the fruit thereof, and did eat, and gave also to her husband with her, and he did eat" (Gen. 3:6). Adam is quick to blame both God and Eve for his own offense: "Then the man said, The woman which thou gavest *to be* with me, she gave me of the tree, and I did eat" (Gen. 3:12).

Claudio casts away the fruit and thus escapes the timeworn fate of men, brought low by the treacherous appetites of women. Like Eve, Hero is both temptress and temptation; rejecting his bride, Claudio preserves his "honor." He and his band of brothers correct the original "biting error" that has plagued humankind since the garden of Eden. But, as *Much Ado* makes clear, the error is Claudio's, and it is this very obsession with honor—in reality simply a coded sort of selfishness—that has fractured the relationship between men and women. The path to redemption, or at least to the reconciliation of sexual and romantic love, does not involve accusation and rejection but is instead contingent upon trust and surrender, both predicated upon the men in the play recognizing that they are victimizers, not victims, as Benedick comes to learn in the remainder of the scene. The *Oxford English Dictionary* cites C. S. Lewis in defining a "Beatrician" experience: "the recovery (in respect to one human being) of that vision of reality which would have been common to all men in respect to all things if Man had never fallen."[32] Even if one does not hold that Shakespeare read Dante, or that he knew Dante's Beatrice at some remove, *Much Ado*'s Beatrice undeniably *operates* as a Dantean Beatrice, bestowing blessing, as Benedick's name indicates—the blessing that corrects the warped view of the world shared by the men in the play.

The mutual confession of love between Beatrice and Benedick, which is precipitated by the rejection of Hero by Claudio, embraces the language of consumption:

> BENEDICK. By my sword, Beatrice, thou lovest me.
> BEATRICE. Do not swear it, and eat it.
> BENEDICK. I will swear by it that you love me, and I will make him eat it that says I love you not.
> BEATRICE. Will you not eat your word?
> BENEDICK. With no sauce that can be devised to it. I protest I love thee.   (*Ado*, 4.1.265–70)

The proverbial notion that one might eat one's own words by going back on an oath has a particular resonance in this context. Swearing on one's sword, the hilt and blade of which form a cross, is a declaration of one's adherence to a code of honor, grounded in martial and masculine values. To avenge the dishonor done to her cousin, Beatrice is counting on what she had derided before—the proclivity of men to vanquish and consume. She wants him to swear an oath to her, a promise that will supersede all the obligations he has to his male companions. Earlier she had mocked his claims of bravery by saying that she would eat all of his killing. Now, when he seems to bear out her claims that he is less than valorous, and worse, that his love for her is delimited by his bonds to his companions, she responds, "O God, that I were a man! I would eat [Claudio's] heart in the market place" (292–93). With sincerity bred in the crucible of emotional crisis, Beatrice hits square upon the truth of this play: men are eaters of hearts. Their radical selfishness, cloaked in codes of honor and allegiance, is bound to a bestial appetite that can accommodate neither empathy, sympathy, nor, especially, love. And this as well is what Benedick has proven to her in denying her appeal—he has, as she had always feared, eaten *her* heart. Yet witnessing his beloved's grief, Benedick is transformed. As Leonato notes, "Men / Can counsel and speak comfort to that grief / Which they themselves not feel; but, tasting it, / Their counsel turns to passion" (5.1.20–23). Benedick experiences, *tastes,* the deep pain that Beatrice feels for Hero, the compassion that one person can feel for another and, through the medium of his own feelings for Beatrice, finally understands passion, and love. When he concedes, "Enough, I am engag'd" (4.1.310), he agrees not only to engage Claudio but finally to be engaged, bound fully and selflessly to the will of another.

Confronting Claudio, Benedick declares, "You have kill'd a sweet lady, and her death shall fall heavy on you" (5.1.140–41). Benedick adopts the epithet "sweet," by which Claudio had called Hero repeatedly; Benedick understands the sweetness that can attend upon love, while Claudio has lost his taste for it. Don Pedro either mistakes the gravity of Benedick's challenge or, recognizing it, attempts to diffuse the situation: he makes light of the proposed duel: "What, a feast? A feast?" (142). Claudio responds in earnest, however: "I'faith, I thank him, he hath bid me a to a calf's head and a capon, the which if I do not carve most curiously, say my knife's naught" (144–45). The feast has turned deadly. A banquet is predicated upon hunting and killing; food is flesh. Now the revelers are prepared to carve one another. The symbol of concord in Shakespearean comedy—a feast—has become the site of conflict. In a world of abundance, we have reached the point of *naught*, of nothing.

Providentially, through the intervention of souls as honest "as ever broke bread" (3.5.30), named after foods of simple sustenance, dogberries and oatcakes, the world of Shakespeare's comedy rights itself. (A "dogberry" is the fruit of the wild cornell, a common shrub, an oatcake a customary treat, and "verges" the sour juice of unripe grapes.) It can only do so, however, if those who have denied love can find a way back into love's graces. The truth must be acknowledged if reconciliation is to be achieved. In the song "Hey nonny, nonny," the fickleness of men—"To one thing constant never" (*Ado*, 2.3.57)—is remarked upon; the men who listen, however, fail to note the notes (as Balthazar suggests they should). Their blitheness is the source for "sounds of woe" (61) among all women. At Hero's tomb, singers intone,

> Pardon, goddess of the night,
> Those that slew thy virgin knight;
> For the which, with songs of woe,
> Round her tomb they go.   (5.3.12–15)

It is now the men, repentant, who sing "songs of woe." Their self-awareness is subtly yet sublimely marked by Don Pedro, who commands, "Put your torches out. The wolves have prey'd" (24–25). Those who have just *prayed* at Hero's monument are finally recognized for what they are, or have been—wolves that have *preyed*. The bestial, appetitive, selfishness of men is not simply exposed for what it is, but has been acknowledged by the men themselves. Claudio's love for Hero is embodied by an act of surrender. Having turned his will over in probate to her father, for "reckonings" (5.4.51), he concedes willingly, "I am your husband, if you like of me" (59). The choice is hers, not his, and as the choice, in fact, is Hero's all appears to turn out well. At the play's conclusion, Shakespeare turns a critical thread of action in this play—eating, consumption, ingestion—into a gesture of eloquence. Beatrice teases Benedick that she yielded, "partly to save your life, for I was told you were in a consumption" (95–96). "Peace!" he retorts, "I will stop your mouth" (96), and in this moment mouths conjoin to taste the strangest dish of all.

Part 2

BODY AND STATE

Chapter 4

Fluid Mechanics: Shakespeare's Subversive Liquors

KAREN RABER

Like other characters in his plays, Shakespeare's alcoholic beverages have "their entrances and exits," and each in its time plays many parts. As Rebecca Lemon discusses in chapter 6 of this volume, sack, wine, and beer were complexly and contradictorily understood to not only enhance physical health but also to create disease; to encourage convivial community yet provoke antisocial behaviors; and to inspire creativity but at the same time debilitate the spirit and soul. Peter Kanelos observes in this collection that "eating lies at the conjunction of desire and necessity," making food choices a particularly fraught domain of life; strong drink, however, not only adds the element of inebriation, which seems to defeat regimes of bodily and cultural control and even to lead to self-destruction, but also puts into question the whole subject of what counts as necessary. For a country embroiled in competition over trade, in wars of empire, and in religious conflict, the question of where and how desire might trump need is crucial.

In this essay I introduce a new paradox centered on the presence of sack and other forms of wine, one that revolves around the association of wines with economic, religious, and political encounters and transactions. In this paradox, the divergent potential that allows wine to operate as both illness and remedy is repeated and expanded when wine functions as a product that enables travel and trade by

75

making possible long sea voyages, thus becoming one instrument for creating the wealth of a nation. At the same time, however, imported wine, which medical and moral treatises agree can corrupt individual health and behavior, operates both as a material *national* toxin and as a figurative device for expressing the problems that transnational trade poses for the collective economic, religious, and political body of the state: the trade in wine specifically, and the global exchanges that wines in turn make generally possible, encourage England's contamination by foreign goods and ideas, threatening the establishment of a coherent and stable national identity.

Every time wine appears in Shakespeare's plays, I suggest, it activates "England" and "Englishness" as concepts—at once newly revivified yet still fluid—that rely on a body/state analogy. When Falstaff lauds the powers of his sherris-sack in *2 Henry IV*, audiences would recognize that his personal addiction is implicated in a national failing: it is a legacy of foreign wars and an ongoing danger for England's *corpus economicum*. Clarence's death in a butt of malmsey in *Richard III* not only engages with his particular history to reflect his fluctuating loyalties, but taps into English ambivalence about the nation's relationship to its continental wars, its former possessions in France, and its appetite for imperial expansion. Likewise, that providential cask of sack that saves Stephano and transports Caliban in *The Tempest*, the very sack whose preservative powers helped make voyages to the New World possible in the first place, ends up raising questions about the consequences of discovery and conquest for religious integrity. Shakespeare's literary references to wines thus saturate his plays with allusions to religious, philosophical, medical, ideological, and mercantile discourses that can only be fully distilled if we consider the broader individual, national, and international dimensions of wine consumption.

In *2 Henry IV*, Falstaff offers this infamous paean to the virtues of sack:

> A good sherris-sack hath a two-fold operation in it. It ascends me into the brain; dries me there the foolish and dull and crudy vapours which environ it, makes it apprehensive, quick, forgetive, full of nimble, fiery, and delectable shapes, which delivered o'er to the voice, the tongue, which is the birth, becomes excellent wit. The

second property of your excellent sherris is the warming of the blood, which, before cold and settled, left the liver white and pale, which is the badge of pusillanimity and cowardice. But the sherris warms it and makes it course from the inwards to the parts extremes. It illumineth the face, which as a beacon, gives warning to all the rest of this little kingdom, man, to arm; and then the vital commoners and inland petty spirits muster me all to their captain, the heart, who, great and puff'd up with this retinue doth any deed of courage; and this valour comes of sherris. So that skill in the weapon is nothing without sack, for that sets it a-work; and learning, a mere hoard of gold kept by a devil till sack commences it and sets it in act and use.[1]

Borrowing Galenic medical theory about the dry, hot nature of liquor, Falstaff makes the case that sack can invigorate the necessary courage for war in a soldier like himself, can muster his wit, raise the temperature of his blood, and so free the circulation of both bodily fluids and acquired skills. Drinking sack lets a man rise to the defense of his kingdom.

But for Falstaff the argument is always larger and grander, of course, and in this case what is at stake is not merely his own performance on the battlefield under the influence of sack, but the role of liquor in the health of the kingdom. Jonathan Gil Harris has charted English transformations of the body/state analogy that evolved in response to the advent of international trade, observing that literary and cultural artifacts reflect a struggle to keep that body open to exchange, while protecting it against infection by foreign economic corruptions and diseases.[2] Where trade had once been seen as an "activity less of nation-states themselves than of people or trading associations," and the commonwealth referred to the moral condition of the nation, by the seventeenth century new economic conceptions of nationhood took hold. Through a discourse of mercantilism, the responsibility for the "commonwealth," now the wealth of the nation, was gradually transferred to state.[3] Meanwhile, the body-state analogy that obtained in political discourse, the idea of the *corpus politicum*, expanded to include economic activity as well. In general, the "body" of the nation was a humoral one, and health was conceived of as a balance among the humors. However, while there was no germ theory to account for assaults on the nation's financial health, other medical concepts allowed authors on finance and trade to include images of invasion and attack: the notion of "seeds" as the source of disease, along with observations on the infectious nature of plague, and associations that linked venereal disease with travel and traffic with other nations, contributed to anxieties about the potential pathology in transnational commerce.

Reading *The Merchant of Venice* for the way it creates Jewish identity as "far more refractory and transnationally palimpsested" than usually supposed, Harris finds Shylock to be a hybrid figure who encompasses Dutch, Spanish, and other nations that are perceived to pose an economic/pathological menace to England.[4] And wine plays a part here: Dutch immigrants, Harris argues, are alluded to in the play's references to Rhenish wine, which, although German, was more commonly associated in London with that city's Dutch community.[5] Harris is most interested in the use of the wine to distinguish between types of blood in Salerio's comment that "there is more difference between your bloods than there is between red wine and Rhenish" (*MV*, 3.1.36-8). Salerio's effort to make Jessica Venice's own, and Shylock its other, is defeated by syntax and custom in this line, argues Harris, since the logic of this sentence actually aligns the Jew with the "generically Mediterranean" red wine, Jessica with a foreign import. But it is also worth remembering that the play's first mention of Rhenish comes in Portia's description of her suitors. When Nerissa asks how she likes the German duke, Portia replies, "Very vilely in the morning when he is sober, and most vilely in the afternoon, when he is drunk" (1.2.84-85). To distract him from choosing the correct casket, she considers "set[ting] a deep glass of Rhenish wine on the contrary casket" to entice him away. Rhenish wine establishes a link between consumption and the erasure of distinction on both an individual and a national level—the German drunkard is blinded to distinctions between the caskets, just as he fails to note different times of day. So Salerio's analogy of differentiation by blood fails to differentiate; the nature of all wine is to make distinction fail. Avoiding this confusion would require eschewing wine altogether, foreign or domestic, whether as a beverage or as a metaphor.

Ben Bertram, also writing about Falstaff's celebration of sack, argues that discourses that wedded the circulation of money and commodities to a strong, even puritanical ethic of sobriety provided one comforting answer to anxieties about economic trade and the nation's susceptibility to imported pathologies, especially (as Lemon notes in her essay for this volume) through a degrading and enfeebling addiction to imported goods. In Bertram's analysis, Prince Hal's considered, calculating use of conviviality to further a national agenda, which famously proposes that "if all the year were playing holidays, / To sport would be as tedious as to work" (*1H4*, 1.2.197–98), is just such a prophylactic.[6] Bertram observes that Falstaff proposes economies of pleasure and community that analogies between the abstract, de-individuated body and the state were meant to reject: bodily temperance, the balance of humors, the careful monitoring and, if necessary, suppression of fleshly appetites, dominate the literature of the *corpus politicum*.[7] The dangers of England's participation in global economic trade, Bertram goes on to point out, are figured through Falstaff's enormous, bloated roundness: he is a "huge hill of flesh" (2.4.241), a "tun of man" (2.4.443), a "bombard of sack"(2.4.446), a "globe of sinful continents" (*2H4*, 2.4.285) with a "whole merchant's venture of Bordeaux" (2.4.64–65) in him. Bringing the drift of Harris's model to a focus on Falstaff, Bertram finds the fat man's engagement in private, plebeian, pleasure-maximizing trade results in "poor circulation when trade increases the consumption of imports and the private profit for merchants without adding to the industry and increased gain of the nation as a whole."[8]

Contemporary commentators saw a similar set of dangers in English addiction to foreign wines such as sack. George Gascoigne's 1576 *A Delicate Diet for Daintiemouthde Droonkards*, written "at the height of the Elizabethan era of nation-building in the political, military and cultural spheres," sees excessive drinking as a threat to the nation's status, rather like that represented by the import of other luxuries to which the English have become addicted: drunkenness is "a monstrous plant, lately crept into the pleasant orchards of England," that threatens to make the English no better than the Germans, the continent's "wardens" of drunkenness.[9] Peter Parolin notes elsewhere in this collection that even the most apparently English of drinks, small beer, was originally a Dutch beverage, adding to anxieties about trade and alcoholic consumption. Thomas Young writes in *England's*

Bane; or, The Description of Drunkenness (1617) that "the great drinkings of forraine Countries compared to ours are but sippings."[10] The prefatory poem to Thomas Heywood's *Philocothonista; or, The Drunkard Opened, Dissected, and Anatomized* (1635) proposes that "warrelike Brittaine" should expel wine altogether. While the Danes brought the custom of drinking "healths" or salutes into England to the detriment of sober society, the French continued to exploit the English, Heywood argues, by sending their "refuse" to England, keeping the best wine for themselves.[11] And the English, because they dwell in a cold climate, are "most forward to commit drunkenness," but also seem to have become addicted to foreign fare: in a chapter titled "What forraine Wines and sundry sortes of drinks are now frequent in this kingdome," Heywood decries the fact that other countries are content to consume their own wines, but the English "as if doting upon insatiety, borrow from them all."[12] The implication is that the English not only cannot produce their own wines because of climate but also cannot produce original and valuable goods because they have become used to borrowing from others, a syndrome for which wine is both cause and symptom.

If we return to Falstaff's praise of sack, however, we find that one critical component is missing from the picture we have drawn so far: Falstaff is specifically a soldier preparing for war—"skill in the weapon is nothing without sack," he says, suggesting that English military might is enhanced by this imported drink. But precisely because there is no such thing as English sack, we must wonder how dependence on a foreign substance (foreign not only to the individual body, but to the national body) to muster military energy reconciles with the preservation and expansion of English objectives through military domination. The trajectory of the tetralogy's wars is, after all, also foreign—having suppressed rebellions at home, Henry V will conquer French territories for England. In addition, then, to imperiling English national corporeal identity with the wrong kind of trade and consumption, sack is implicated in the politics of England's involvement in continental military actions.

Sack, sherry, and other fortified wines actually surged in popularity during and after the Anglo-Spanish wars, when soldiers returning from Europe brought with them the habits of their temporary hosts in Europe. As Barbara Sebek notes in her essay for this collection, sack and other strong wines were the product of "nautical conflict and uneasy alliances" in the early modern world: Spanish religious anxieties generated by growing Protestantism in Europe overlapped with concerns about smuggling and commercial competition in the war's many skirmishes between English and Spanish forces. Privateering figured prominently in the repertoire of tactics the English used against their Catholic enemies. In 1587 Francis Drake captured as part of his raid at Cadiz nearly 3,000 barrels of sack. He staged a public drinking celebration on his return to England, boosting the appeal of the wine especially among England's burgeoning navy. To alleviate the siege of Antwerp, Elizabeth signed the Treaty of Nonsuch in 1585, committing England to supplying a substantial number of troops and horses, and an annual subsidy to the Dutch, keeping the relationship alive, but at a cost to the English treasury. By 1590, however, William Camden was linking the wars to bad drinking habits and blaming the Dutch, not the Danes, for the pernicious habit of drinking "healths": "The English in their long wars in the Netherlands first learnt to drown themselves with immoderate drinking, and by drinking others' healths to impair their own. Of all the Northern nations, they had been before the most commended for their sobriety."[13] To drink deep was, in the parlance of the day, "Upsee Dutch," or "opzee [over sea] Dutch," to drink like a Dutchman.[14] Thomas Nashe's *Pierce Penniless* places the blame for English drunkenness squarely on these foreign wars, blasting English "superfluities in drink, a sinne that ever since we have mixt our selves with the Low Countries is counted honorable, but before we knew their lingring warres, was held in the highest degree of hatred that might be." The country would be better served by "sowring the wine in the cellars and merchants' storehouses that our countrymen may not pisse out their wit and thrift against the walls."[15]

As the end of the century approached, England also faced competition at sea and in trade from Dutch ships, which were overtaking the Portuguese in long voyages and so cornering global trade. By 1600 the Dutch were the largest spirit traders on the Continent; in 1604, James I issued an ordinance limiting the consumption of sack at court, probably prompted by fears that trade in the wine would line either Dutch or Spanish pockets.[16] *Henry IV, Parts 1 and 2*, written in the late 1590s, thus link Shakespeare's portrait of Falstaff not only to fears about the economic consequences of increased importation of foreign wines but also to political and social weariness over involvement in Dutch defense and new doubts about the shift of global power represented by Dutch trade. Toward the end of the century, Elizabethan foreign policy, which relied on heavy conscription and taxation, was "carried out against a backdrop of economic depression, dearth and plague."[17] The "physic" of war, its capacity to remedy England's conflicts with powerful neighbors like Spain and France, had paled significantly for a populace soured by resentment over its costs; the Elizabethan solution, requiring investment in foreign ventures, seemed merely to result in the strengthening of other nations and the debilitation of the English. Just as the health benefits of the continental war's by-products, imported liquors, were no longer signs of English trade strength but evidence of the plague of luxury that weakened English society, importation of sack and other European wines thus signaled England's dangerous entanglement in foreign religious conflicts and power struggles.

As every Shakespeare student is taught, Falstaff is a notoriously bad soldier whose role in defending English interests comes second to his maximization of pleasure, suggesting a link between his indulgence in sack and his indulgence in near-treasonous incompetence. Having "misused the king's press" and gained a company of cannon fodder (*1H4*, 4.2.12) rather than fit soldiers, Falstaff is forced to admit after the actions at Shrewsbury that "there's not three of my hundred and fifty left alive," the rest of his men gone as he'd predicted to "fill a pit" (5.3.36–37, 4.2.12, 4.2.65). On the battlefield, instead of a sword he hands Hal a bottle, substituting an instrument of individual pleasure for one of national defense. As Rebecca Lemon hints in her essay on addiction in chapter 6, by the time Falstaff makes such a substitution he has demonstrated that his loyalties are compromised by drinking—that, in fact, he has become more committed to the rituals of conviviality than he can ever be to any definition or representation of the state. And, of course, Falstaff crowns his actions with theft from the crown—a theft of credit for Percy's death, who was actually killed by Hal. As Heywood and Nashe would have agreed, Falstaff's vices—his lying, cheating, and stealing—are linked not only to his mistaken celebration of sack, but to the nation's moral debility caused by its addiction to foreign drinks, foreign goods, and foreign wars. The reading of Falstaff's relationship to sack I've proposed so far, though it may temporarily validate Prince Hal's model of restraint, should, in the long view of the tetralogy as a whole, make us careful about assuming that Shakespeare endorses the trajectory that culminates in Henry V's possession of French territory. Any triumph represented by Hal is short lived: his conquests would, after all, eventually lead to searing civil conflict during the Wars of the Roses.

Well before he portrayed Falstaff's betrayal of his office in the second tetralogy, Shakespeare had already considered many of the same connections between liquor and fluid, treasonous loyalties as they influenced those wars. In *Richard III* Clarence is stabbed and then drowned in a butt of malmsey rather than beheaded, which was the usual practice for royal offenders. The First Murderer plans to "Take him on the costard with the hilts of thy sword, and then throw him into the malmsey butt in the next room," his co-conspirator responds, "O excellent device! And make a sop of him" (R3, 1.4.156–60).[18] After pleading his case at length, Clarence is stabbed once by the First Murderer, who again exclaims, "If all this will not do, I'll drown you in the malmsey butt within" (1.4.273), dragging away the body presumably to do so.

Rehashing the tale of Clarence's fate allows Shakespeare to convey the slipperiness of Clarence's political allegiances. Before he is murdered, Clarence dreams of an accident at sea:

> Methoughts that I had broken from the Tower
> And was embarked to cross to Burgundy,
> And in my company my brother Gloucester,
> Who from my cabin tempted me to walk
> Upon the hatches
>
> ....
>
>   As we paced along
> Upon the giddy footing of the hatches,
> Methought that Gloucester stumbled, and in falling
> Struck me (that thought to stay him) overboard
> Into the tumbling billows of the main.
> O Lord, methought what pain it was to drown!
>
>   (R3, 1.4.9–13, 16–21)

This opening already encompasses all the symbolic and metaphorical connections to Clarence's several betrayals of his brothers and father-in-law. The historical Clarence fled England for Calais to join

Warwick in a plot against Edward; disillusioned with Warwick's maneuvering, however, Clarence returned to England to be forgiven for his temporary treason. These events are adapted in *3 Henry VI* when Clarence first abandons his brother, Edward, for Henry's side and marries Warwick's daughter. He then defects yet again, suborned by Gloucester's arguments (who, the audience understands, is already plotting to remove him), announcing:

> I throw my infamy at thee.
> I will not ruinate my father's house,
> Who gave his blood to lime the stones together,
> And set up Lancaster. Why, trowest thou Warwick,
> That Clarence is so harsh, so blunt, unnatural,
> To bend the fatal instruments of war
> Against his brother and his lawful king?   (*3H6*, 5.1.82–88)

Of course, the oath that Clarence now swears merely repeats the several he has already violated in the course of that play, with the same outcome.

The giddy sea voyage to Burgundy that Clarence recalls at his death not only invokes Clarence and Warwick's journey to France in *3 Henry VI* (not to mention the important role of Burgundy in supplying arms and men in England's conflict), but it seems to repeat the trajectory of that last shift of loyalties from Warwick back to Edward, registering the fact that endlessly shifting Clarence is pitched into the sea—that is, betrayed—by the yet more supple, shifting Gloucester. Such a reading is confirmed by the end of Clarence's dream, when he is reproached by the ghost of his father-in-law and hailed by Prince Edward, "Clarence is come, false, fleeting, perjured Clarence" (*3H6*, 1.4.55).[19]

At first glance, Clarence's dream seems to have little to do with death-by-malmsey. Malmsey, however, like sack, was a wine directly linked to sea trade and sea travel, first made popular by its ability to withstand long shipboard voyages. Because it did not deteriorate in rough conditions or over time, this Greek sweet wine (later made in the Madeira Islands, and sometimes called "Canary" wine) was carried far and wide in the holds of European trading vessels.[20] "The Goode Gossippes Song" from the Chester plays has the speaker advising a "pottill full of Malmsine" to cure the fear of drowning as Noah's flood encroaches, while Chaucer's "Shipman's Tale" has Brother John bringing a butt of malmsey as a gift to his friend the merchant, indicating the English appreciated malmsey at least as early as the fourteenth and fifteenth centuries.[21] Further, these two examples hint that the drink was always connected to sea voyages and mercantile identities. As Clarence's dream proceeds, the relationship between his death for treason, his past deceptions and shifting allegiances, and his end in the butt of malmsey are linked more clearly with images of shipwrecks of both trade and state:

> Methought I saw a thousand fearful wracks:
> A thousand men that fishes gnawed upon;
> Wedges of gold, great anchors, heaps of pearl,
> Inestimable stones, unvalued jewels,
> All scatt'red in the bottom of the sea.   (*3H6*, 1.4.24–28)

He recounts to the keeper the physical terror of being both unable to breathe and unable to die:

> often did I strive
> To yield the ghost, but still the envious flood
>   ...would not let it forth
> To find the empty, vast, and wand'ring air,
> But smothered it within my panting bulk,
> Who almost burst to belch it in the sea.   (1.4.36–41)

Through Clarence and his dream, Shakespeare offers a parable about containing the energies of political and economic ambition. To prevent those "wracks" with their attendant waste of life and treasure requires an act of stifling akin to Clarence's own physical smothering by the treachery of the "envious flood." The butt of malmsey Clarence is fated to cork with his dead flesh becomes at once a parodic sign and reductio ad absurdum of an appropriate response to grasping political and military designs, and he dies in an ironic metaphorization of his very real fears of drowning in the course of trading (goods, secrets, political influence) at sea.

English relationships with France in particular, that nation so heavily implicated in the first tetralogy, were complicated by appetite—for possession and conquest, for luxury goods, for funds to further English plots. Protestants like Sir Philip Sidney and Francis Walsingham dreamed of a religious war on the Continent, while at home French meddling in nearby politics inspired fear, even loathing: in 1560 William Cecil wrote, "How Long tyme [the French] have bene enne-meyes to England; how brickle, how false, how dooble there pacts of peace have bene, the storyes be witnesses. Theis seven hondred yeres was there never king of England, with whom they have not made warres.... The Insolency of the French nation, being in hope of victory, is not unknowen."[22] In his *An Harborow for Faithful and Trew Subjects,* Bishop John Aylmer warned the Scots to join with England instead of the French to avoid being "subjected and slaved to the proudest, untruest and the mooste tirannicall nacion, under the soone."[23] Indeed, French interference in Scotland continued to preoc-cupy the English until at least the early seventeenth century. That does not mean that France was uniformly scorned or suspected—at least some in England felt themselves brethren especially to French Protestants, a sentiment expressed in John Eliot's *Ortho-Epia Gallica* (1593) in terms of shared tastes in wine: "I love a cup of new Gascon or old Orleans wine, as wel as the best French of you all." As David Womersly argues, however, the abjuration of Protestantism by Henri IV more clearly settled English opinion against the French by the time Shakespeare wrote his plays.[24]

Rowland Cotterill's reading of both tetralogies posits France as a wound that threatens English cohesion and a promised cure for that same wound. So he argues that in the second tetralogy, conquest of France (and the marriage to a French princess) restores England to itself; legitimizes its monarch Henry V; quells national division by turning divergent interests of Welsh, Irish, or Scottish rabble toward a common end; and makes whole what was sundered by Richard II's death.[25] Yet the first tetralogy has established the cyclical, repetitive nature of this structure: there, the interrupted negotiations for a mar-riage between Lady Bona and Edward IV, and Edward's secret mar-riage to Lady Grey, inspire both Clarence's and Warwick's rebellions. Edward wants to assert English self-sufficiency in setting his "will" ("It was my will and grant / and for this once my will shall stand for law" [4.1.49–50]) above national dependence on French goodwill, but his choice "bur[ies] brotherhood" (4.1.55), not only with France but with his own brothers: "Leave me or tarry, Edward will be king, / And not be tied unto his brothers' will" (4.1.65–66). The common tastes of French and English found in John Eliot's work make them brothers of a sort, but political and imperial interests set them at odds, infecting and transforming English political alliances.

England's unrestrained appetite, leading to its implication in political maneuverings in France, does little to advance English power abroad, however much a French conquest may temporarily deflect social unrest within the nation; rather, a more sober approach to the attractions of expansionism at home and abroad promises to keep England whole. To Montague's proposition that England is "the safer when 'tis backed with France," Hastings retorts, "The better using France than trusting France. / Let us be backed with God and with the seas / Which He hath giv'n for fence impregnable" (*1H6*, 4.1.41–44).

By the conclusion of *2 Henry IV*, Prince Hal has repudiated Falstaff's plebeian liquidity, restoring economic systems "based on the abstractions of money and credit." Falstaff's failure to sacrifice appropriately for the national good at Shrewsbury will be punished, and as Henry V, Hal will go on to engage in the "larger world" of England's European ambitions. Thus, as Bertram observes, "Hal can control circulation in a money economy that will extend the reach of royal power."[26] While Bertram allows that Falstaff's ghost is not so easily dismissed, remaining after his banishment to "mock the future-oriented calculation of exchange guided by moral restraint" that relies on fantasies of national totality, he does not clarify what the consequences of that revenant might be. I suggest that the logic of the two tetralogies supplies an answer: while Henry may appear to enable an eternal body of the state, in contrast to Falstaff's all-too-temporal corpus, in truth he merely plants the seeds of the state's future disintegration with his conquests in France. That is, Hal appears to "cure" England with the physic of expansionism in the second tetralogy; in fact, to playgoers familiar with the story of Clarence, Burgundy, and the malmsey butt, he might also accurately be estimated to have rendered the English corpus yet more perilously porous. Cotterill's description of France as *pharmakon* also seems to describe the function of wine itself—the more you drink for health, the more you invite addiction and dependence. The *corpus politicum* of the first tetralogy, like the *corpus economicum* of the second tetralogy, is best defended by rejecting foreign influences. Had the historical Clarence been prevented from his ventures at sea, the Wars of the Roses might have ended differently; had the fictional Falstaff's sack-swilling sixteenth and seventeenth century alter egos been retained for strictly English defenses, they'd have ended up less utterly pickled and ineffective as agents of English global power.

According to John Spargo, Clarence's fate in the malmsey butt was not entirely unprecedented. Although historians were, and are, skeptical of the tale's authenticity, Spargo finds a number of similar uses of wine barrels in punishments on the Continent during the sixteenth through the eighteenth centuries. "Most of the victims," he notes, "were condemned to execution by drowning in a vessel of water for committing the crime of heresy, frequently of the Anabaptist variety."[27] Water, of course, is not wine, at least not for Protestants.[28] But then that's precisely the point of the method here: those convicted of heresy were religious reformers and were also being punished for treason because they rejected key aspects of Catholicism—and that usually extended to the issues of transubstantiation and the nature of the sacraments. While there is no reason to think that Clarence was a proto-Anabaptist, the set of connections made available by his death does remind us that the sacramental and transformative power of wine would have been a major factor in audience reactions to its staged interventions. By the late sixteenth and early seventeenth centuries English global ambitions had altered to include not just encounters with enemies like Catholic Spain or Protestant allies on the Continent, but the exploration and the settlement of far-flung colonies in the New World and elsewhere. This drive toward new spheres of influence, new territories to incorporate, had its own set of attendant anxieties, again realized in the plays through the device of liquor. Wine's role in religious conflict and competition links the history plays' mobilization of malmsey and sack to wine's appearance in *The Tempest*, where its potential to both save and corrupt are again at work.

Shakespeare's decision to make *The Tempest's* Caliban susceptible to the lure of wine is generally taken as the playwright's way of signaling the creature's "essential" monstrousness—the fish-man's indulgence in Stephano's butt of sack transforms him (rather like Bottom) into a more complete version of what he is, an irrational beast acting on base desires whether for drink or sex or violence. Although many continued to defend drink for its medicinal properties and its ability to inspire conviviality, drunkenness was usually identified as a plague on reason: "Drink beastiates the heart, and spoils the brains, / Exiles all reason, all good graces stains" exclaims a poem warning

of the dangers of drink.[29] Walter Raleigh advises his son to avoid the
"beastly infection" of drunkenness; "a Drunkard will never shake off
the delight of beastlinesse," warns Raleigh, and it will make a man
"not only a beast, but a madman; and if thou love it, thy own Wife,
thy Children and thy friends will despise thee."[30] Thomas Young lists
versions of drunkenness associated with animal characteristics: "Lyon
drunke" involves acts of destruction of property, "ape drunk" leads to
capering and leaping around, "sow drunke" results in vomiting, and
so on.[31] Where Clarence's monstrously labile loyalties were subtly but
powerfully characterized through his reputation for addiction to drink,
and his eventual fate drowned in malmsey, Caliban's affiliations and
obligations are directly assaulted through the medium of liquor—he
moves in an instant of drunkenness from resentful servant to murderous subject.

But while all three characters who imbibe in *The Tempest* are corrupted by the act, Caliban's particular lineage and its national and religious associations suggest that the religious context for his attachment
to drink is most important. His temptation and fall is represented as a
perversion of faith through entrapment by a false sacrament imported
to the island by two European Catholic layabouts whose intervention
mimics the trickery employed by New World explorers. Caliban's
behavior thus introduces another set of English anxieties regarding the
nation's role in global patterns of travel and discovery. Clarence and
Falstaff, and their preferred liquors, are bound up in English concerns
about national identity, bodily and military robustness, and potential contamination of both body and identity through international
exchanges; Caliban extends the scope of such fears to include English
imperial aspirations, which are also always necessarily linked to religious identity in the early modern world. From concerns about body
and country in the earlier plays, then, *The Tempest* moves the debate
into the realm of the soul.

Caliban's origins link him to any number of contemporary discourses: he's been identified with New World colonialism, natural
histories of hybrids, Irish natives, the wild man—the list is long and
diverse, leading one commentary to brand him "a loose end."[32] His
mother's story is equally fascinating since it speaks in several ways
about gender and power—and wine. In *The Tempest*, Sycorax is often
connected in early modern references to the classical Circe, whose

potions reduced men to beasts. Like both Circe and Medea, Sycorax is a sorceress with magical powers that she uses to ensnare others to her "earthy and abhorred commands" (*Tmp.*, 1.2.275). She occupies an island in both the Homeric original and the Shakespearean revision, a place outside the usual social controls of court or country and a space that has no clear affiliation or national identity.[33] Although she doesn't transform others into swine with a magic potion like her classical counterpart, Sycorax does "litter" a "freckled whelp, hag born—not honored with / A human shape" (1.2.285–86). As Marina Warner points out, the beast that most haunts the play "is the pig that links the play to its Homeric shadow self."[34] Caliban is forced into the pig's place, which he recognizes when he complains to Prospero, "here you sty me / In this hard rock" (345–46); having tried to reverse Caliban's swinish condition, Prospero gives up when Caliban threatens to rape Miranda, abandoning the humanist European project of redressing through education the shortcomings of a spiritually and appetitively bestial being.

Sycorax's association with Circe provides one justification for Caliban's fondness for drink. Literary Circes, Karen Britland points out, embody the dangers of sensual appetite, especially those represented by wine, which "poses a threat to masculine coherence, both personal and social."[35] In other words, Circe's threat was not much different from that we saw posed by Falstaff to the more sober, disciplined, properly "masculine" (because skilled in battle), Hal. What Circe provides in the Homeric original is excessive hospitality, again in the same fashion that Falstaff's tavern-going "opens" both the knight and the prince to inappropriate associations with low company. The luxury and self-indulgence that Circe encourages wipes the memories of Odysseus's men so that they forget their national, even their species, origins. By the sixteenth century, the image of Circe's cup was being tossed back and forth in the religious and political propaganda of the Reformation: if Catholics saw the wine of the Eucharist as material and symbolic life for the community, Protestants deployed the idea of Circe's wine to attack Catholic faith in transubstantiation. For Protestants, belief in the transformation of the Eucharist was, first, equivalent to the superstition of ancient peoples who did not have the benefit of God's enlightenment and, second, debasing to the church's followers, who "consumed" religious error at their masses when they witnessed this supposed miracle. For Protestants, Circe's cup overlapped the golden cup carried by the whore of Babylon, who in turn was commonly seen as a representation of Rome. William Fulke makes use of that connection when he rails against Catholicism's ability to convert the ignorant through the encouragement of superstition: "even so Babylon hath enticed all men lyke an other Circe, to drink the cup of her delectable error."[36]

But Circe's cup also migrated into the literature of wine and alcohol, often carrying with it religious as well as social connotations. Gascoigne's *A Delicate Diet for Daintiemouthde Droonkards* repeatedly personifies drink as a Circe: "I thought not impertynent to name this vice of droonkenness, the Circe or Medea, which metamorphoseth and transformeth men into most ugly and monstrous shapes and proportions."[37] Thomas Heywood's *Philocothonista* opens on a frontispiece illustration of a tavern table surrounded by drunken revelers. Each of them has been transformed into an animal (in the same vein as Thomas Young's list of bestial characters)—a lion head on a threatening drunkard lifting his cup as if to strike a fellow, a swinish head vomiting in the front. The full poem that accompanies the image is as follows:

> Calves, Goates, Swine, Asses, at a Banquet set,
> To graspe Health's in their Hoost's, thou seest here met;
> Why wonder'st thou oh Drunkard, to behold
> Thy brothers? In whose ranke thou art inrowl'd,
> When thou (so oft, as tox't at any Feast)
> Canst bee no better held, then such a beast,
> Since, like Cyrcean Cups, Wine doth surprise
> Thy sences, and thy reason stupifies,
> Which Foe, would Warre-like Brittaine quite expell,
> No Nation like it, could be said to excell.[38]

Given the ubiquity of the Circean connection to religious controversy, it is not a huge leap to imagine that when Heywood describes the "Foe" who will be expelled from "Warre-like Brittaine," he is hinting that both the "Cyrcean Cup" of foreign liquor and the "Roman Whore" who wields the cup would be so treated in a good Protestant country.

Sycorax is identified as a follower of the god Setebos: according to Caliban, Setebos was "my dam's God" (*Tmp.*, 1.2.376), to whom Caliban also prays (5.1.263). Setebos was from European mythology about Amerindian culture, a god associated with sexual promiscuity, degradation, and violent perversions of natural order. Shakespeare may have borrowed Setebos from Richard Eden's sixteenth century works on Magellan's voyages, in which he describes Patagonian natives, confronted with the explorer, calling on their god Setebos to help them.[39] The god is also described in Antonio Pigafetta's *A Briefe Declaration of the Voyage or Navigation Made Abowte the Worlde* (c. 1511) as "a greate devyll."[40] Whatever the origins of Setebos in *The Tempest*, the god's nature cooperates with the play's depictions of both the classical Circe and of Caliban as a monstrous and bestialized quasi-human.

When Caliban discovers drink, therefore, it's possible that he embraces elements of his own heritage associated with pagan gods, witches, and destructive magic. But I want to emphasize another aspect of Caliban's experience with sack—namely, the often overlooked story of its arrival on the island. No drink, after all, is available to Caliban, regardless of his "natural" tendencies, until it is imported to his home through the agency of the butler, Stephano, who survives the shipwreck through the intervention of that "celestial liquor" (*Tmp.*, 2.2.117): "I escaped upon a butt of sack, which the sailors heaved o'erboard" (2.2.120–23). Unlike poor Clarence, whose dreams of drowning presage his fate, Stephano is able to announce, "the sea cannot drown me" (3.2.13), yet in both instances the treacherous liquidity of the sea, mobilizing confused loyalties and slippery allegiances, threatens more than mere individuals. Having experienced his own version of salvatory transubstantiation (he should have swallowed seawater and drowned, but instead was granted a cask of wine), Stephano becomes a convert: "Swear by this bottle...which I made of the bark of a tree with mine own hands since I was cast ashore" (2.2.122–23). Later he says, referring to the bottle, "kiss the book" (2.2.129). These scenes are clearly a parody of religious ritual; but what is being parodied, and in whose interests? Initially, it seems obvious that Caliban is demonstrating the necessity that he be ruled, justifying Prospero's seizure of "his" island, as well as his subsequent slavery. Given an opportunity to free himself, all Caliban does is subject himself to a supremely unworthy pair and gin himself up for a murderous attack on his former master.

But it is Stephano, the Neapolitan Catholic, who makes claims for the wine's salvatory powers. Surely, then, an English Protestant audience would identify him as a superstitious believer in Roman "myth," and so a suitable imbiber from Circe's cup. Not only does he carve a reliquary for his precious wine, but he testifies to its spiritual healing effects: "He shall taste of my bottle; if he have never drunk wine afore, it will go near to remove his fit," says Stephano of the shaking Caliban, and later, "If all the wine in my bottle will recover him, I will help his ague." Giving Caliban the bottle, he concludes: "Amen" (2.2.75–76, 93–94).

Stephano's misrepresentation of the wine as magical, and Caliban's instant worship of the two Europeans based on their misuse of ordinary sack, echo Fulke's fears about conversion and, at the same time, reproduce themes familiar from accounts of early modern New World encounters.[41] European ventures in the Americas relied on the translation of economic appetites into moral and religious imperatives; exploitation of natural resources could thus be justified by the simultaneous importation of Christianity. Explorers often mistook native reactions to their appearance, tools, and other attributes as worship—Hernán Cortés, for instance, interpreted Moctezuma's gifts to the Spanish as bribes and pacification of creatures the Aztecs considered godlike, as he reported in his *Letters of Relation*.[42] Such errors, to English Protestant minds, confirmed the introduction of religious abuse and wrongdoing on the part of Catholic countries engaging in discovery and exploitation.

English exploration and settlement sought to overcome an initial sense of belatedness in arriving at the feast of global conquest and, at the same time, tried to distinguish English practices from England's much more advanced Catholic competitors, especially the Spanish and Portuguese. We find exactly this combination of sentiments in Richard Hakluyt's dedicatory preface to his *Divers Voyages:* "and that the nakedness of the Spaniards and their long hidden secretes are now at length espied, whereby they went about to delude the worlde, I conceiving great hope that the time approacheth and now is, that we of England may share and part stakes...both with the [S]paniards and the Portigales, in part of American and other regions, as yet undiscovered."[43] Walter Raleigh's *Discoverie of Guiana* also encourages Elizabethan exploration and settlement in that country in part by using the example of evil Spanish influence, marked by atrocities and oppression. Raleigh recounts native laments about their mistreatment, which lets him plead for Elizabethan intervention on the natives' behalf, arguing that they would respond with gratitude for better treatment: even the cannibals are united with other nations, "all holding the Spaniards for a common enimie." Once natives discover that Raleigh's party might help liberate them from Spanish rule ("of whose cruelty" they had already "tasted"), they offer cooperation with the English.[44] Raleigh harps on England's relative material shortcomings in his preface, the result of delays in conquering distant possessions like Guiana, and in stark contrast to the looming wealth of Spain in particular, which, Raleigh notes, "beginneth againe like a storme to threaten shipwracke to us all." It is Guiana's gold that will make England as strong as Spain: "we shall finde that these abilities rise not from the trades of sackes, and Civil Orenges, nor from ought else...it is his Indian Golde that indaungereth and disturbeth all the nations of Europe."[45] As Raleigh well understood, England's sense of imperial mission revolved around its belief in a global destiny tied up in assumptions about its spiritual superiority, and its material vulnerability, to Catholic Spain, Portugal, and other European nations.

The Spanish, however, had already discovered that there were dangers attached to global exploration and conquest.[46] Pedro de Quiroga, for instance, remarks in his 1555 dialogue, *Los colloquios de la verdad,* that "this land [the New World] weakens the judgment, disturbs the spirit, harms and corrupts good customs, and creates in men effects contrary to those which they previously had."[47] European explorers were transformed by their New World experiences, while New World influences of all kinds opened the national body to change, sometimes positive (as with the infusion of treasure, more imagined than real), but more often negative (encouraging rebellion, lawlessness, and the attenuation of religious orthodoxy). The English, in attempting to accomplish acts of global "discovery" in a different way from their Catholic precursors, nevertheless ran the same risk of contamination, even the risk of becoming replicas of their archenemies by suborning natives with superstition and false gods. Raymond Urban makes the case that when Stephano encourages Caliban to worship him as "the Man i' th' Moon," and Caliban falls for the ploy, the butler is actually inviting the native to join "a religion of drunkards—a comic Bacchanalian sect that took the man in the moon as its god and the liquor bottle as its Bible."[48] London had, Urban points out, three taverns called "The Man in the Moon," and Shakespeare's playgoers would have been familiar with the parodic tradition that turned taverns into churches, the drunken masses within into congregations of the faithful.

Reading Caliban's corruption by Stephano's sack against these historical developments shifts culpability away from the monstrous half-man and onto the Neapolitan butler and the Milanese jester. Once transported to the island, these two characters are set free from the normal social and political constraints that in their homelands might otherwise more profitably channel their behavior. Making their own "discovery" of a new world, and aided by Stephano's providential butt of sack, they turn Caliban into a drunk who can be converted to a new religious faith—in wine.

Having abused sack by mobilizing it in a false ritual that results in communal drunkenness, the three conspirators are inspired to become agents in a plot to overthrow Prospero. "Monster, I will kill this man," promises Stephano; "His daughter and I will be king and queen—save Our Graces—and Trinculo and thyself shall be viceroys" (*Tmp.*, 3.2.106–08). Influenced by the wine and by Caliban's poisonous descriptions of Miranda's beauty, the two invaders turn into rebellious subjects, helping Caliban aspire to repeat his first attempt to resist Prospero's absolute authority, when he attempted to rape Miranda, as well as appropriating and extending Caliban's repeated assertions of his own sovereignty. Falstaff's laudatory lines resonate here, if in ironic fashion: "great and puff'd up" with "this retinue" of sack's physical changes to the body, sack (filtered through Caliban's liberated desires) arouses Stephano and Trinculo to martial deeds. The two "foreigners" behave like typical conquerors; their actions speak as much to their own superstitious "delusions" and "nakedness" (to borrow Hakluyt's language) as to Caliban's nature as a child of Circe and a follower of Setebos. Like other Europeans on the island, the New World invaders are tested and found, like Antonio and Sebastian, to be ready to convert or else revert to the basest level of behavior.

It would be convenient to dismiss Stephano and Trinculo as merely simple, crowd-pleasing portraits of wicked papists. But the fact that sack, transmuted into a parody of sacramental wine, is the vehicle that alerts the reader/playgoer to these critical insights strongly connects Stephano's, Trinculo's, and Caliban's treasons against Prospero with the treason-marked wines that appear in the two historical tetralogies.

The fluid mechanics of strong "spirits" corrupt as easily as they for-
tify. Wine degrades bodies and characters, makes spuriously righteous
those who are otherwise morally reprobate, and makes unreliably vol-
atile what should be solid and categorically stable. English dominance
and moral righteousness are always at risk in competitive, appetitive
excursions from the geographical, economic, and social body of the
nation. Each voyage made possible by the demand for, and the properties of, wine becomes a potential source of infection, subversion, and
pathology; each investment in foreign lands, foreign goods, and foreign
liquors becomes a sign of appetites out of control, further opening the
national body to substances, behaviors, and desires outside its usual,
healthful, strictly delimited boundaries.

Sack, malmsey, and other strong European wines of the Renaissance
are, then, not merely inert props in dramatic works by Shakespeare,
nor can their meaning be summed up entirely through the description of their influence on the human body, since that body is always
linked metaphorically and materially to the condition of the nation's
political and economic corpus. Wines are simultaneously instruments
of trade (since their natural resistance to spoilage makes long voyages
possible) and objects of trade (since England had to import all its wines
throughout the Renaissance), as well as threats to the coherence of
ideologies spelling out the boundaries of individual, and national, bodies. What the three vinous episodes outlined above suggest is that for
Shakespeare, strong drink keeps company most often with treason
and heresy rather than with health and vitality, despite what so many
medical writers (and Falstaff) might maintain. In each case, wine testifies to the body's openness to outside influence—which in religious,
political, and economic terms almost always gives rise to anxieties
about the coherence of English identity.

Chapter 5

Feeding on the Body Politic: Consumption, Hunger, and Taste in *Coriolanus*

ERNST GERHARDT

Coriolanus famously opens with a food protest. Hungry citizens have taken to the streets in order to redress what they see as market manipulation: their starvation results from others' hoarding of grain. Although their starvation is literal, they cannot articulate it in literal terms. Their language slips away from their action into metaphor, and their embodied suffering serves instead as a sign within a political economy. As one of the protesters notes, "The leanness that afflicts us, the object of our misery is as an inventory to particularize their abundance."[1] Food and hunger's ambiguous nature—their literal and figurative significations—generates one of the main tensions of the play and proves to be one of the play's structuring elements. The opening scene, for instance, insists on the literal nature of food even as it compels its characters and audience to interpret and refigure it. As soon as the citizens disclose their starvation, they subject it not simply to interpretation but also to figuration. Declaring that his call for rebellion originates in "hunger for bread, not in thirst for revenge" (1.1.19–20), the First Citizen contrasts his literal hunger with an alternative motive figured in food imagery. He denies his figurative motive—his thirst for revenge—and insists instead on a physical and physiological one. Yet the play insistently repurposes literal and physiological food as metaphoric food, turning physiological hunger to ideological purposes.

The play's treatment of food has long attracted critical attention, ranging from formalist readings of the play's imagery to studies of the play's relationship to corn dearths as well as to republicanism.[2] Others have understood the play's food imagery as key to unpacking Martius's psychology, locating his desire for an impossible self-sufficiency in a contradictory desire to eat and a fear of being eaten.[3] In his brilliant essay on the play, Stanley Cavell interprets the hero as an extreme instance of an individual alienated from his political and social context, a man who refuses to be incorporated into a collective body. Cavell sees Martius—and, in broader terms, the play itself—as caught up in a paradoxical dilemma "of hungering not to hunger, of wanting not to want, of asking not to ask."[4] Because food signifies metaphorically as well as literally, language itself appears as a paradoxical substitute for food, at once sating and unsatisfying. As Cavell argues, "The play presents us with our need for one another's words by presenting withholding words, words that do not meet us halfway. It presents us with a famine of words."[5] Food itself is a language caught up by multiple discourses.

Many also have noted that the play's language veers at times toward meaninglessness, failing to address its context appropriately and that Martius's inability to engage in civil discourse proves symptomatic of his failure or inability to accommodate himself to the collective body of the polis.[6] Arthur Riss maintains that the play "stages a rebellion not only by the plebs but also by literality itself."[7] Contending that *Coriolanus* critiques the way that the patricians appropriate the citizens' embodied experience of hunger to ideological discourse, Riss valuably traces how the figuration of the body politic subsumes and obscures the citizens' physical, hungry bodies. Cavell highlights this issue, too, noting that Brecht's adaptation of the play succeeds precisely "in getting us *not* to interpret...but to stay with the opening fact of the play, the fact that the citizens of Rome are in revolt because there is a famine.... Not to interpret this means, in practical or theatrical terms, that we come to see that this cluster is of human beings...who work at particular trades and who live in particular places where specific people await news of the outcome of their dangerous course in taking up arms."[8] By attempting "*not* to interpret," Cavell foregrounds the literality of the citizens' physical—and physiological—situation: they are hungry because they lack food. The call *not* to interpret is a demand that food's literal signification supersede—or at least exist alongside—its figurative signification.

In this essay, I examine the intersection between the play's figuration of the body politic and of food, particularly the play's repurposing of material food production as the limit of the body politic. Because *Coriolanus* emphasizes alimentary consumption, food production remains invisible yet staged as the horizon against which the body public is imagined in this play. Beginning with the play's opening scene, I examine the several ways in which Menenius figures Rome's political situation as a metaphorical relation to food. In variously turning the citizens' physiological hunger to ideological and psychological dependency, Menenius's body politic begins the play's figuration of politics as feeding and of Martius himself as the communal dish Rome tastes.

While Menenius's "notorious" belly fable expresses a commonplace Renaissance model of social order, it does so by sketching the contours of a food distribution system, tracing the way food—the "viand" (1.1.89)—enters, moves through, and arrives at its various destinations.[9] Significantly, this food distribution system elides both the geographic and productive origin of food; in Menenius's formulation, the "viand" allegedly hoarded by the stomach exists as a thing already given. Menenius's model thus assumes food to be a ready-at-hand convenience, an item that appears without any labor.

To counter the citizens' accusations, Menenius relates the belly's defense of itself to the rest of the body's members, which have accused the belly of remaining "I'th' midst o'th' body, idle and unactive, / Still cupboarding the viand, never bearing / Like labour with the rest" (1.1.88–90). The belly responds to these accusations by defining its central, distributive role in the body:

> 'True is it, my incorporate friends'...
> 'That I receive the general food at first
> Which you do live upon, and fit it is,
> Because I am the storehouse and the shop
> Of the whole body. But, if you do remember,
> I send it through the rivers of your blood

> Even to the court, the heart, to th' seat o'th' brain;
> And through the cranks and offices of man
> The strongest nerves and small inferior veins
> From me receive that natural competency
> Whereby they live.
>
>   . . . .
>
>   'Though all at once cannot
> See what I do deliver out to each,
> Yet I can make my audit up that all
> From me do back receive the flour of all
> And leave me but the bran.'   (*Cor.* 1.1.119–29, 31–35)

As Menenius explains, "The senators of Rome are this good belly" and should the citizens "examine" and "digest things rightly," they "shall find / No public benefit which you receive / But it proceeds or comes from them to you, / And no way from yourselves" (1.1.138–43). While Menenius's belly fable provides an analogy of Rome's social and political order, it also "makes the body a city with many essential features of city life—storehouses, workshops, rivers, offices, a central court—and almost suggests intricate topography in the winding distribution of the general food supply."[10] Yet the topography of this food system does not include the space of food's production, mapping only the spaces in which food is stored and distributed. The belly passively receives the "general food at first" and then distributes it throughout the body. Only once the food has entered the city and been "cupboard[ed]" in the "storehouse and the shop" (that is, the belly) can it be distributed throughout the city. Food appears here ready-made, a product conveniently available for the body politic's consumption; the ingestion of food into the body politic originates the political order Menenius describes here. By representing food production as exterior to the body politic, Menenius's fable presents this particular relationship to food as a marker that signals incorporation into the body politic.

The context in which Menenius delivers his speech is significant here for three reasons. First, Menenius's belly fable speaks so directly to the citizens' hunger that it threatens to collapse his entire fable into a literal description of the body politic's present failure, and Menenius's metaphorical food threatens to designate precisely the thing the citizens lack: material food. Collectivizing the physiological location of this hunger, Menenius reconfigures the literal (and moral) demands stemming from the citizens' hunger, thus divorcing individual hungering bellies from the collective sated one. In doing so, he attempts to undermine the citizens' moral claims, casting the citizens' literal demand for food as an attack on the collective self.

Second, Menenius's belly fable represents food as a ready-made product available for the body politic's consumption, and in doing so the belly fable excludes the labor necessary for food's provision to the body politic. By depicting distribution as the only labor required for the sustenance of the body politic, Menenius "mystif[ies] a doctrine of social inequality and...obscure[s] the actual labor that is part of the production and distribution of provisions."[11] Situating the consuming body politic in relation to an external production of food, the belly fable renders productive food labor alien and invisible yet nevertheless constitutive of the body politic: the body politic must eat to survive, but it does not produce food for itself.

It is worth comparing this version of the body politic with that articulated by Thomas Starkey in the first half of the sixteenth century. In his *Dialogue between Pole and Lupset*, Starkey describes a body politic in which food production figures prominently:

> For when al thes partys thys couplyd togyddur, exercyse with dylegence theyr offyce & duty, as the plowmen & labuererys of the ground dylygently tyl the same for the gettyng of fode, & necessary sustenance to the rest of the body, & craftys men worke al thyngs mete for mayntenance of the sane [*sic*], ye and they hedys & rularys <by just pollycy> mayntene they state <stablyschyd in the cuntrey> ever lokyng to the profyte of they hole body, then that commyn wele must nedys florysch, then that cuntrey must nedys be in the most prosperouse state, <for> there you schal see ryches & convenyent abundance of al thyngys necessary, ther you schal see cytes & townys so garnyschyd wyth pepul, that hy schalbe necessary, in placys deserte to byld mo cytes castellys & townys.[12]

Starkey here depicts several types of laborers as necessary to the body politic's self-sufficiency. Significantly, the provision of food proves essential to the body politic's sustenance, and "the plowmen & labuererys of the ground" receive equal praise for their contributions, as do other members.

Menenius appropriates not only the image of the citizens' hungry bodies but also the ethos of productive labor that Starkey's plowmen and laborers possess.[13] For Menenius, the work of grain brokers and distributors becomes central (in literal and metaphoric terms) to the body politic's sustenance. By representing agricultural labor as exterior to the body politic, Menenius's fable renders that labor invisible. Yet the circulation of that labor's product—grain—nevertheless identifies the constituent parts of the body politic itself, implicating dependency and permeability in the very constitution of the body politic.

By making food distribution constitutive of the polis, Menenius imagines a fundamentally urban and mercantile body politic, a body incorporated not so much through its members' production or provision of food (or other goods, for that matter) as by their dependency on the belly's food shipments to them.[14] Rather than sustain itself through mutually beneficial labor, as Starkey's does, Menenius's body politic sustains and organizes itself through the distributive work of merchants. While this reliance on exterior labor suggests dependency, Menenius reshapes that dependence as self-sufficiency, mythologizing marketing and distribution as self-sufficient, fundamental labor.[15]

The context of Menenius's belly fable is significant for a third reason. By imagining food production as exterior to the body politic, and by emphasizing the belly's invisible work in organizing the contours of the body politic, Menenius's belly fable replicates the uncertainty of Rome's corn market. While the play offers two explanations for the grain shortage, neither satisfactorily accounts for the dearth. The citizens claim that the patricians hoard grain. As the First Citizen argues of the patricians, "They ne'er cared for us yet: suffer us to famish, and their storehouses crammed with grain" (*Cor.* 1.1.70–72). However, Menenius attributes the dearth to natural causes, explaining to the citizens that "The gods, not the patricians, make it, and / Your knees to them, not arms, must help" (1.1.64–65). It is impossible to decide which explanation has the greater claim to the truth here, and in fact the play moves away from this question, leaving it "behind, isolated and unresolved, as a sign of the division between idea and actuality."[16] Yet while the question of dearth indeed becomes less important to the play's actions, the mysterious functioning of the corn market remains an issue.

The point may not be so much who is correct as it is about the opacity of the corn market itself. Indeed, dearth's causes were not always clear, and while contemporaneous explanations increasingly accused grain brokers for dearth, there remained uncertainty as to dearth's causes. Official attempts to survey and distribute grain stocks throughout England downplayed "both the weather and its prime mover, the hand of the Almighty, as causes of dearth," and official remedies for dearth such as county searches of grain stores "themselves implied that the problem did not lie in a national deficiency of grain but in its faulty distribution."[17] John Walter and Keith Wrightson note that the Privy Council shared the popular understanding that dearth was the product of the activities of brokers.[18] When food riots occurred, rioters often appealed to authorities' sense of the "moral economy," with much of the riots and grain seizures directed against brokers, whom local authorities also blamed for dearth.[19]

Even so, popular understandings of dearth's causes varied. Often, three causes for dearth were asserted. These included, understandably, the weather (often understood as God's judgment), hoarding, and export of grain out of the region.[20] A 1586 "remedy in this dearth" noted the two causes identified in *Coriolanus:* "It must be granted that this present dearth doth grow either by the want of corn itself within the realm, utterly failing in this last year's season; or else by the wretched covetousness of the cruel cornmasters."[21] Ballads published in response to the 1608 Midland Rising offered "diametrically-opposed assessments of the causes of high prices," at once interpreting dearth as a manipulation of the market by *"Greedy Fermours"* and as a providential judgment of sin.[22]

In his response to the 1596 dearth, Hugh Plat identified multiple causes of it. Assuming that the dearth was, at least in part an instance of divine judgment, he recommended praying that God "forget and forgiue our manifolde sins and transgressions, which haue turned his fauorable countenance so long from vs, and brought downe from heauen so many clowdes of wrath vpon the fruites of the earth."[23] Moreover, Plat advised the moderation of individuals' diets, noting that "if euerie rich man would spare but one meale in a weeke, and confer the estimate vppon the poore of the parish...I saie euen this one meale would serue wel to mend a whole weekes commons of a poore *Subscisor.*"[24]

Among other remedies, including increased poor relief and the proper execution of the Privy Council's orders for grain distribution, Plat urged the cessation of speculative price inflation. Proposing a series of innovative substitute foods for those suffering hunger, Plat aimed to "frustrate the greatest parte of these couetous complots, and by new, and artificial discoueries of strange bread, drinke, and food, in matter and preparation so full of variety, to worke some alteration and change into this great and dangerous dearth."[25] While Plat emphasized the "covetous complots" increasing dearth, he nevertheless asserted several causes, suggesting a reluctance to settle on a singular cause.

It is this uncertainty that Shakespeare stages in *Coriolanus*, and the different explanations for the dearth proposed do more than represent antagonistic political positions. As the cause of dearth remains unresolved in the play, these competing explanations stage the market's uncertainty in a realistic fashion, constructing the market as unknowable. In his revision of his source material, Shakespeare eliminates causal explanations of the dearth, heightening the uncertainty regarding its causes.[26] As critics have noted, Shakespeare revised Plutarch's account of the citizens' uprising: whereas in Plutarch the citizens protest outrageous rates of usury, in *Coriolanus* a scarcity of corn motivates the citizens' protest.[27] By foregrounding dearth, the play echoes those riots and protests motivated by dearth that occurred in England, most notably the 1607–08 corn dearth and the 1608 Midlands insurrection against enclosure and corn scarcity.[28] Yet in Plutarch the citizens stage a second insurrection because of the "extreme dearth they had emong them."[29] Moreover, the war against Corioles caused the dearth: "Bicause the most parte of the errable lande within the territorie of Rome, was become heathie and barren for lacke of plowing, for that they had no time nor meane to cause corne, to be brought them out of other countries to sowe, by reason of their warres which made the extreme dearth."[30] Shakespeare recasts this second revolt as the initial revolt in *Coriolanus*, eliminating the causal connection Plutarch establishes between the two insurrections.[31] By increasing the uncertainty regarding the dearth's causes, Shakespeare introduces a third limit within the body politic: the citizens'—and the audience's—inability to know the cause of the scarcity of corn.

In fact, Martius mocks the citizens' explanations, emphasizing their inability to assess the dearth's causes. Responding to the citizens' claim that the "city is well stored" with corn, Martius scoffs,

"They say? / They'll sit by th'fire and presume to know / What's done i'th' Capitol" (1.1.178–81). Martius condescendingly reports their demands:

> They said they were an-hungry, sighed forth proverbs—
> That hunger broke stone walls, that dogs must eat,
> That meat was made for mouths, that the gods sent not
> Corn for rich men only.   (1.1.194–97)

Yet even as Martius characterizes the citizens' demands as empty words grounded in deficient knowledge, the play reveals Menenius's belly fable to be empty. Menenius aimed to offer the citizens words as a substitute for food. However, while the citizens may be willing to take words for food, the play instead stages their acceptance of another substitution: political representation for food.

Whereas Plutarch's Menenius successfully pacifies the revolt by relating the belly fable and by offering tribunes, Shakespeare's Menenius simply stalls the citizens, his words having little persuasive effect. Plutarch emphasizes Menenius's successful oration as the senate's representative; Shakespeare separates him from the senate, suggesting that his speech is ineffectual precisely because he does not speak on the senate's behalf.[32] Indeed, Shakespeare stages Menenius's speech *at the very moment* the senate grants tribunes to the citizens, thereby emphasizing the emptiness of Menenius's address.

Petitioning for food, the citizens instead receive tribunes. Coupled with the need for war preparations, the granting of tribunes deflates the food protest, and the citizens return to their homes. The granting of tribunes appears here as a substitute for distributing food, with the citizens receiving political representation instead of corn. In granting tribunes to the people, the senate thus metaphorically produces and distributes food to the citizens.

While the play implicitly figures this granting of tribunes as a form of feeding, it later makes this figuration explicit in Martius's equation of food and political representation. Angry that he has not been approved for the consulship, he complains that

> In soothing them we nourish 'gainst our Senate
> The cockle of rebellion, insolence, sedition,
> Which we ourselves have ploughed for, sowed, and scattered
> By mingling them with us.   (*Cor.*, 3.1.73–76)

In his view, the republic feeds the citizens with the political power that Martius holds identical to the patricians as a ruling class.

Interestingly, Martius figures the senate's actions in terms of agricultural labor, the work of plowmen and sowers. Whereas Menenius's belly fable excluded agricultural work, Martius here integrates this work into Rome's body politic, attributing this productive labor—albeit in negative terms—to Rome's ruling class. In both Menenius's and Martius's versions of Rome's body politic, the production of food remains at the limit: while Menenius excludes food's production, Martius integrates it in order to demonstrate its harms. For Martius, the senate metaphorically produces food for the citizens; the body politic feeds itself.

Martius revises Menenius's image of the body politic. Objecting to the giving of free corn to the people, Martius argues that "Whoever gave that counsel to give forth / The corn o'th' storehouse gratis...I say they nourished disobedience, fed / The ruin of the state" (*Cor.*, 3.1.116–17, 120–21). Martius's language registers inversely to the language of the opening protest. There, the scarcity of corn led to Menenius's metaphorical appropriation of the citizens' hungry belly as the patricians in the body politic. Here, however, the literal distribution and consumption of corn is transfigured as a metaphorical nourishment of discord in the body politic.

Perhaps because he figures political representation as food, Martius objects to it in terms of its taste. Protesting the citizens' political representation, he laments its leveling of hierarchy. He tells the senators, "You are plebeians / If they be senators, and they are no less / When, both your voices blended, the great'st taste / Most palates theirs" (3.1.104–07). Martius associates "voice"—that is, political power—with taste, arguing that the citizens' voices will overpower the senators'; the stronger the breath, the more it governs the palate, or, possibly, the stronger it tastes (on the palate).

The image figures a communion of sense in which senators and citizens simultaneously taste and are tasted, the resulting flavor satisfying the palate of the citizens rather than of the senators. Martius's language here echoes the play's representation of the citizens' political participation via a complex of oral associations that conflate breath, tongue, and voice. In this register, food signifies via a cluster of bodily

associations: the citizens' breath, for example, is marked by plebeian food—onions and garlic. And it is precisely plebeian breath that
Martius eschews in the marketplace: in the political forum, the value-
less (from Martius's point of view) plebeian political voice is marked
by its inferior palate, its inferior culinary taste.

Just as voice marks the citizens' approval of Coriolanus as consul,
it also marks their political power. As Sicinus declares, "the people /
Must have their voices" (*Cor.*, 2.2.136–37). Indeed, the citizens also
figure their approval as voice: the First Citizen declares that "if he do
require our voices we ought not to deny him" (2.3.1–2), and he confirms to the tribunes that Coriolanus "has our voices" (2.3.145). One
citizen wonders whether the others will "give your voices" (2.3.33),
and another declares that the citizens "give you our voices heartily"
(2.3.96). As though he were a vendor, Coriolanus contemptuously
invites the citizens to exchange their votes for his services, which
are signified by his wounds: "Your voices! For your voices I have
fought, / Watched for your voices, for your voices bear / Of wounds
two dozen odd; battles thrice six / I have seen and heard of for your
voices" (2.3.116–19). Preparing to display his wounds in the marketplace, Coriolanus objects to displaying "th'unaching scars, which I
should hide, / As if I had received them for the hire / Of their breath
only" (2.2.145–47). Moreover, the Third Citizen notes that "every one
of us has a single honour in giving him our own voices with our own
tongues" (2.3.39–40). Earlier in the scene, this citizen informs his fellows that if Coriolanus "show us his wounds and tell us his deeds,
we are to put our tongues into those wounds and speak for them"
(2.3.5–7).

This last image figures two things. First, Coriolanus's wounds appear
as mouths to which the citizens lend their tongues. These mouths
then speak on behalf of Coriolanus, collectively approving his nomi-
nation. Coriolanus's wounds incorporate the citizens' tongues to form
here a second body politic, one in which the citizens' and Coriolanus's
political power become interdependent: Coriolanus's wounds cannot
speak without tongues (or voices), and the citizens' tongues and voices
require mouths to house them.

Second, the image hints at an oral interaction between the citizens
and Coriolanus as though the citizens lick Coriolanus, tasting his

wounds. In this light, Coriolanus appears as a communal dish presented to and assessed by the citizens' tongues. While it stops short
of figuring Coriolanus as eaten (as opposed to tasted), the image is
underwritten by a more general threat that the citizens will devour
him.[33] Indeed, Coriolanus later informs Aufidius that the citizens
"hath devoured" (4.5.75) all of him, saving his name. In any case, the
citizens' tongues tentatively assess Coriolanus's worth, a political
assessment figured as taste, both in sensory and aesthetic terms. That
they do devour him, in Coriolanus's view at least, suggests a turn from
corporate speaking—the citizens' tongues speaking in Coriolanus's
wounds—to a consumption, as though Coriolanus's exile were a form
of feeding. The body politic feeds on itself.

As I have noted, the play conflates breath with voice, voice with
political power. The play describes the citizens' breath as offensive
because it stinks, often of food associated with lower ranks. For example, in a passage that again equates political action, voice, and breath,
Menenius charges the tribunes as having "stood so much / Upon the
voice of occupation and / The breath of garlic eaters" (*Cor.*, 4.6.100–
02).[34] The association of garlic breath with the citizens also lies
behind the First Citizen's proverb, "They say poor suitors have strong
breaths" (1.1.51–52). Brutus reports to the citizens that Coriolanus
refuses to "beg their stinking breaths" (2.1.222), a point reiterated
when Coriolanus later identifies the citizens as those "whose breath
I hate / As reek o'th'rotten fens" (3.3.124–25). When threatened by
Coriolanus's advance on Rome, Menenius accuses the tribunes of having "made the air unwholesome when you cast / Your stinking greasy
caps in hooting at / Coriolanus' exile" (4.6.138–40).

The play associates political participation—the citizens' giving of
their voices—with taste, or as Coriolanus puts it, with the citizens'
"palate." Coriolanus conflates voice, tongue, and taste, advising the
senators to "at once pluck out / The multitudinous tongue; let them
not lick / The sweet which is their poison" (3.1.158–60). By pluck-
ing out the "multitudinous tongue," the senators would revoke the
power granted to the tribunes. Yet while one might expect Coriolanus
to elaborate the figure "multitudinous tongue" by referring to political
speech, he turns instead to its sense of taste, noting the sweetness of the
poison it would no longer lick. Here the political power of the tribunes

("The tongues o'the'common mouth" [3.1.23]) and, by extension, of the citizens, appears as a tasting tongue, an image that echoes the citizens' licking of Coriolanus's wounds in the marketplace. This conflation operates also in Coriolanus's complex image of blended voices discussed briefly above. In that image, the blended voices of the senators and citizens govern what the collective mouth tastes. It remains productively ambiguous whether Coriolanus refers to the palate's preference for the "great'st taste" as a function of the citizens' "reeking" breath, of their majority of voices, or of both.

In a play concerned with the power of the citizens' voice—and the origin of that voice in its substitution for food—Martius's association of political voice with taste emphasizes the significance of food in the play's imagination of the body politic.[35] Menenius defines the body politic by the consumption of food it does not produce itself. In this model, food delivers itself to the collective, consuming body, acquiring significance not by the productive labor that provides it but by the mercantile labor that distributes it. Because food production remains exterior to the body politic, Menenius's fable makes food consumption the mechanism by which the body politic incorporates individuals into its collective body. Eating, coded as a passive reception of food, becomes a core signifier of one's membership in the body politic.

As the rioting citizens make evident, there is little food in Rome. While Menenius does invite Volumnia and Virgilia to dine with him, Volumnia rejects his offer and proposes a metaphorical dinner in its stead: "Anger's my meat, I sup upon myself, / And so shall starve with feeding" (*Cor.*, 4.2.53–54). Like Menenius, Volumnia turns a desire to eat literally into an image of metaphorical eating. Moreover, she figures herself as both producer and consumer of this metaphorical meat.

In contrast, the Volscians have plenty of food. As Martius insultingly puts it, "The Volsces have much corn. Take these rats thither / To gnaw their garners" (*Cor.*, 1.1.240–41). Indeed, the play's Antium scenes stage food as plentiful, satisfying, and available to eat, contrasting Antium's plentiful commensality with Rome's corn dearth as well as with Volumnia's solitary self-consuming dinner. Martius enters Aufidius's house during a feast, interrupting the servants' preparation and service of food. The scene presents a well-ordered household, reflecting Aufidius's command of a more stable, ordered, and hierarchical environment than that which occasioned Martius's exile. The order is represented through food service, and, for the first time, food actually appears on stage. In contrast to his disdain for the unruly breath of Rome's garlic eaters, Martius associates the pleasant aroma of cooking food with the orderliness of Aufidius's household: "A goodly house. The feast / Smells well" (4.5.5–6). Whereas in Rome Martius had been accused of causing dearth, in Antium he becomes associated with plenty. A lieutenant reports to Aufidius that "Your soldiers use him as the grace fore meat, / Their talk at table, and their thanks at end" (4.7.3–4). Noting that Coriolanus would win "should we encounter / As often as we eat" (1.11.9–10), the praise echoes Aufidius's earlier praise of him.

The Antium scenes also blur the line between figurative and literal food labor, linking war and service with food labor. For example, Coriolanus's agreement to attack Rome is characterized as a dish served at Aufidius's table: "'Tis as it were a parcel of their feast, and to be executed ere they wipe their lips" (*Cor.*, 4.5.213–14). Moreover, when he enters Antium, Coriolanus mockingly fears the "wives with spits" who would seek "in puny battle to slay me" (4.4.5–6). In fact, Coriolanus's service to Aufidius becomes identified as the sort of cookery the "wives with spits" might perform. Aufidius's servants liken Coriolanus's previous battles to preparing and grilling meat, noting that he "scotched him [Aufidius] and notched him like a carbonado" (4.5.185–86). Another adds that had Coriolanus "been cannibally given, he might have broiled and eaten him too" (4.5.187–88).

A third servant depicts Coriolanus as an agricultural laborer who "will mow all down before him, and leave his passage polled" (*Cor.*, 4.5.199–200). The image recalls Volumnia's depiction of Coriolanus as "a harvest-man that's tasked to mow / Or all or lose his hire" (1.3.33–34). Aufidius too understands Coriolanus in these terms, noting that "he bears all things fairly / And shows good husbandry for the Volscian state" (5.1.21–22). In praising "husbandry" Aufidius praises Coriolanus's military management; yet, the term connotes agricultural labor as well.[36] Later, Coriolanus himself understands the Volscian advance he leads in terms of agricultural labor. Steeling himself against his wife's and mother's petitions, he vows not to abandon the attack on Rome:

> Let the Volsces
> Plough Rome and harrow Italy! I'll never
> Be such a gosling to obey instinct, but stand
> As if a man were author of himself.   (5.3.33–36)

From the Romans' point of view, Coriolanus appears to be an agricultural laborer who must destroy rotten grain. As Cominius notes, Coriolanus has asserted he

> could not stay to pick them [his friends] in a pile
> Of noisome, musty chaff. He said 'twas folly,
> For one poor grain or two, to leave unburnt
> And still to nose th'offence.   (5.1.25–28)

The play figures Martius as the sort of laborer Menenius's body politic excludes and renders invisible. As an agricultural laborer, Martius appears here as a provider rather than consumer, a characterization made ironic because, as Cavell points out, the citizens "maddeningly accuse him of *withholding* food."[37] The image of Martius as agricultural laborer also proves ironic because his exile mirrors Menenius's exile of food labor; at the moment Rome requires food, it finds that its supplier—the "greedy fermour" thought responsible for dearth in the first place—has been exiled only to serve its enemy.

Coriolanus is caught up in a social imaginary in which food-as-object gives way to food-as-metaphor. Yet the play foregrounds the political stakes surrounding this representation of food: food production stands at the limit of the body politic and serves as a crucial motif in the body politic's imagination of itself. Where the production of material food marks the boundaries of the body politic, this exteriorization sets in motion a metaphoric logic by which the republic comes to feed itself with political representation and by which Rome's communal tasting of its members becomes a means to know its limits.

Chapter 6

Sacking Falstaff

REBECCA LEMON

In a climactic battlefield moment near the end of *2 Henry IV*, as rebel and crown troops fiercely engage, the play veers away from historical rebellion to trumpet the benefits of alcohol. Falstaff delivers his famous mock encomium, praising sack: "If I had a thousand sons, the first human principle I would teach them should be to foreswear thin potations, and to addict themselves to sack" (4.2.1010–13).[1] Falstaff's defense of the dry—*sec*—white wine from Spain is at once tongue-in-cheek and entirely heartfelt, promoting the drink's benefits for both physical and mental health, its "twofold operation" (88).[2] Offered in the form of a classical defense, the speech supports sack drinking as an ethical pursuit. Shakespeare's character uses his skills of argumentation to uphold not folly, as Erasmus does before him, but drunkenness. The sack speech, as Joshua B. Fisher argues, turns "the conventional discourse about the dangers of intemperate drinking squarely on its head."[3] But like Erasmus, and in good humanist tradition, Shakespeare invites the audience to dismiss the speech as mere play—it is, after all, an extended joke, a fact amplified by the speech's delivery on the battlefield by a drunken man defending his favorite pastime. Yet, as with Erasmus's mock encomium, so too with Falstaff's speech: the comic presentation contains a serious insight, one that this essay seeks to tease out.

This speech offers two defenses of drinking familiar to Shakespeare's audience: drinking fosters health and encourages convivial community. Yet even as Falstaff defends and eagerly consumes sack, by this point in *Henry IV* he exhibits neither the health nor the successful community promised by alcohol's defenders. Instead, one of the theater's most beloved drinkers helps to reinforce contemporary attacks on drunkenness as a source of disease and poverty.[4] For against the knight's rhetorical argument in his sack speech stands his theatrical trajectory. His drinking shifts over the course of the Henriad: what begins as an apparent choice to drink turns, precisely as the physician Galen warns his readers, into a habit and then a necessity. The contradictions in Falstaff's character are part of the play's exploration of how alcohol, even as it holds the power to forge community, over time might also threaten such community, particularly in circumstances where a social pastime devolves into a habit and an illness. The substance promising inspiration and community can—when misused, overused, or misunderstood—rot and isolate the consumer.

In staging this devolution of drinking practices, *Henry IV* reveals the power of alcohol as a rebel force undermining monarchical sovereignty in this unstable kingdom.[5] Sack becomes, as Karen Raber writes in chapter 4 of this volume, a sign of England's "moral debility" and national failing as drinkers exhibit dangerous attachments to foreign drink and goods at the expense of the country's exchequer. Falstaff's drinking proves especially problematic in this regard: not only does he choose to imbibe a foreign rather than a domestic beverage, but also his manner of consumption proves increasingly antisocial as the plays continue. Falstaff's gluttony has attracted a degree of critical attention, yet it is his drinking rather than eating that proves oppositional as the plays develop.[6] The knight eats less and less, while continuing to drink. Eventually this appetitive opposition turns from a sign of good fellowship into a potentially treasonous attachment to drink. Loyalty to sack trumps his other commitments—to Hal, Eastcheap, and England. As Falstaff becomes increasingly preoccupied and even controlled by sack, the tavern subculture, so often read by critics as a site of carnivalesque festivity and good fellowship, condenses to the singular spectacle of the lone drinker.[7] Inspiration turns to isolation, not because Falstaff is banished but because earlier in the play he pursues, as he counsels his "thousand sons" to do, his addiction.[8]

THE JOY OF SACK

Falstaff's mock encomium opens by lampooning Prince John, who fails to appreciate a good glass of wine:

Good faith, this same young sober-blooded boy doth not love me, nor a man cannot make him laugh—but that's no marvel: he drinks no wine. There's never none of these demure boys come to any proof, for thin drink doth...over-cool their blood....They are generally fools and cowards, which some of us should be too, but for inflammation. A good sherry-sack hath a twofold operation in it: it ascends me into the brain, dries me there all the foolish and dull and cruddy vapours which environ it, makes it apprehensive, quick, forgetive, full of nimble, fiery, and delectable shapes, which delivered o'er to the voice, the tongue, which is the birth, becomes excellent wit. The second property of your excellent sherry is the warming of the blood, which before, cold and settled, left the liver white and pale, which is the badge of pusillanimity and cowardice. But the sherry warms it....So that skill in the weapon is nothing without sack, for that sets it a-work, and learning a mere hoard of gold kept by a devil, till sack commences it and sets it in acts and use. Hereof comes it that Prince Harry is valiant, for the cold blood he did naturally inherit of his father he hath like lean, sterile, and bare land, manured, husbanded, and tilled, with excellent endeavor of drinking good and good store of fertile sherry, that he is become very hot and valiant. If I had a thousand sons, the first human principle I would teach them should be to foreswear thin potations, and to addict themselves to sack. (*2H4*, 4.2.80–113)[9]

The sack speech, most obviously, trumpets the benefits of drinking. Falstaff defends drinking on essentially two levels. He insists that alcohol cures humoral imbalances, "warming the blood, which before, cold and settled, left the liver white and pale" (94–95). Galenic theory counseled that good health lay in the proper management of the four humors through diet and exercise—and alcohol played a crucial role in this management. English medical writers follow Galen's practice of prescribing alcohol, including wine, ale, and beer, to patients.[10] Nicholas Culpepper (1653) writes how "hops...open obstructions of the liver and spleen to cleanse the blood,...to cure the French disease and all manner of scabs, itch, and other breakings out of the body," and Timothy Bright (1586) writes, "wine, and strong drinke...have a power to comfort the braine, and hart, and affect all our bodie throughout with celeritie and quicknesse."[11] Sack is particularly advised for the elderly since their veins "waxe cold" and this wine helps to warm them.[12] For these writers a beverage like sack is cleansing and comforting; it helps cure and protect the drinker, a point Michael Schoenfeldt and Gail Kern Paster amplify in their studies of the humors and health.[13] Falstaff clearly draws on such health literature, making a humoral defense of alcohol ingestion, as if his primary reason for drinking were physical well-being.[14]

The mock encomium moves to another register when Falstaff assures the audience that sack produces mental as well as physical health, in the form of increased wit and sociability. This link between drinking, wit, and fraternal community was well established for Shakespeare's audience. Classical precedents such as Anacreontic verse supported urbane drinking culture, as both Joshua Scodel and Stella Achilleos have illuminated.[15] And Michelle O'Callaghan's work has been particularly helpful in uncovering and analyzing the drinking communities of witty gallants in Shakespeare's England.[16] Despite the resonance of Falstaff's speech with such contemporary modes of urbane consumption, the knight's drinking more obviously recalls raucous, unruly communities of drunken soldiers, less interested in convivial conversation than consumptive excess. With the knightly bombast and heavy drinking habits typical of soldiers he cries, "Gallants, lads, boys, hearts of gold, all the titles of good fellowship come to you! What, shall we be merry?" (*1H4*, 2.4.253–54).[17] Falstaff rallies the troops, inviting his good fellows to be "merry," a term signifying drunkenness. Sack, he argues, helps to prepare "the rest of this little kingdom, man, to arm" (*2H4*, 4.2.99). Formerly armed with weapons, now with sack, returning soldiers upheld excessive drinking as a rite of passage, evident in health drinking and other rituals: drunken excess offers one means of establishing clannish loyalty.[18]

Contemporary examples of raucous drinking are legion. One group, known as "the Damned Crew," earned notoriety for beating up the watch in 1600 after drinking heavily at the Mermaid, where the group's leader, Sir Edmund Baynham, allegedly "affirmed with great oaths at that time, that if he had but fifty horses, he could overrunne the said citty, and that he cared not a fart for the Lord Maior or any Magistrate in London and that he hoped shortly to see a thowsand of the citizens throats cut with divers other most vile and opprobrious words."[19] Falstaff's boast at the Gadshill robbery, "Cut the villains' throats!" (*1H4*, 2.2.74), anticipates Baynham's cry, as both men drink heavily, threaten violence, and deride authority, be it the lord mayor or the lord chief justice.[20] Falstaff evokes this martial subculture in his link of sack to valor, "skill in the weapon is nothing without sack," a line ripe with masculine bravado, sexual innuendo, and comic irony. However, Falstaff's speech also hints at (even as it represses and denies) the frequently noted tension between masculine performance and alcohol; as the Porter puts it in *Macbeth*, "it provokes the desire but it takes away the performance" (2.3.24–25).

Recent studies of the material practices of drinking illuminate Falstaff's ethos. B. Ann Tlusty highlights the "exaggerated norms of masculine behavior" evident among soldiers drinking in taverns.[21] Here soldiers goad one another to overdrink or to brawl. Bernard Capp also illuminates the masculine culture of boisterous drinking and fighting: "The world of drink, gaming and roistering condemned by the conduct books represented an alternative model of manhood, always attractive to some."[22] Gina Bloom is even more pointed in her analysis of heaving drinking, drawing attention to the dissenting possibilities of intoxication: for "working men of lower or middle status and youths… disorderly behaviors like heavy drinking could constitute a bid for an antipatriarchal, countercode of masculine conduct."[23] Finally, my own study of health toasts and Adam Smyth's study of drunkenness both draw attention to the pleasures of heavy drinking for certain male communities.[24]

What makes Falstaff's speech especially witty, in light of these recent studies, is the way he combines two opposite defenses of drinking familiar to Shakespeare's audience members. He yokes the martial drinking practices that promote excess to the medicinal ones demanding moderation. First, he argues that drinking fosters physical health through moderate consumption; and second, that alcohol promotes community and courage when ingested in larger quantities. The result of this witty promotion of sack has been a long critical tradition of celebrating Falstaff for his humor and good fellowship. To William Hazlitt, "Falstaff's wit is an emanation of a fine constitution; an exuberance of good-humour and good-nature; an overflowing of his love of laughter and good-fellowship."[25] Falstaff is known for his "wit, humor, laughter, good-fellowship, insatiable zest for life."[26] Further, "Falstaff conquers us with his irresistible humor and good-fellowship."[27] This praise trumpets Falstaff's excess: his good fellowship overflows, his humor is "irresistible," his zest for life "insatiable." Alcohol, by this logic, serves as an ethical elixir, countering distance, isolation, and sober moralizing.

Since Falstaff appears to be the consummate good fellow, drawing critical attention to those less congenial aspects of his character might seem moralizing or puritanical. Yet teasing out the insight of the sack speech requires risking such a charge. For even as Falstaff rehearses discourses in support of drink in his encomium, his physical character trumpets the warnings familiar from anti-alcohol polemic, to which the next section turns. This is yet another reason why Falstaff's speech reads as an extended joke, although this aspect of the joke comes at Falstaff's expense: he defends drinking as companionship even as he drinks alone, and he links alcohol and good health even as his body is riddled with disease. To view Falstaff as a celebration of tavern culture thus requires ignoring aspects of his character that threaten conviviality, signing on to Falstaff's comic logic while ignoring his tragic trajectory. Ian Moulton puts it, "Shakespeare goes to great lengths to show us just how serious Falstaff's corruption is."[28] Indeed, given Falstaff's jovial productivity and his immense popularity with audiences, why does the play repeatedly draw attention to the more troublesome characteristics of this beloved knight?[29]

Sick with Sack

Falstaff lacks the good health that should come with managing humors through alcohol. To use the language of *Henry IV* to describe him, Falstaff is a "whoreson obscene greasy tallow-catch" (*1H4*, 2.4.208–09), a "bolting-hutch of beastliness" (409), "stuffed cloak-bag of guts" (411), a "roasted Manningtree ox" (411), a "swollen parcel of dropsies" (410), a "globe of sinful continents" (*2H4*, 2.4.257), a "sanguine coward" (*1H4*, 2.4.221–22), a "whoreson little tidy Bartholomew boar-pig" (*2H4*, 2.4.204), a "huge bombard of sack" (*1H4*, 2.4.410), "fatkidneyed" (2.2.5), "short winded," (*2H4*, 2.2.108), "surfeit-swelled" (5.5.48), "rheumatic" (2.4.52; *H5*, 2.4.33); one who "sweats to death" (*1H4*, 2.3.16) and who suffers from "diseases" (*2H4*, 1.2.3) and "consumption of the purse" (1.2.216–17). As the doctor claims at the start of *2 Henry IV*, Falstaff's "water itself was a good healthy water but, for the party that owed it, he might have more diseases than he knew for" (1.2.2–4).

These descriptions point to Falstaff's body as a site of infirmity: suffering from "diseases" and "dropsies," he is "rheumatic" with "consumption." Such specific medical ailments reinforce contemporary arguments linking drink and disease. Indeed, early modern pamphleteers catalogue precisely the infirmities exhibited by Falstaff. In *A Looking Glasse for Drunkards*, the writer describes how drunkenness creates "multitudes of diseases in the body of man, as apoplexies, falling sicknesses, palsies, dropsies, consumptions, giddinesse of the head, [and] inflammation of the blood and liver."[30] Similarly, Dr. Everard Maynwaring writes, "That drunkenness is a disease or sickness will appear in that it hath all the requisites to constitute a disease...; the stomach perhaps vomites or nauseates; his legs fail...an unwholesome corpulency and...plentitude of body does follow:...as well as imbecility of the nerves."[31] Finally, William Fulbecke expands on the dangers of excessive drinking, which can provoke "a great number of diseases: as Catarres, rewmes, swellinges, goutes, dropsies, doe shake the foundation of our healthe."[32] Lack of courage ("imbecility of the nerves"), as well as unwholesome corpulency, dropsies, palsies, and consumption characterize Falstaff in precisely the manner these pamphlets on drunkenness suggest.[33]

Falstaff's diseases are abundant, both verbally and physically. They are also, arguably, spiritual, and resonate with contemporary critiques of sinful drinking. He is "Sir John, Sack-and-Sugar Jack" who, as Hal claims, has sold his soul to the devil for "a cup of Madeira and a cold capon's leg" (*1H4*, 1.2.109–10); he is a notorious debtor; he is a knight who cares nothing for time itself unless, as Hal famously puts it, "hours were cups of sack, and minutes capons" (1.2.6–7). This language of damnation, debt, and sloth typifies that of moralizing pamphlets. In *Woe to Drunkards*, for example, Samuel Ward writes that drunkenness is the "utter undoing...of health and wealth," and it is "the deadly poison of this odious sinne." Furthermore, "wine takes away the heart, and spoyles the braine, overthrowes the faculties and Organes of repentance and resolution."[34] The drinker, according to Ward, ruins his or her physical and financial health, as well as compromises the ability to reform and repent.

Falstaff's defense of drinking comes under increasing pressure as *Henry IV* develops, not only because of the knight's obvious physical and spiritual impairments but also more palpably because the coupling of love and alcohol fails to uphold good fellowship as promised. At first, the relationship of Hal and Falstaff is supported by shared drinking, the "cups of sack" (*1H4*, 1.2.6) for which Hal "hast paid all" (46). Such devotion to sack appears in comic form early on, as Hal reads the debtor's tally he pinches from Falstaff's pocket. It includes two gallons of sack, anchovies and sack after supper, a capon, bread and sauce. As the prince remarks, "Oh, monstrous! But one halfpennyworth of bread to this intolerable deal of sack" (2.4.491–92). Even drinking companions acknowledge the "monstrous" nature of Falstaff's drinking. If such imbibing is initially humorous, by the time *Henry IV* ends Hal no longer drinks with the knight. Instead he desires the low-alcohol beverage small beer, a desire rife with class and national resonances as Peter Parolin explores in chapter 1 of this volume. Falstaff, by contrast, continues to imbibe sack and in doing so exhausts his friendships with others by preying on their purses to fuel his appetites. His drinking becomes, as Hal claims, "intolerable." Falstaff notoriously has made "three hundred and odd pounds" out of those "toasts-and-butter" men who bought their way out of military service. Commanding a regiment of "scarecrows" who are "food for powder," Falstaff increases his purse and supports his drinking (*1H4*, 4.2.13–14, 19, 35, 59–60).

Uncomfortably turning military service into a fundraising campaign for himself, Falstaff preys on his friends to garner even more funds. He owes Bartolph an angel for his battlefield drinking (*1H4*, 4.2.6), Master Shallow a thousand pounds (*2H4*, 5.5.71), and Mistress Quickly a hundred marks; driven into debt, Quickly is forced to sell her tavern's plate and tapestries to keep from prison. As she claims of Falstaff, he has taken "all I have. He hath eaten me out of house and home; he hath put all my substance into that fat belly of his. But I will have some of it out again" (*2H4*, 2.1.62–64). Thanks to his silver tongue, however, Falstaff convinces Quickly otherwise, and she continues to supply him even to the point of her arrest. Beyond Bartolph, Shallow, and Quickly, Falstaff most obviously draws on Hal, who serves both as the payer of his debts and as security for the knight's credit.

Falstaff's love of drink drains rather than sustains his tavern community. So too does sack fail to produce the valor Falstaff champions. He is a notorious and hilarious coward, as revealed at Gadshill and in battle. In fact, against his logic in the sack speech, drink and courage work in opposition with him, as Hal realizes to his dismay.

Encountering an idle Falstaff on the battlefield, the prince chides him and Falstaff responds:

> FALSTAFF: Take my pistol, if thou wilt.
> PRINCE: Give it me. What, is it in the case?
> FALSTAFF: Ay, Hal, 'tis hot, 'tis hot. There's that will sack a city.
> *The Prince draws it out, and finds it to be a bottle of sack.*
> PRINCE: What, is it a time to jest and dally now?
> *He throws the bottle at him. Exit.*　　　　　　　　　(*1H4*, 5.3.49–52)

Not only does Falstaff fail to fight in battle, but also in replacing his pistol with liquor he inverts what his speech promises—sack, which should lead to weapon-wielding, instead substitutes for it. Here Falstaff reveals his inability to move beyond his appetite for drinking, even in the emergency of wartime. His allegiance to sack proves stronger than his allegiance to Hal or Henry IV, for whom he is meant to be fighting.

SACK ADDICTION

The sack speech embeds contradictory views on drinking, resulting in an argument that exists in tension not only with itself but also with its speaker. It is the significant shift in Falstaff's character over the course of the Henriad that produces this tension between speech and speaker. This shift appears at the levels of both plot and staging, as suggested above: Falstaff stands alone and impoverished by the time he delivers the speech, having once enjoyed the friendship and credit the speech promises. Yet the shift in Falstaff's character also appears through changes in the play's lexicon of conviviality. The tension and transformation condensed in the sack speech unfold in another register, and more gradually, as key words associated with Falstaff shift, resonating over the course of the Henriad. As this section will explore, the use of terms like "sack," "consumption," "company," and "addict" transform as the play proceeds. Their altered signification is one of the ways in which the play charts the change in Falstaff's drinking from choice to compulsion.

For example, Falstaff deploys the key word "sack" differently in his exchange with Hal on the battlefield, in contrast to the sack speech. Falstaff brags of his pistol case, "There's that will sack a city" (*1H4*, 5.3.51). His pun, in drawing attention to the double resonance of sack as liquor and ruin, cleverly turns attention away from the violence surrounding him and toward his convivial community. Here weapons become libations. This popular knight turns the battlefield into a tavern, death and destruction into merriment.[35] Equally, however, Falstaff's statement serves not to deflect violence but instead to collapse the ostensibly opposite impulses of drink and destruction into each other. The noun and verb forms of "sack" have come to accord with each other: the knight's love of drink has drained the resources of his closest friends. His excessive drinking bankrupts his allies and prompts the sacrifice of impoverished men in battle; Falstaff sacks or plunders his own community.[36]

Just as the term "sack" embeds simultaneous notions of alcohol and wreckage, so too do the other terms key to the play's convivial lexicon—namely, "consumption," "company," and "addict." Falstaff's sack speech is a tribute to the benefits of vigorous consumption. Indeed, the comedy throughout *Henry IV* depends on scenes of consumption, in locations from Eastcheap to the prince's quarters. The play's use of the term "consumption" associates not with pleasant ingestion, however, but with wasting disease. As Falstaff complains, "I can get no remedy against this consumption of the purse. Borrowing only lingers and lingers it out, but the disease is incurable" (*2H4*, 1.2.216–18). Here consumption and disease are synonymous.

As with "sack" and "consumption," so with the term "company": it initially signifies community but in the end denotes death. At the start of *Henry IV*, "company" references the tavern, albeit the criminal elements of tavern life: the term first appears in relation to the company of men at Gadshill enjoying supper. Falstaff complains of Hal that he has been "bewitched with the rogue's company" (*1H4*, 2.2.15). But of course, his attack on company is tongue in cheek. To claim, as he does, that "company, villainous company, hath been the spoil of me" (3.3.8–9) is to invite audience laughter—Falstaff delights in Hal's company, as evidenced in his plea to "banish not him thy Harry's company" (2.4.436). But while the term initially designates tavern communities, and particularly Falstaff's attachment to Hal, the term comes to signify an alternate meaning—namely, a military unit. When Falstaff impresses the weakest and poorest soldiers into his unit in act 4, scene 2 of *1 Henry IV*, they literally become his company. He takes no pride in his ragged troops; indeed, as he admits, he is "ashamed." He notes, "There's not a shirt and a half in all my company, and the half-shirt is two napkins tacked together and thrown over the shoulders like a herald's coat without sleeves" (4.2.38–40). This impoverished crew is mere "food for powder," he notes, signaling their dispensability. The company of the tavern, with its abundant food and friendship, becomes the impoverished company of wartime; the "napkins" that might accompany a meal serve as pathetic, inadequate clothing stock. Company is not merely martial, but also physical—it is, as with consumption, linked to disease, such as when Falstaff warns that "men take diseases one of another. Therefore, let men take heed of their company" (*2H4*, 5.1.65–66). Finally, the term appears in the banishment scene when the prince informs Falstaff, "I have turned away my former self. / So will I those that kept me company" (5.5.56–57). This last use of the term drives home its density, with "company" invoked by Hal as a polluting force and a sign of his former corruption, even as the term might also remind the audience of its first usage, in describing Falstaff's tavern community.

The final joke in Falstaff's sack speech—"If I had a thousand sons, the first human principle I would teach them should be to foreswear thin potations, and to addict themselves to sack"—deploys the notion of "addict," which also had double resonance for early modern audiences. The term "addict" in the final line is crucial to the speech's triumph, crowning the argument's comic hyperbole. But what does it mean to "addict" oneself to sack circa 1600? Most commonly, the term "addict" designated one devoted or bound to a person or pastime. From the Latin *addictus*, the term was used in Roman law to signal the delivery of a person in accordance with a judicial decision, such as one "addicted" to a creditor; "addict" also meant devotion to an activity, occupation, or object.[37] Early modern "addiction" draws on this Latin usage. The dominant understanding of addiction throughout the sixteenth century posited it as a form of devotion or dedication. Thus, in his *Thesaurus linguae Romanae et Britannicae*, Thomas Cooper uses "addict" as a synonym for "vow": "To vowe: to addict or giue: solemnly to promise," while John Florio in *World of Words* links "addict" and "dedicate": "*Dedicare*, to dedicate, to consecrate, to addict" and "*Dicare*, to vowe, to dedicate, to addict, to promise."[38] In addicting themselves to sack, Falstaff's sons would devote themselves to the life-affirming beverage.

Yet even as Falstaff draws on the devotional resonances of addiction, boasting that his addicted sons would be faithful worshippers of sack, his tongue-and-cheek delivery also betrays a joke: the audience recognizes that sack addiction is more diseased than devotional. If the terms "sack," "consumption," and "company" initially appear convivial, only to signify damage later in the plays, the word "addict" appears only once, but it is similarly dense in signification. Evoked as a devotional practice, addiction as deployed by Falstaff also hints at its emergent modern meaning: compulsive consumption of drugs or alcohol. In fact, the early modern understanding of the term "addict" appeared at the moment of the play's first performances, as polemicists debated the dangers of alcohol. In anti-alcohol pamphlets, writers deployed—for the first time ever—the term "addiction" to describe the phenomenon of drinking excessively. For example, John Downame, a godly minister, writes of drunkenness that "many of our people of late, are so unmeasurably addicted to this vice, that they seem to...spend the greatest part of their time in carousing, as though they did not drink to live, but lived to drink."[39] Downame catalogues the ways in which drinkers abuse themselves, illuminating the dangers of addiction's inversion: one does not drink to live, but lives to drink.

Falstaff's apparent contradictions become more comprehensible when viewed in relation to such contemporary discourses on drunkenness, and specifically in relation to writings on habit and the compulsion to drink. What at first seems to be a choice becomes instead a habit, a transformation resonant with the portrait of Falstaff in *Henry IV*. To use the language of the pamphlets, through repetition or "custom," delight turns into "necessity" and infirmity.[40] Richard Young, for example, writes in *The Drunkard's Character*, "for by a long and desperate custome, they [drunkards] turne delight and infirmity into necessity, and bring upon themselves such an insatiable thirst, that they will as willingly leave to live, as leave their excessive drinking."[41] The author of *Condition of a Drunkard* repeats this precise language: "by a long and desperate custome, they have turned delight, and infirmity, into necessity; so that without wine they cannot live."[42] Ward's *Woe to Drunkards* also draws on this formula of "desperate custom," writing of drunkenness, "if once a Custome, ever necessity."[43] In *The Trial of Tabacco*, the author and physician E. G. invokes it as well: "How great the force & power of this cruell tyrant Custome is, that creepeth in by little & little, insinuating and conveighing himself slily into our natures, so that at length he will be so malepart, as to vendicate the whole rule and government of our bodies, prescribing and limiting new lawes, even such as it selfe pleaseth, and abrogating old ancient orders, constitutions, and fashions."[44] The new habit or custom creeps in, assuming "rule and government of our bodies" and establishing "new laws," a process associated with tyranny in custom-governed England. Finally, Downame invokes the phrase twice in the following passage:

> the drunkard by his much tipling maketh himself a slave to his vice, and by long custome bringeth superfluity into urgent necessity: for as it is in other sinnes, so in this; before it is admitted, it creepeth and croucheth, flattereth and allureth, like a lowly vassall; but being entertained, it straight sheweth it selfe, not onely a master, but also a Lordly tyrant, which raigneth and ruleth with great insolence. First sinne is committed, then practiced, and often practice bringeth custome, and custome becommeth a second nature, and hath in it the force of a law which must be obeyed, not in courtesie but upon necessity.[45]

The phrase repeated in each of these texts—custom (i.e., habit) turns delight into necessity—comes from Galen: *habitum, alteram naturam,* or "custom alters nature." Writers adopt this Galenic medical formula as an explanatory device in accounting for habitual, excessive drunkenness.[46] The phrase helps turn what might otherwise seem to be oppositions—between choice and compulsion, freedom and necessity, delight and disease—into a continuum. One moves from custom, through habit, into necessity, to the point where "without wine [one] cannot live."

Ingesting alcohol begins, much as *1 Henry IV* itself, with conviviality: it is described, as the pamphlets chronicle above, as a "delight," "superfluity," or "entertaining." But the custom of drinking is "insinuating," and "flattering." Sneaking in as a humble servant, facilitating good times, drink slowly gains power: the formerly "lowly vassall" of drinking becomes the "Lordly tyrant." Then, drinking "raigneth and ruleth with great insolence," establishing its own form of law. "Abrogating" tradition and upsetting the natural order, it has "the force of a law which must be obeyed." Indeed, it proceeds with "prescribing and limiting new lawes." The law of drink is not, of course, the law of nature or of the commonwealth but, rather, the innovative law of the usurping tyrant. It takes away one's senses and pleases itself instead.

Formerly self-sovereign, the habitual drinker becomes overtaken, enslaved, and addicted. "Drunkards" suffer from a "slavish condition," tied to the "tap-house"; the drinker, as Downame writes, "maketh himself a slave."[47] The language of tyranny and enslavement illuminates the strange condition of drunkenness in which a subject both is and is not himself, as this essay's final section explores. The drinker holds some agency—he enslaves himself, just as he addicts himself, in Downame's formulation cited earlier. The hesitancy on the issue of will and agency is telling. These authors struggle between moralizing and diagnosing, unsure precisely where to credit the will—to the drinker, to the force of custom, or to the power of alcohol itself.

Tyrannous Sack

The early modern view of the habitual drinker enslaved by the usurping power of alcohol helps to illuminate why Falstaff appears evacuated of agency, even as he repeatedly asserts his own desires up to the end. As the writer of *Diet for a Drunkard* poignantly puts it, "A Drunkard is a man, albeit in his drunkennesse little better than a painted man: as Ambrose said, *What is a Drunkard, but a superfluous creature?*"[48] It is this superfluity of the drinker, the sense of him as emptied out of any purpose beyond drinking, which the play's representation of Falstaff draws on in the final acts of *Henry IV*. Falstaff becomes, Barbara Everett explains, "an outer man only."[49] His superfluity (in the sense both of his excess and his lack of substance) becomes, as this section will explore, both politically and theatrically problematic.

Falstaff's habitual drinking helps to foster the ailments chronicled in this article's second section, even as his consumption appears, at least initially, to operate under the guise of fellowship, thereby collapsing what are otherwise dichotomous cultural views on alcohol. Drinking is, in Falstaff, *both* fellowship *and* disease: "Here, Pistol, I charge [toast] you with a cup of sack" (*2H4*, 2.4.98–99); "I'll give you a health for that anon" (5.3.21–22); "Health and long life to you, Master Silence!" (48). Falstaff no longer eats food but only drinks. As Davy reassures him, "What you want in meat, we'll have in drink" (25–26), and as Falstaff tells Shallow, "Come, I will go drink with you, but I cannot tarry dinner" (3.2.173–74).[50] Food is here associated with abundance and leisure, making Falstaff's refusal to eat seem to be a sign of impoverishment: his supply of meat is lacking, his time for eating has passed. He no longer feels pleasure in drinking but instead necessity. He thus spends most of 2 *Henry IV* preoccupied with cash and his supply of sack. His scenes with Master Shallow are hardly funny; they instead demonstrate his fixation with his shrinking purse and its inability to sustain his appetites.

In a play so preoccupied with questions of governance, Falstaff might initially offer meaningful dissent through the humor of tavern culture: at the start of 1 *Henry IV* he satirizes the king, robs his exchequer, and outwits justice. As the play progresses, however, Falstaff's custom of drinking turns to habit. Falstaff no longer rebels against court culture; he is instead compelled by drink, a rival regime. As a result, he is more loyal to his drink than to his king. His threat to monarchy is hardly the most familiar form of dissent; it is not the political and religious opposition offered by aristocratic upstarts or dissident Catholics. His threat is instead embodied by his appetitive opposition. He is, Hal argues, "the tutor and the feeder of my riots" (*2H4*, 5.5.60), banished for his "surfeit" and "gormandizing," as the prince puts it in his final speech to Falstaff (48, 51).[51] Under the sway of alcohol, he transgresses the regulatory boundaries of royal sovereignty and professes loyalty to a foreign substance, as Raber argues in chapter 4 of this volume. While a long critical tradition condemns Hal for blindsiding Falstaff by banishing him, the knight has proved an oppositional subject unable to integrate himself into the polity. His disloyal actions determine Hal's response every bit as much as the rebels' armed rising does earlier. In both cases, Hal must respond to disruptive dissent.

Unlike the rebels, however, who willfully choose armed opposition, Falstaff's relation to his own oppositional behavior is more complex. Even as Falstaff appears to revel in his cups, increasingly the Henriad reveals that drinking governs him. Choice has turned, as the Galenic formula cautions, through habit into necessity. When Falstaff announces, on learning of Hal's ascension, that "the laws of England are at my commandment" (*2H4*, 5.3.124), he speaks as if free. But Falstaff is not, as the audience well knows, under his own command. He is governed by appetite, "the force of a law which must be obeyed." The custom of sack drinking, in "prescribing and limiting new lawes" for this character, has left him unresponsive to his environment, unaware of the terrain that has shifted beneath his feet, and incapable of anticipating the inevitable rejection.

If Falstaff imagines the connection of sack to heroism, valor, and wit, the play upends this association by linking drink to disease and indeed addiction by the end of *Henry IV*. Falstaff exhibits less, not more, freedom than other characters; he is more constricted and constrained, whether financially, physically, or theatrically. Even Falstaff's much-vaunted verbal skills show some signs of degeneration by the end of *2 Henry IV*. Of course, Falstaff delivers some clever set speeches in the latter portion of this play, particularly when he selects his soldiers and justifies his choice of lean, impoverished men. Furthermore, he offers his notorious sack speech toward the end of the play. But even as his wit remains evident, he increasingly repeats himself in short, punctuating phrases. Rather than offering the extended imaginative fantasies typical of *1 Henry IV* (as he imagines himself to be prince or king, or as he improvises his way out of the Gadshill robbery), he instead defends himself through repetitious pleading. "Come," he says to Doll, furious at the knight for his debts, "thou must not be in this humor with me. Dost not know me? Come, come, I know thou wast set on to this" (*2H4*, 2.1.131–33). "Go with her, with her; Hook on, hook on" (140–41). "What's the news, my lord? ... What is the news, my lord" (145, 148–49). "We catch of you, Doll, we catch of you. Grant that, my poor virtue, grant that" (2.4.41–42).

Falstaff's legendary power of transformation — he transforms himself from coward to hero on the battlefield where he claims to fell Hotspur, or from thief to Diana's minion when he justifies his thieving — breaks down under the alluring power of sack itself. He will not pretend indifference to it; his interest in drinking sustains him through his various locations and communities: "An I had but a belly of any indifferency, I were simply the most active fellow in Europe. My womb, my womb, my womb undoes me" (*2H4*, 4.2.18–20). That *this* character, with his great theatrical range, is unable to shift, change, or adapt to new circumstances in battle or at court — circumstances that demand moderation — suggests how the material tyrannies of alcohol can overpower even theatrical and verbal talent. A consummate actor, Falstaff began the Henriad able to transform himself through imaginative feats. This transformative ability proves crucial not only for Falstaff as a character but also for the man playing him onstage:

an actor was deemed capable of changing not merely his speech and costume but also, as Joseph Roach brilliantly explores, his humorological body, "precisely controlling the instantaneous transitions between passions."[52] Figures like Richard Burbage and Edward Alleyn were famous for their ability to shape-shift on stage: exhibiting "Ovidian alterations of bodily state," these players demonstrated a range of passions through manipulation of their humors, a dangerous practice that allowed transformations from role to role, and at different moments within a single role. As Thomas Heywood writes of Alleyn, he is a "Proteus for shapes, and Roscius for a tonge / So could he speak, so vary."[53]

Falstaff might begin *Henry IV* as a skilled actor, shifting from thief to prince to king to favorite to witty gallant. But, as the play proceeds, he becomes more of a caricature, less of a character. Falstaff opens *2 Henry IV* by boasting, "a good wit will make use of anything" (1.2.226). He can turn his "consumption of the purse," his "gout" and his impoverishment into profit—as he claims, "I will turn diseases to commodity" (216–17; 222; 226–27). Such transformations, however, become less convincing as the play progresses. Stuck in his own desires, Falstaff's early choices become habits, which become tyrannical appetites, ruling him despite his manifest talent and skill of transformation. Falstaff might promise to swear off sack at the end of *1 Henry IV*— as he claims in his last lines of the play, "If I do grow great, I'll grow less, for I'll purge and leave sack and live cleanly, as a nobleman should do" (5.4.157–58)—but no one takes his claim seriously. His line is tongue in cheek, of course. But by the end of *2 Henry IV*, that final line—"If I do grow great, I'll grow less"—has been inverted. Instead of greater courtly status and diminished size, he ends the Henriad with an increased body and deflated standing. The reports of his demise acknowledge, even as they attempt to suppress, the knight's constraining habits. He dies, Nym claims, from "bad humours" (*H5*, 2.1.113), a reference to the prince's ill humor but one that also evokes the humorological excesses of Falstaff leading to his inflexibility and death. Furthermore, if Falstaff dies of a broken heart as his friends and critics claim, he nevertheless spends his final moments thinking not of Hal but of sack: "They say he cried out of sack," Nym reports—and the hostess confirms, "Ay, that 'a did" (2.3, 24–25). In railing against sack, Falstaff acknowledges what others might not: drinking over-came him.

Falstaff's fate has the unfortunate effect of fulfilling godly polemic, a surprising outcome given Shakespeare's presumed hostility toward his Puritan detractors. Why might Shakespeare offer such an unexpected, frustrating, moralizing portrait? Richard Strier provides one persuasive, and indeed moving, answer: Shakespeare stages, in the rejection of Falstaff, a moral position he does not necessarily embrace. Even if the plays demand the rejection of Falstaff to facilitate the rise of Hal, Shakespeare is not comfortable with such a moral position. In the Henriad, "prudence, order, and morality had to prevail, and Shakespeare never forgave himself for that. He never again put himself in a position of seeming to favor (as Falstaff puts it) 'Pharoah's lean kine.'"[54] As a result, Strier argues, in a subsequent play such as *King Lear*, the foolish old man becomes the hero, and those daughters who chide him with foolishness are the villains.

Closer, however, to *2 Henry IV* than *King Lear* is *Twelfth Night*, a play embracing transformation in all its theatrical possibilities. And it is the theatrical cost of Falstaff's drinking, finally, that might finally account for why Shakespeare brings his popular knight to such an apparently moralizing end. The performance of good fellowship through drunkenness onstage is initially full of possibility, a point Tobias Doring illuminates in chapter 8 of this volume. If Sir Toby, Doring argues, represents both the cultural memory of festive ritual, and the drunken forgetting that might allow for transformation, so too does Falstaff. Initially the capers, gags, and witty exchanges of the tavern exhibit the playful imagination of the playwright, who is freed from the more constraining historical narrative of the plays' other plot lines. But the compulsion to present the knight's drunkenness perhaps wears thin as it extends over the course of two plays. The transformative possibilities of alcohol—inspiring verse and action—diminish. In his attachment to sack, Falstaff proves not only disastrous as a political subject but also, more pointedly, debilitated as a transformative actor. Falstaff's theatrical trajectory includes nearly novelistic character development, through which Shakespeare reveals a sustained commitment to the power of transformation: he shows precisely why an actor's craft is crucial for the theater, and for its audiences. Even the most convivial activities become dangerous when compulsory, and even the most comic figures turn tragic as a result.

The play's end thus stages the heartbreaking spectacle of Falstaff— the man who strove to "foreswear thin potations and to addict [himself] to sack"—condemned. What was once a human principle—namely, sack addiction—is now claimed by Hal as Falstaff's *only* principle. The audience, of course, desperately wishes it were otherwise, since Falstaff's drinking produces the play's fanciful lyricism and comic wit. But through Hal, Shakespeare represents the point at which Falstaff is no longer recuperated as artist, jester, or loving friend; in other words, he reveals the point at which Falstaff has become a "*superfluous creature*"—and that point is Falstaff's addiction.

Part 3

THEATER AND COMMUNITY

Chapter 7

Cynical Dining in
Timon of Athens

DOUGLAS M. LANIER

It is not news that feasting and food are central to Shakespeare and Thomas Middleton's *Timon of Athens*. Two banqueting scenes, arguably the most elaborate in the Shakespearean canon, punctuate Timon's biography in the play's first half. Even so, at first glance it is not obvious why dining, real or metaphorical, should play so prominent a role, for this element hardly appears in the Timon myth as it was received in early modernity. In the play's classical sources there is scarcely any mention of feasting or food, and indeed few details of Timon's pre-misanthropic past. In Plutarch's "Life of Marcus Antonius," we learn only that Timon feasted with Alcibiades in an attempt to woo him and that he had a nasty exchange with Apemantus during the Choae, the Athenian feasts of the dead.[1] Lucian's *Timon, or the Misanthrope* offers even less. Two of Timon's suitors, Gnathonides and Philiades, mention dining, but only in a passing phrase. When Mercury details how Timon's prodigality undid him, he stresses the bestial ravenousness of his so-called friends (likely the source of this image cluster in the play), but this metaphor doesn't appear elsewhere in Lucian's dialogue and doesn't specify that Timon's prodigality included banqueting. When in Lucian Timon recalls his ruin, feasts figure not at all; later he speaks of being undone by "voluptuous pleasures," but those pleasures are never designated as culinary.

135

In an important study, Robert Miola situates *Timon of Athens* in the context of classical discourses that associate the decadence of Athenian symposia with the ills of democratic liberty. Miola concludes that Shakespeare (and Middleton) deploys this association to express his own "contempt for democracy," a contempt founded upon "man's infinite capacity for self-delusion, the universality and bestiality of his appetites, and his need for political and moral controls, however imperfect and uncertain."[2] *Timon*, an anonymous play James Bulman convincingly established as a source, includes two banquet scenes, the first a lavish feast for friends hosted by Timon, the second a wedding feast for Timon and his erstwhile bride, Callimela, broken up by news that Timon's ships have been lost, rendering him destitute.[3] The structure of these banquet scenes—the first essentially comic, the second disrupted and satirical—may have suggested to Shakespeare and Middleton the structure of the two banquet scenes in *Timon of Athens*.

Without discounting the importance of these sources, I want to consider another context for the prominence of banqueting in *Timon of Athens:* early modern "banqueting ideology," those ethical and sociopolitical ideals that in theory were embodied by Renaissance banqueting practices.[4] With the consolidation of court culture under the Tudors, the sixteenth century in England saw a significant shift in banqueting ideology, away from the humanist model of the *convivium*, based on an idealized vision of the classical *symposium* melded with components of monastic and pedagogical practice, and toward an aristocratic patronage model that increasingly and uncomfortably mirrored capitalist practices of investment and usury. Several fine studies have traced how Timon's compulsive largesse seems to reflect the behavior of King James I, whose early years on the throne were marked by what was for many a troubling political practice of currying favor through gift-giving.[5] While it is certainly true that James's royal example accelerated the change in banqueting ideology, James was by no means the only catalyst for this ideological shift. This discussion seeks to trace a longer arc in the cultural function of banqueting and to explore how and why that change is linked to Timon's fall into misanthropy. I want to situate *Timon of Athens* more firmly within the wider phenomenon of humanist disillusionment in the late sixteenth and early seventeenth centuries, with the banquet serving a privileged symbolic role in the play's portrayal of escalating disenchantment with humanist ideals.

In book 2 of the *Utopia,* Thomas More devotes several pages to the eating patterns of his fictional citizenry. A number of details bear upon the humanists' investment of the banquet with sociopolitical significance. Attention to seating arrangements, for instance, suggests More's desire to balance adherence with the principle of hierarchy with that of equality. The head table honors the duly designated and religious political authorities, the syphogrant (seated with his family) and the priest, and separates them from the crowd.[6] Otherwise, the dominant principle of order is age, a principle More correlates more with emotional maturity and wisdom than with patriarchal authority. Indeed, More's utopian feast honors the principle of meritocracy, where the wisest, not those of high inherited political status, are given precedence; the meal is pointedly not about the display of status or wealth. The seating arrangements also consciously work to promote the principle of convivial communality. Though the precedence of elders is recognized in the serving of food (they are served first and given the best food), they are distributed throughout the dining hall so that they can stimulate lively conversation, conversation being the most conspicuous sign of a temporary suspension of social differences and the creation of commensality. Though More says that he wants to strike a balance between hierarchy and equality, the creation of festive communality, a quality rooted in the sharing of food and table talk, is of higher value than the marking of differences of status, as More's phrasing indicates: "nevertheless equal commodity cometh to every one" (*Utopia,* 67).

Equally noteworthy in More's description of this ideal banquet is his emphasis on moral education. The Utopians, he tells us, "begin every dinner and supper of reading something that pertaineth to good manners and virtue" (67). This public reading is followed by general conversation prompted by the elderly, "to the intent that they may have a proof of every man's wit and towardness or disposition to virtue, which commonly in the liberty of feasting doth show and utter itself" (67). The uplifting reading that accompanies the utopian banquet is reminiscent of the secular, philosophical, or heroic discourse humanists encountered in classical descriptions of banqueting in texts like the *Aeneid*. The conversation afterward is subtly guided or at least urged on by the wise elders scattered throughout the hall, with the intent of developing each person's intellect, social sensibility, and spirit. For More, the banquet is an occasion for communal moral edification set in motion by a public text and reinforced by its communal contemplation through discussion. If food nourishes the body, the reading and its communal digestion through conversation nourish the spirit; the reading converts an event potentially and problematically associated with bodily pleasure into an intellectual, moral occasion. This is not to say that More imagines something dour. Each meal includes music and dessert as well as several other elements that make the occasion festive, for "no kind of pleasure [is] forbidden whereof cometh no harm" (67). More emphasizes that the aesthetic elements of the banquet, the sensual delights of food and music, and the stimulating nature of witty dinner talk are entirely compatible with—and indeed mutually reinforce—the didactic intent of the dining experience, its fashioning of intellect and morality. The banquet, in short, exemplifies the humanist reassessment of the relationship between pleasure and virtue that ideologically underpins so much of *Utopia*.

More's discussion of dining customs is a definitive statement of the early English humanist ideal of the communal meal, an ideal that had its precedent in the substantial humanist literature of conviviality practiced by such figures as Dante, Ficino, Castiglione, Boccaccio, Bouchet, Erasmus, Guazzo, and Bruno.[7] This literature traces its lineage primarily to two sources. First, and principal among them, are classical portrayals of the Greek *symposium* and Latin *convivium*, an after-dinner drinking party that was the occasion for extended philosophical or witty conversation, a space distinguished from the realm of *negotium*.[8] Plato's *Symposium* provides the template for the many examples that followed, including the most important—Xenophon's *Symposium* and Plutarch's *Symposiaka*.[9] Classical representations range from the staid to the stuporous. By contrast, early humanists strongly preferred idealized representations of *convivia*, though there are certainly examples of more raucous versions, such as Erasmus's so-called *Profane Colloquies* or Rabelais's *Gargantua and Pantagruel*.

At *convivia*, wine is not just a required source of sensual pleasure; it also prompts free speech, provides divine inspiration, and loosens social distinctions.

The other source of humanist banqueting literature is the monastic practice of communal dining, a practice taken up in modified form in schools. Chapter 38 of *The Benedictine Rule* specifies that meals be taken in silence as an edifying text is read to the diners. Distantly behind this practice lies the Eucharist, that ur-meal that converted the act of taking sustenance into a quintessential scene of instruction and sacramental communalism.[10] The ghost of sacramental community often haunts humanist convivial discourse, giving its disruption or symbolic violation the force of secular blasphemy. The fiercely satirical force of Rabelais's Abbey of Thélème, to take one familiar example, derives in part from its insistence upon the un- and antisacramental qualities of monastic feasting. Paradoxically, such iconoclastic discourse has a long pedigree in medieval monastic literature, such as in the *Carmina Burana*.

If, as Michel Jeanneret argues, humanists conceptualized the banquet as an ideal site where cultural opposites might be reconciled, in *Utopia* we sense some of the abiding tensions in humanist ideals of the *convivium*—between hierarchy and mutuality, between sensual indulgence and virtuous instruction, between maintaining a social space free of *negotium* and regarding the banquet as an institution symbolically central for the polis. Unlike Utopian conceptions of banqueting, however, actual banqueting practice was often, perhaps even typically, quite different. Throughout the sixteenth century as court culture consolidated itself, the banquet was increasingly treated as an instrument of royal or aristocratic privilege. Banqueting provided an occasion for the display of the magnificence, bounty, and political power of the elite, a setting in which social hierarchies were reinforced and aristocratic status mystified, a site of patronage where competitive exorbitance and gift-giving, not festive communality and moral education, were the norm. What is more, in order to maintain the ever-escalating levels of expenditure, nearly the entire aristocratic class had to become involved in literal and figurative forms of usury. Elite largesse was often financed by loans and, perhaps even more disturbing, patronage became increasingly regarded as a system for investing cultural, political, or economic capital in pursuit of some future return in the form of sponsorship, gifts, promotion, or fame.[11] These elements had, of course, also long been part of classical banqueting discourse—Latin moral philosophers and satirists, and in particular the Roman poet Martial, target them.[12] The gap between the banqueting ideal and its actual practice widened during James I's reign, as he used extravagant court entertainment (along with lavish gifts and unwarranted elevation) to secure his hold on the throne and perhaps, so argues Coppélia Kahn, to satisfy a primal need to identify with unlimited maternal bounty.[13] Though the Jacobean court's development of the masque (an extension of royal culinary entertainment, after all) provided a focus for discontent with the ideal of the humanist banquet, there is considerable evidence that the perception of a troubling gap between theory and practice was well established by the late sixteenth century.[14]

Developing disillusionment with banqueting mirrors the more widespread souring of humanism in early modern England, what William J. Bouwsma dubs the "waning of the Renaissance."[15] Ben Jonson, for example, addressed the widening gulf between the ideals of humanism and political realities by both denying and accentuating it. He was willing to provide a veneer of humanist idealism for the Jacobean masque, representing James's prodigality as a form of natural bounty, with the king as the animating sun. At the same time, he often treated the practice of private feasts as a separate institution that promised to reinstate the classical ideal of the *convivium*. On the early seventeenth century stage, representations of aristocratic banquets, particularly in tragedies, often call attention to the gap between the idealized appearances and the sordid subtexts of these banquets and entertainments, reflecting a growing skepticism about utopian humanist representations of social order. These representations draw upon an anti-convivial classical tradition, where banquets are sites of excess, extravagance, or immorality, or are mechanisms for intrigue or vengeance.[16]

Kyd's *The Spanish Tragedy* helped to define court entertainment as the preferred venue in which a disaffected protagonist might take revenge upon an oppressive, hypocritical elite. Early in his career Shakespeare offered his own version in *Titus Andronicus*, with a protagonist who, devoted to a recognizably humanist ideal of ethical rectitude, comes to discover the malicious clientage behind the "love-day" banquet that ends the first scene and who takes revenge by feeding the sons of his tormenters to them at another feast of "peace,...love,...league and good to Rome" (*Tit.*, 5.3.23). Middleton (and perhaps Thomas Dekker) amps up this grisly motif in the final scene of *The Bloody Banquet*, in which a tyrannical king forces his adulterous bride to eat the flesh of her murdered lover in public, in a banqueting hall festooned with his bloody limbs.[17] In a city comedy like *A Chaste Maid in Cheapside* (1613), Middleton empties the culminating banquet of its connotations of social order and recuperated amity. Yellowhammer's grudging acceptance of the comic resolution is shot through with irony and parsimony: "So Fortune seldom deals two marriages / With one hand, and both lucky. The best is, / One feast will serve them both!" (5.4.118–20).[18] One need only compare this to the final banquet in Dekker's *The Shoemaker's Holiday* (1599)—with its bounty, mirthful wit, and utopian politics—to sense growing skepticism about the banquet as an emblem of social order.

Typically, Shakespeare favors the motif of the "broken banquet," in which a feast is begun and then somehow disrupted or delayed.[19] This motif too has both classical and Christian provenance. The arrival of uninvited or unruly guests to a *convivium* was a well-worn narrative motif in classical convivial discourse, the most famous example of which is the late arrival of the drunken Alcibiades to Plato's *Symposium*. The accusation of Judas during the Last Supper provides another authoritative example. The Shakespearean motif of the "broken banquet" first appears in *The Taming of the Shrew* in the form of two disrupted feasts, one the wedding feast cut short by Petruccio and Kate's precipitous exit, another the "burnt meat" episode Petruccio engineers upon the couple's arrival at his home. The play's final scene offers the much-delayed "proper" wedding feast, but even there the festive communality of the gathering is interrupted by squabbling among the guests and the improvised obedience contest between the husbands. The forest feast of Duke Senior and his exiled companions in *As You Like It*, act 2, scene 7, offers another example. As the group is entertained by Jaques's tale of the fool he met in the wood, they are interrupted by Orlando, who, sword drawn, rudely demands food for himself and Adam. This "broken banquet" is mended when Duke

Senior, eschewing rank and showing pity, welcomes Orlando to their table, one of the few moments in Shakespeare's canon where banqueting is portrayed in its ideal form and, tellingly, where the diners are isolated from court.

Elsewhere in the Shakespearean canon, the "broken banquet" is associated with tragedy. *Macbeth* features a coronation feast that might at first seem to exemplify the banqueting ideal—Macbeth declares his intention to "mingle with society / And play the humble host" and encourages those assembled to "be large in mirth" (*Mac.*, 3.4.3–4, 11). Yet the appearance of Banquo's ghost destroys the feast's superficial merriment and makes clear the tyrannical, guilt-ridden reality behind all the magnanimity. The harpy episode in *The Tempest* also partakes of this pattern. This sequence begins with "several strange shapes, bringing in a banquet" and beckoning the marooned Neapolitan court to eat; Gonzalo takes this to be a gesture of native hospitality, as if in recognition of their privileged status. After Ariel, attired like a harpy, sweeps away the feast, Prospero's speech reminds Alonso, Sebastian, and Antonio—"three men of sin" (*Tmp.*, 3.3.53)—of the nefarious way in which they usurped his power, violating the ideals of communal trust and magnanimity exemplified by the banquet. Particularly in the tragedies and romances, the broken banquet and the banquet-as-revenge motifs restore the feast's function of moral education, for the disrupted or revenge banquet becomes an ethical exemplum, albeit a negative one. These broken, bloody, or poisonous banquets thereby register how fully humanist convivial ideals have been violated and how powerfully many early modern English people longed to restore the banquet to its function as a mechanism for social order.

TIMON'S HUMANIST BANQUET

Timon of Athens is the most extended consideration of humanist banqueting ideology and its latter-day corruption in the Shakespearean canon.[20] Several commentators have noticed that the play's first two scenes offer markedly different perspectives on Timon's character.[21] The opening scene, principally by Shakespeare, establishes Timon's largesse as seeming to be genuinely noble. Timon presents his freeing of Ventidius from prison as an act of loyalty to a friend, a loyalty he intends to maintain after Ventidius's release; his dowry gift to Lucilius

rewards his honest service and prevents a greedy father from block-
ing his daughter's romance; and his acknowledgment of gifts from the
artisans is appropriately gracious. Timon's admiration of the verisi-
militude of the painter's portrait–"since dishonour traffics with man's
nature, / He is but outside; these pencilled figures are / Even such as
they give out" (*Tim.*, 1.163–64)—suggests that Timon is somewhat
but not utterly naïve, aware of the existence of hypocrisy but poorly
equipped to detect it. Timon's invitation to all to his banquet at scene's
end seems to be a culminating gesture of liberality and community
building. By contrast, Apemantus is initially presented as a malicious
refuser of festivity whose discontent seems relatively unmotivated.
After insulting Timon and his circle of friends, he vows to attend the
banquet merely "to see meat fill knaves, and wine heat fools" (1.264).
Nonetheless, eating metaphors hint that Timon has himself become
an object of communal consumption. When Timon asks Apemantus,
"Wilt dine with me, Apemantus?," he willfully misreads the invitation
and replies, "No, I eat not lords" (1.207–08); Alcibiades greets Timon
with the remark, "I feed / Most hungrily on your sight" (1.256–57);
the First Lord, anxious to attend the feast, remarks, "Come, shall we
in, / And taste Lord Timon's bounty?" (1.76–77). As Timon's betrayal
unfolds, these initially unremarkable metaphors grow in cannibalistic
significance.

   Timon's promised banquet in the second scene, principally by
Middleton, profoundly changes our impression of his values, his friends,
and the banquet's significance. The nonmutuality of Timon's generosity is immediately established by his refusal to accept Ventidius's
repayment of his debt. "I gave it freely ever," he tells Ventidius, "and
there's none / Can truly say he gives if he receives" (*Tim.*, 2.10–11). His
distortion of Scripture—Acts 20:35 reads, "it is more blessed to give
than to receive"—suggests that there is something absolutist about
Timon's generosity. His refusal follows a pattern seen several times
throughout the scene: Timon enmeshes his friends in gift-obligations,
placing himself at the center of power, while cloaking those obligations in a rhetoric of altruism. His initial exchange with Apemantus
also complicates our view of Timon's psychology. The ancient Cynics
actively courted rejection in order to highlight conventional society's
incipient savagery and to test the strength of their own dissidence, and
so does Apemantus, true to Cynical tenets.[22] To Timon's welcome, he

retorts, "I have come to have thee thrust me out of doors" (2.25). Yet though Timon sees Apemantus's curmudgeonly behavior as blameworthy, he does not eject him from the feast, instead seating him at a separate table. Apemantus is, Timon declares, "an Athenian, therefore welcome" (2.35–36), a remark that links the banquet to Timon's vision of an ideal, inclusively democratic polis. However, Timon adds, "I myself would have no power; prithee, let my meat make thee silent" (2.36–37). Here again Timon seeks to use a gift—the banquet itself—to enmesh Apemantus in a web of obligation so as to silence his dissident tongue, all the while denying that he is engaged in any exercise of power.

We are presented with two views of Timon's banquet. On the one hand, it exemplifies the ideal of commensality, at least superficially. Timon specifies that the guests dispense with niceties of rank, for "where there is true friendship, there needs none" (*Tim.*, 2.18); for him, the gathering is a model of social order, a space of brotherhood free from self-interested maneuvering. Timon's speech on friendship, with its vision of virtue, mutual duty, and amity, turns the banquet into a moral exemplum: "We are born to do benefits; and what better or properer can we call our own than the riches of our friends? O, what a comfort 'tis to have so many like brothers commanding one another's fortunes!" (2.97–101). Certainly circulation of property in the form of intracommunal gifts resembles the practice of potlatch,[23] but it also smacks of the communistic notions of property described in More's *Utopia*. Timon's understanding of economics privileges a humanistic ideal of communalism over the pursuit of profit. (Economic realities emerge only in the play's third scene, when his financially stretched creditors call in Timon's loans.) The maudlin tears that Timon sheds at the end of his speech indicate that this is an ideal in which he fervently believes and with which early modern audiences, weaned on classical-humanist discussions of friendship, might sympathize.

On the other hand, Timon's speech is yet another example of his use of gift-obligation to bind others to him while denying doing so. What prompts it is the First Lord's request to "express some part of our zeals" (*Tim.*, 2.83), that is, to engage in genuine reciprocity with him as host. But Timon will have none of it. His speech pushes the lord's request off into an indefinite future when he will have need of them: "O, no doubt, my good friends, but the gods themselves have provided that I shall have much help from you. How had you been my friends else?...'O you gods,' think I, 'what need we have any friends if we should ne'er have need of 'em? They were the most needless creatures living, should we ne'er have *use* for 'em'" (2.85–86, 91–94; emphasis mine). "The word "use"—with its implication of usury—suggests how despite Timon's evident altruism, he seems to be conceptualizing friendship in terms of financial investment and emotional return. With this sequence, Middleton reminds his audience of the humanist banqueting ideal while teasing out some of the latent psychological and financial elements that undermine it.

Apemantus is crucial to the play's emerging double perspective on banqueting. In the second scene his withering comments more clearly proceed from ethical principles, one of which is vegetarianism.[24] The Cynics of antiquity reduced their diet to the basics of water and uncultivated vegetables in an effort to return to a natural, animal state of existence and thereby avoid the corrupting effects of "civilized" behavior such as the eating of cooked flesh. Apemantus highlights his diet's moral superiority by holding high his glass of water as others drink toasts of wine; the parodic grace he offers to the gods praises his own refusal to be taken in by "civilized" hypocrisy, ending with a pithy contrast that stresses the relationship between culinary practices and virtue: "Rich men sin, and I eat root. / Much good dich thy good heart, Apemantus" (*Tim.*, 2.71–72). As a abstainer of meat, Apemantus seems especially sensitive to the carnivorousness that pervades Timon's banquet, a meal that in the early modern period would be dominated by roasted flesh.[25] Returning to the eating metaphor of the first scene, he equates the seeming amity of Timon's feast with cannibalism: "I scorn thy meat. 'Twould choke me, for I should ne'er flatter thee. O you gods, what a number of men eats Timon, and he sees 'em not! It grieves me to see so many dip their meat in one man's blood; and all the madness is, he cheers them up, too" (2.38–42). This crucial passage reverses the significance of the banquet in several ways at once. Where Timon intends the banquet to be an outward sign of amicable harmony and unconsciously seeks to "consume" his guests' admiration and dependency, in reality, Apemantus suggests, it is Timon's wealth—and with it Timon himself—that the diners consume.[26] The doubled carnivorousness of his guests—they eat bloody flesh dipped in blood—hints at cannibalism. The implicit identification of the diners with Judas, the betrayer Christ refers to as "he that dippeth his hand with me in the dish" (Matt. 26:23), makes clear just how fully their false fellowship violates the sacred bond this meal is intended to establish.[27] Apemantus even obliquely references the culminating banquet of revenge tragedies, noting, "there's much example" for scenarios in which "the fellow that sits next him, pledges the breath of him in a divided draught, is the readiest to kill him" (2.46–48). Reference to this kind of scenario reveals in another form the savage subtext of this as yet idyllic scene.

During the masque, the banquet's pièce de résistance, dining images again convey disgust for what Apemantus regards as a perverse display of hypocritical love and sensual indulgence. Doubtless Timon's masque aims at the Jacobean court's penchant for ostentatious entertainments, and Apemantus only magnifies the "sweep of vanity" by contrasting the masque to the culinary emblem of his resistance to excess, his "little oil and root" (*Tim.*, 2.131). Extending the dining metaphor, Apemantus then laments the folly of "spend[ing] our flatteries to drink these men / Upon whose age we void it up again / With poisonous spite and envy" (2.133–35), analogizing the cycle of creating and consuming displays of false amity to decadent Roman feed-and-purge cycles reported by Seneca, Cicero, and Suetonius.[28] Given this concatenation of references, otherwise empty culinary metaphors take on a sinister tone. Fending off Alcibiades's declaration of loyalty to him, Timon quips, "you had rather be at a breakfast of enemies than a dinner of friends" (2.75–76), to which Alcibiades answers, "so they were bleeding now, my lord, there's no meat like 'em" (2.76–77); the ambiguous antecedent (are "they" enemies or friends?) points up the unwittingly cannibalistic values of Timon's banquet. Alcibiades's final line, "I could wish my best friend at such a feast" (2.78), extends the ominous ambiguity, for it applies to Timon, and in a way that leaves unresolved whether he is guest or meat.

Apemantus's phrase "spending flatteries" encapsulates how fully the banquet ideal has been displaced by an essentially capitalistic relationship between patron and client: the host "spends" his wealth on gifts in hopes of an emotional profit and political status, and the guests venture empty expressions of intimacy expecting that the patron will redouble their gifts for financial gain. Timon's tragedy is that he mistakes the civilized amity of the humanist banquet for the emergent, cannibalistic world of capitalist self-interest and consumerism.[29] The play's attitude toward the banquet is divided. On the one hand, the humanist banquet ideal remains an ethical standard against which the behavior of Timon's friends is judged. Their violation of bonds of hospitality and amity proper to the banquet makes their subsequent ingratitude all the more appalling and sufficiently traumatic that Timon's response in the play's second half seems plausible. Nevertheless, the play also recognizes that banqueting as Timon practices it has become (and perhaps always was) a form of aristocratic prodigality. Underlying the gift economy of Athens is an armature of financial and affective debt unacknowledged in humanist idealizations of the banquet. Even as the play thereby offers a proto-Marxist critique of a central symbol of humanist ideals, it does not entirely abandon the banquet as a symbol of ethical aspirations. Like humanism itself, Timon simply refuses to acknowledge the economic realities underpinning his ideals until he is forced to do so. Tellingly, when first approached by creditors, Timon's steward bids them "cease till after dinner" (*Tim.*, 4.41), as if Timon would rather remain at the banquet table than confront brute economic reality.

TIMON'S ANTICONVIVIAL BANQUET

At first glance, Timon's penchant for denial also seems to lie behind his otherwise incomprehensible response to his friends' betrayal by planning yet another banquet. As the second banquet scene opens, the senators surmise that Timon's request for funds may have been just a test of their friendship. Their unlikely hypothesis signals that they have moved to the position of the naïf once occupied by Timon, for it allows them to maintain their own illusions of Timon as endless source of bounty and themselves as master manipulators. Earlier oblique allusions to revenge tragedy and Timon's identification of his former friends as "luxurs" and "rascals" (*Tim.*, 9.8–9) hint that a revenge banquet may be in the offing. That expectation is compounded by the sound of trumpets on which Timon invites them to "feast their ears" (11.32), a sound appropriate to the battlefield, not the banqueting hall. News of Alcibiades's exile, which arrives as the guests move to sit, also indicates that the amity of the earlier banquet has been broken even before the meal begins. Nonetheless, Timon insists, as if repeating the earlier banquet, that his meal will not stand upon hierarchical principle: "Your diet shall be in all places alike" (11.65). This time, however, he pointedly goes on to compare the gathering to "a City feast" (11.66), in effect linking those in attendance to figures of commerce. As before, the meaning of the banquet is defined by an extended speech by Timon, an acidic prayer mirroring Apemantus's earlier parodic grace. In it, Timon methodically inverts the banquet ideal: instead of regarding bounty as generating gratitude, Timon counsels parsimoniousness lest "deities be despised" (11.71–72); instead of focusing on the amity of his fellow diners, Timon suggests that food will be far more beloved; instead of the banquet being a site of moral education, Timon wishes it were a scene of vengeance. His final line dubs his guests "present friends," that is, those whose friendship depends upon gifts, and he uses the occasion to undo the bonds he knit together at the earlier banquet: "they [his friends] are to me nothing, so in nothing bless them; and to nothing are they welcome" (11.81–83). If Timon's first banquet was designed to create a fraternal community, this banquet is an antiritual designed to purge those impure relationships, thereby restoring to the banquet its moral function.

The antibanquet's nonfoodstuffs are crucial to its message. Though stage directions specify only that the uncovered dishes contain steaming water, Timon's taunt, "take thy physic first. Thou too, and thou" (*Tim.*, 11.99), and the fourth senator's parting line, "one day he gives us diamonds, next day stones" (11.114), imply that the dishes also contain stones with which Timon pelts his guests. Apemantus had already established that water is the Cynic's substitute for wine, an unfestive potable "nothing" proper for animals and the poor. The water's lukewarm temperature corresponds to his friends' tepid loyalty. The "smoke" Timon calls his guests' "perfection" mirrors the insubstantiality of their friendship (he later calls them "vapours" [11.96]), but it may also indicate an awareness of one of the central concepts of Cynicism, τῦφος (tÿphos; literally, "smoke"). Τῦφος designates the foolishness, self-deception, and pride brought on by one's immersion in civilized convention. It is a condition remedied only by ascetic practices—such as drinking only water—that bring one back into alignment with unadorned, elemental nature.[30] Timon's offering of "smoke" and water thus provides an object lesson in Cynical principles. More immediately apparent to the early modern audience would have been the sacramental resonances. Given the eucharistic undertones of the banquet, where humble food and drink are transformed into attributes of the divine, Timon pointedly desacramentalizes the meal's ingredients. The oblique allusion to Christ's divine power to change water into wine and bread into stones (John 2:1–11; Luke 4:3) suggests that Timon is undoing the spiritual efficacy of the earlier banquet. His tossing of water on the diners involves the inversion of an ecclesiastical ritual, the sanctification of the faithful with holy water, an association brought into play by Timon's word "sprinkle," the English translation of *asperges*.[31] In Timon's hands, this ritual of blessing becomes a curse, a means by which Timon can cleanse himself of the taint of their false amity:

> This [feast] is Timon's last,
> Who, stuck and spangled with your flatteries,
> Washes it off, and sprinkles in your face
> Your reeking villainy.   (*Tim.*, 11.89–92)

The epithets Timon heaps upon his guests inaugurate several themes he will pursue in his exile: humankind's essentially carnivorous, bestial nature ("affable wolves, meek bears" [11.94]); humankind's deception and servility in the pursuit of profit ("Cap-and-knee slaves,…minute-jacks" [11.96]); Timon's desire that humankind be plagued with disease ("the infinite malady / Crust you quite over" [11.97–98]). Of special interest is the phrase "trencher-friends" (11.95), which encapsulates Timon's outrage that the bonds of banqueting extend no longer than the meal itself; the phrase that follows, "time's flies" (11.95), cuts even deeper, for it casts his guests as carrion flies waiting for an opportunity to feed, with Timon implicitly as the meat. His curse quickly escalates:

> Henceforth be no feast
> Whereat a villain's not a welcome guest.
> Burn house! Sink Athens! Henceforth hated be
> Of Timon man and all humanity!   (11.101–04)

This sudden broadening of his outrage has seemed to be unjustified to many commentators, a mark of Timon's immaturity, wounded ego, or all-or-nothing mindset. It is important to notice, then, that Timon's tirade is framed by specific references to banqueting. The logic of Timon's misanthropy turns on his—and humanist culture's—investment in the communal meal as an incarnation of humanism's central aspirations. Timon's traumatic recognition that the banquet has been corrupted and that this corruption has become institutionalized suggests that the humanist project of cultivating virtue has been fatally compromised. This is not to ignore Timon's complicity in this corruption but only to suggest that the precipitous extension of his curse from dinner guests to Athens to humankind makes sense given the symbolic weight attached by humanism to the *convivium*. This link appears in Timon's repetition of his curse, where he singles out banqueting as a signal form of human community:

> All's obliquy;
> There's nothing level in our cursèd natures
> But direct villainy. Therefore be abhorred
> All *feasts*, societies, and throngs of men.   (14.18–21; emphasis
> added)

In short, the addition of banqueting to the Timon story is crucial to connecting his legendary loss of faith in humanity with the growing crisis of humanist idealism in the early seventeenth century.

Timon's Cynical "Banquet"

Though Timon's "broken banquet" does not give us the climactic revenge we may have expected, it does set in motion Timon's descent from disillusionment with civilized ideals into full-blown misanthropic rage. A full discussion of that descent is outside this essay's scope, but I want briefly to explore the implications of what replaces the banquet for Timon—the root. At Timon's first banquet Apemantus establishes the root as the signature foodstuff of Cynics, and so as Timon begins his life as a cynical outcast it is appropriate that he dig for roots. Shakespeare does not specify the root for which Timon digs, but root vegetables in general bore several connotations.[32] At the bottom of the early modern hierarchy of foodstuffs, roots—in particular the wild roots Timon seeks—were regarded as food for animals (especially pigs), associated with the earth and the dung heaps in which they were often cultivated.[33] In Timon's case, the root's rawness sets it in primal opposition to the cooked cuisine that suggests civilization. Timon's search for roots thus signifies not just his descent into poverty but his embrace of philosophical Cynicism, a rejection of corrupting social convention by willingly becoming animal, using nature to create contempt for "human" nature (see *Tim.*, 14.6–8). Timon's asceticism is emphatically *not* that of the Christian monastic tradition, where bodily denial is a means for transcending earthly life. Timon's initial goal is *immersion* in the natural world so as to purge the falsity of social custom. His digging for roots completes the process of cleansing he begins at the broken banquet.

There is a second, more historically specific context for understanding Timon's search for roots. The 1590s and early 1600s had seen a series of disastrous grain harvests, with the result that grain and bread were suddenly far more expensive and in short supply.[34] This fact was particularly ruinous for the urban poor, who risked starvation. Shortly before this time, textile workers from the Low Countries who had immigrated to East Anglia brought to England skills at growing root vegetables in gardens as well as new varieties of roots from their homelands. They soon began to sell their surplus crop locally, and by the turn of the sixteenth century they were shipping them to London, taking advantage of the need for edible vegetables. There is evidence that under pressure of these circumstances, the cultural status of root vegetables began to be reevaluated. Before this period, roots warranted hardly any mention in dietaries or cookbooks, other than the radish (the so-called *radix radicum*, "root of roots," described as an aid to digestion and speaking) and the carrot (often described as an aphrodisiac because of its phallic shape).[35] By the early seventeenth century, roots were becoming regarded as basic sources of nutrition. Richard Gardiner's *Profitable Instructions for the Manuring, Sowing and Planting of Kitchin Gardens* (1603) is at the vanguard of this change, focusing almost exclusively on the cultivation of root vegetables.[36] Gardiner's praise for the carrot is especially fulsome. He chastises English city dwellers for allowing foreign nations to capture the emerging market for this root, and he explicitly argues that "the benefit of Carret rootes are profitable" for the poor's "better reliefe," proclaiming, "carrets in necessitie and dearth, are eaten of the poore people, after they be well boyled, instead of bread and meate. Many people will eate Carrets raw, and doe digest well in hungry stomackes: they give good nourishment to all people, and no hurtfull to any, whatsoever infirmities they be diseased of, as by experience doth proove by many to be true" (D3). Anticipating the idea of the victory garden, Gardiner urges his readers to "sowe Carrets in your Gardens," for the carrot is vital to England's national defense: "Admit it should please God, that any City or towne should be besieged by the enemy, what better provision for the greatest number of people can bee, then every garden to be sufficiently planted with Carrets?" (D3). In his 1587 *Description of England*, William Harrison remarks that the revival of gardening in the late sixteenth century led to root vegetables once regarded as "unknown or supposed...more meet for hogs and savage beasts" being "resumed among the poor commons" and even appearing on the tables of the upper classes, grown from "new seeds out of strange countries."[37] To be sure, Timon's diet of roots signifies resistance to the more luxurious temptations of the banquet table, but it also participates in a wholesale revaluation of the root's place in the English diet.

The quasi-redemptive capacity of the root helps to explain why Timon finds his discovery of gold instead so traumatic. After he implores mother earth to yield him roots so that he can purge himself of banqueting's contamination by the profit motive, the earth instead supplies him with the very symbol of greed: glittering, precious, inedible gold.[38] His exasperated exclamation, "No, gods, I am no idle votarist: / Roots, you clear heavens" (*Tim.*, 14.26–27), suggests that he thinks the gods have misunderstood his plea for "roots" and sent him instead "the root of all evil," as if Timon had really been praying to be reinstated as host of the banquet. But this dark pun quickly collapses into a cry of existential despair:

> Thus much of this will make
> Black white, foul fair, wrong right,
> Base noble, old young, coward valiant.
> Ha, you gods! Why this, what, this, you gods?   (14.27–30)

Launching here into his famous tirade against gold, Timon's speech culminates in a savage rejection of the earth, once maternal, now "damned," a "common whore of mankind, that puts odds / Among the rout of nations" (14.42–44) by supplying them, as it now does Timon, with gold. Timon's pun on root/rout underlines how the earth's gift of gold, its root, has the degradation of civil society, the disorderly rout, embedded at its very heart, as if the word "root" (as well as the redemptive potential it stood for) were homophonically corrupted. In any case, at this moment Timon reaches a new nadir of hopelessness. Betrayed by his friends and their gold-lust, he is now betrayed by the very Nature that might have been a means for his redemption. Timon's initial response, as it was in the play's first half, is repression—he vows to rebury the gold as a way of forcing the earth "do thy right nature" (14.45). But he quickly decides instead to *use* gold for what he sees as perversely ethical ends. Once again, Timon will become the gift-giving host to those who visit him in the wood, only now he offers gifts to finance the destruction of Athens.

After Alcibiades and the prostitutes leave him, Timon again digs for roots, but this time his appeal to nature is different. Now nature is a *"common* mother" (*Tim.*, 14.178; emphasis mine), a grotesque, amoral principle of bounty entirely indiscriminate in creating human beings, animals, and monsters, and providing for all of them. Even Timon's pangs of hunger—generated by nature—partake of the unsettling link between glut and emptiness, amoral bodily needs and moral nausea: "that nature, being sick of man's unkindness, / Should yet be hungry!" (14.176–77). Timon's plea—"From forth thy plenteous bosom, one poor root" (14.187)—is the desperate cry of a poor, famished man, absent the ethical program of philosophical Cynicism. When nature arbitrarily obliges, Timon acknowledges the gift sardonically ("O, a root! Dear thanks" [14.193]), but then immediately calls on nature to withdraw its overfertile bounty, for nature, he recognizes as he gnaws his root, is ultimately the source of the decadent banqueting that so corrupts Athens:

> Dry up thy marrows, vines, and plough-torn leas,
> Whereof ingrateful man with liquorish draughts
> And morsels unctuous greases his pure mind,
> That from it all consideration slips!   (14.194–97)

Tracing the problem of corrupting bounty back to its roots, Timon concludes that nature as a principle of ethical purity is no cure for what ails the human spirit; rather, its fecundity feeds the disease.

Though this is also yet one more example of Timon displacing responsibility for his own failings upon others, it clarifies why Timon lapses more deeply into misanthropic despair in this and subsequent scenes. The propensity for nature indiscriminately to supply both kinds of roots—golden and edible—robs Timon of one last avenue for positive, ethical action. When the debate between Apemantus and Timon comes to the issue of food, Timon now imagines the root solely in terms of revenge, reversing Athens's eating of him by his symbolically eating Athens: "That the whole life of Athens were in this! Thus would I eat it. *He bites the root*" (*Tim.*, 14.283–84). Later, Timon briefly tries to convert the thieves to a vegetarian diet when they portray themselves disingenuously as "men that much do want" (14.415), but when the thieves declare their unwillingness to live as "beasts and birds and fishes" (14.423), Timon resigns himself to their ineradicably cannibalistic nature—"you must eat men" (14.524)—and he offers a vision of Nature that suggests not the principle of bounteous gift-giving but of universal thievery (14.435–42, culminating in "every thing's a thief"). Given Timon's initial prayer for roots, his characterization of the earth here is noteworthy: "The earth's a thief, / That feeds and breeds by a composture stol'n / From gen'ral excrement" (14.440–42). The emblematic food of Cynics, grown in the earth and in dung heaps, befouled by its origins, cannot escape imbrication in what here becomes a universal economy of thievery, stealing nutriment from one another's shit; at its root, natural fertility and bounty—what enables the banquet—turns out to be the very antithesis of the virtuously uplifting gift.

After the Humanist Banquet

The souring of faith in humanist idealism in the late sixteenth century brought with it the emergence of the fictional malcontent, a new stock figure through which dramatists considered varieties of cultural disaffection tempting to the age. The growing perception was that humanist aspirations to earthly virtue and political utopia were

increasingly unfulfillable, ultimately empty, available only to flatter-
ers, or, worst of all, a screen for nefarious conduct. As a result, some
were drawn to broad skepticism, lowercase *c* cynicism, Machiavel-
lianism, even nihilism. *Timon of Athens* thus contributes to a larger
cultural discussion of soured idealism, staging through Timon's biography the frustrated idealism of a generation. Apemantus's and Timon's
debate between ethical Cynicism and misanthropic fury—the central philosophical controversy of the play—considers, as do so many
other plays featuring disaffected protagonists, how to respond to one
of the period's cultural traumas: the perceived failure of the promise of
humanism. It is noteworthy, then, that the banquet should be so central a motif in this play about the compromise of humanist ideals. As
a model of social order, the banquet figures crucially in Timon's sense
that his and his culture's ideals have been fundamentally violated, and
it helps to explain why Timon seems so fixated on metaphors of food
and eating in relation to ethical practice. If the predominance of banquets and banquet entertainments in revenge tragedies is any gauge,
Timon was not alone in making this connection. For after the degradation of humanist banqueting, the next troubling question is how to
conceptualize a new posthumanist socio-culinary ideal.

Chapter 8

Feasting and Forgetting: Sir Toby's Pickle Herring and the Lure of Lethe

TOBIAS DÖRING

RED HERRINGS

In 1599, shortly before the ban on and public burning of his works, Thomas Nashe published *Lenten Stuff*, a witty and digressive pamphlet in "Praise of the Red Herring," advertised on the title page as "Fitte of all Clearkes of Noblemens Kitchins to be read."[1] A satirical and rather absurd story, Nashe's pamphlet follows the fate of a certain herring caught by a Norfolk fisherman who is convinced he has witnessed a miracle when his catch of fish, left out to dry, suddenly turns from white to red. This change of color causes a great sensation, taking the fisherman first to the court and then to Rome. There he manages to sell his fish at an enormous price to the pope's kitchen, even though the herring, now regarded as a dignitary, is already rotting and quite seriously stinking. Yet the papal chef, with much ado and pious praying in the kitchen, "drest it as he was enioyned, kneeling on his knees and mumbling twenty aue Maryes to himself in the sacrifizing of it on the coales." When, after much culinary and ritual preparation, the famous herring is eventually served to the pope, "the dishes were vncouered and the swarthrutter sowre took ayre: for then hee made such an ayre, as *Alcides* himselfe that clensed the stables of *Agæus* nor any holster was able to endure." This great fishy fart disrupts the banquet and leads the papal household to the charitable thought "that it might bee the distressed soule of some kinge that was drownd, who, being long in Purgatorie, and not releeued by the praiers of the church, and leaue, in that disguised forme, to haue egresse and regresse to Rome, to craue theyr beneuolence of dirges, trentals, and so foorth, to helpe him onward on his iourney to *Limbo patrum* or *Elisium.*"[2] Instead of eating it, the pope therefore provides the herring with a "Christian burial," complete with dirges, masses, and eventual canonization. Henceforth, a saint's day in April will commemorate this holy fish.

In present-day enquiries into early modern culinary culture, Nashe's curious story has found some attention. Most notably, Robert Appelbaum has given it an extended structuralist reading inspired by Lévi-Strauss and his "culinary triangle," establishing why the herring "was in fact one of the more semiotically interesting foodstuffs of the early modern period,"[3] and how its semiotics bear on our understanding of food debates in Shakespeare's comedy *Twelfth Night*. In that play, as any spectator soon notes, Sir Toby Belch emerges as a connoisseur of herring, especially "pickle herring," evidently the source of his eponymous belching (*TN*, 1.5.112).[4] According to Feste's later quip, "fools are as like husbands as pilchards are to herrings" (*TN*, 3.1.29–30); that is, husbands are greater fools than fools. The herring features as a similar trope in other Shakespeare plays, especially in comic contexts, as when Mercutio taunts the lovesick Romeo that he looks "without his roe, like a dried herring" (*R&J*, 2.3.35), meaning feeble and emaciated.

In fact, the herring plays a central role not just in satire and comedy but also in the material culture of eating. Of all fish, it is "the one which has had most influence on the economic and political history of Europe."[5] Widely available across the North Atlantic and best during the autumn months, herring has long been seen to be both nourishing and versatile in styles of preparation, whether it be frying, boiling, steaming, smoking, pickling, or curing. According to *The Oxford Companion to Food*, the red herring of Nashe's story likely refers to fish that have been soaked in brine, then dried and smoked for several days, a traditional practice dating back to the fourteenth century.[6]

Some cookbooks of Shakespeare's time, such as *A Book of Cookrye* (1584) or *A Nevv Book of Cookerie* (1615), do not actually mention herring, an omission that might indicate that its preparation was considered too mundane or familiar to merit special instruction. Yet *The good Huswifes Handmaide for the Kitchin* (1594) contains recipes for herring pie and herring stew—the latter prepared with ale, onions, mustard, raisins, saffron, figs, and bread—and *The Good Huswifes Jewell* (1596), in the only fish recipe of the entire book, tells us how to "boile diuers kindes of fishes" in a brine made of "faire water and vineger, a little salt, and bay leaues," resulting in a form of pickling "so yee may keepe it halfe a yeare."[7] Indeed, the techniques to conserve such a nourishing and tasty, but quickly rotting, foodstuff over time are absolutely crucial—for household purposes as well as for the larger cultural economies at work in early modern England.

Not only material but also cultural modes of preservation are central in Nashe's story, too. The simple fact that all fresh food and produce perish unless specially prepared or cured gives us the most mundane and general yet powerful reminder of the natural transience of things. Fishing, just like husbandry, follows the seasonal, generative cycle of the year. If cooking, according to Lévi-Strauss, is the basic technique of transforming nature into culture, then this practice also involves cultural preservation so as to make provision for the winter season when few or no fresh goods are naturally available.[8] The stinking Norfolk herring served at the festive papal banquet is such a marker of food value over time: it shows both inevitable natural degeneration, which is the fate of earthly matter, and the inordinate symbolic efforts made by all communities to preserve by social means what must otherwise be lost. This is what the canonization of the herring ironically signifies: it offers a mode of cultural survival through an act of annual commemoration. Therefore, as in the famous food-snatching scene of Marlowe's *Doctor Faustus*—which is also, tellingly, set in the Vatican—no actual eating takes place.[9] The fish is not consumed but ceremoniously buried and, in this way, commemorated. Instead of physical ingestion, the pope performs traditional rites of memory in order to placate the royal fish and relieve the herring's soul from suffering. The immediate point, then, of Nashe's antipapal satire was to launch an attack on the Catholic belief in Purgatory, the doctrine rigorously abolished, in a foundational act of the new church, with the Thirty-Nine Articles of 1563 and, since then, routinely railed against by Protestant polemicists.[10] Yet the larger and more fundamental point of *Lenten Stuff* may be, rather, to raise issues of food and time and to encourage new reflections on the ways in which culinary actions work, and interrelate, with practices of cultural memory.

Such complex intersections of culinary with commemorative practices are my central concern in this chapter, suggested by a new reading of Shakespeare's *Twelfth Night*. In traditional accounts, the Shakespearean playhouse has usually been regarded as a cultural institution where memories were preserved and which may in fact have been constructed on the very principles of the *ars memoria*. This is, at any rate, the central argument of Frances Yates's *The Art of Memory*, which draws mainly on rhetorical concepts laid out, for instance, by John Willis in his 1618 treatise, *Mnemonica*, where "the repositories," or topoi, for storing specific memories are described "as an imaginary fabrick...in form of a *Theater*."[11] More recently, this notion has been identified in the strategies by which old religious doctrines, such as Purgatory, discarded by the new theology, could keep some form of cultural presence on the public stage. In *Hamlet in Purgatory*, Stephen Greenblatt argues that distinctive references to pre-Reformation mourning for the dead are suggested by Hamlet's ghost and preserved in his doom "to walk the night" (*Ham.*, 1.5.10). This reading is further underlined by Hamlet's promise, in response to the ghost's tale, to remember him "whiles memory holds a seat / In this distracted globe" (1.5.96–97)—a telling phrase denoting not just his own head and the world at large but also the Globe Theatre as a seat of memory. And yet, against the long tradition of such readings, I wish to propose that the early modern theater, as an institution and a social practice, works not just toward memory but also toward oblivion, and that, in particular, its alliance with practices of food and feasting connects it to cultural functions of forgetting.

Herring offers an appropriate material and symbolic figure to rethink our understanding of the playhouse in this way because of the double valences and different meanings this fish could bear. As Robert Appelbaum argues, herring was a symbol of both poverty and wealth, fasting and feasting.[12] Like all fish, herring was a seasonal or weekly marker of the meatless days prescribed by the Catholic ritual calendar. Yet herring also was an oily and rich dish, much favored by food lovers for their bouts and feasts. For example, as Francis Meres reports, Shakespeare's fellow playwright Robert Greene "died of a surfet taken at Pickld Herrings & Rhenish wine, as witnesseth *Thomas Nash*, who was at the fatall banquet."[13] Double determinations of this fish and its symbolic valences recur. In "The Battle between Carnival and Lent," Pieter Brueghel's magnificent 1559 canvas, an emaciated, gray, and gloomy Lenten figure carries herring as the emblem of meager or ascetic diets, in opposition to the roasted pig brandished by King Carnival. However, in the pageant of the seven deadly sins in Marlowe's *Doctor Faustus*, the figure of Gluttony explains that "Peter Pickle-herring and Martin Martlemas-beef" are its godfathers, thus combining the two sides opposed in Brueghel's painting.[14] This double-sidedness and functional ambivalence may, therefore, prompt us to develop a more nuanced view of early modern theater, beyond only memorial uses.

My broader interest in this argument is to establish a more meaningful and productive perspective through which to view culinary Shakespeare and the manifold interrelations between kitchen culture and the playhouse, beyond simply listing food items referred to in the plays and explaining their provenance[15]—and further, to give a functional perspective that might help us see what cultural *work* these food engagements performed, on and through the stage, for Reformation English culture. *Twelfth Night* is relevant in this respect not just because its entire lexicon—beginning with Orsino's opening lines—is full of alimentary tropes, but because this festive comedy grounds or grafts itself on seasonal entertainment. As with *Lenten Stuff*, its title highlights a specific period in the ritual calendar and, in Shakespeare's case, signals the involvement with traditional pleasures and pastimes of Tudor England, where January 6 was riotously celebrated as the most sumptuous feast of the whole year, the culmination of the 12-day Christmas celebration.[16] What does it mean, however, for a play script, written and produced for the commercial stage, to announce itself like a festive season and refer to culinary habits at this time? What story—or what *stories*—would this play have told contemporary audiences through its strong engagement with food, drink, and physical excess? And what may have been the function of these stories?

To pursue these questions, my argument offers two opposing views on the figure of Sir Toby. The traditional view, which I outline first, sees Sir Toby—the famous drunkard, glutton, misbehaver and upsetter of the household order, great appreciator, as well as instigator of excess—as a memorial character, that is, a festive figure that embodies for Shakespeare's audiences specific memories and tells them of their recent past. In contrast to this view, I suggest that we should also see Sir Toby as a figure of forgetting and forgetfulness, a character who also tells another story by which specific cultural memories might be finally released.

Staging Memory

Twelfth Night comes to its first climax in the so-called "kitchen scene" of act 2, scene 3. Even though the setting here is textually not specified, the kitchen has long been regarded as the logical location in Olivia's household where the nightly drinking and carousing of Sir Toby and his friends takes place.[17] Interestingly, in the entire Shakespeare canon we find thousands of references to food, eating, and cooking, but we find no other single scene set in a kitchen—with the possible exception of the witches and their cauldron in *Macbeth* (a scene, however, that was written and included by Middleton, probably transferred from his own play *The Witch*).[18] This seems remarkable not least because, historically, the connections between theater culture and culinary culture were clearly very close. We find evidence not only in festive banquets and their entertainments but often as major elements of drama.[19] Further historical examples include Richard Tarlton's pub on Gracechurch Street and John Heminges's tavern by the Globe, gastronomic establishments that these well-known actors used to run as business ventures. Playwrights themselves describe their drama in terms of kitchen work: Ben Jonson opened his masque *Neptune's Fortune* with the learned propositions of a master cook, who tells a poet why their arts are essentially the same: "For there is a palate of the understanding as well as of the senses. The taste is taken with good relishes, the sight with faire objects, the hearing with delicate sounds, the smelling with pure scents, the feeling with soft and plump bodies, but the understanding with all these, for all which you must begin at the kitchen. There, the art of poetry was learned and found out, or nowhere, and at the same day with art of cookery."[20] In this speech, the mode is funny, but the point is serious and deserves reflection: what does it mean, in terms of social relevance and status, when the kitchen is made the model of literary production?

In fact, Renaissance cooks were mostly lowly figures, modest artisans who seldom rose to prominence and were rarely named.[21] Despite elite enjoyment of excessive feasts, and despite increased sophistication—even in England—in preparing and celebrating sumptuous banquets, English Renaissance writing seems to give little regard to the cultural, let alone artistic, value of cooks. This may derive from humanistic prejudices against cooking as a deceptive practice, an attitude most famously expressed in classical antiquity by Socrates. In the Platonic dialogue *Gorgias,* cooking is condemned because its artifice tends to supplant the proper art of medicine. As Socrates says, "Cooking assumes the form of medicine, and pretends to know what foods are best for the body; so that if a cook or a doctor had to contend before boys, or before men as foolish as boys, as to which of the two, the doctor or the cook, understands the question of sound and noxious foods, the doctor would starve to death. Flattery, however, is what I call it, and I say that this sort of thing is a disgrace."[22] According to Michel Jeanneret, cooking is condemned here for two reasons, morally and epistemologically: because "it only seeks to please" and because "it cannot explain the true nature of things."[23] On both accounts, cookery operates like rhetoric—and like the playhouse, which was condemned by its early modern opponents for just these reasons, as a fraudulent and immoral institution appealing to the pleasure of the lower senses and obstructing the truth. Puritan writers such as Philip Stubbes in *The Anatomie of Abuses* could therefore attack the extravagances of the stage in just the same terms as the extravagances of the kitchen, both of which Stubbes saw as recent and shared influences corrupting English culture.[24]

Such critiques are relevant for the kitchen scene in *Twelfth Night* because they are echoed and staged through the figure of Malvolio:

"Do ye make an alehouse of my lady's house?" (*TN*, 2.3.83–84), he rebukes the nightly drinkers. An alehouse, to be sure, was a business establishment different from a kitchen, yet like the kitchen it offered a place where physical needs and sensual pleasures were the main concern. It was a gastronomic institution, moreover, which also played a role in the prehistory of the London playhouses, the architectural structure and theatrical practice of which partly developed from early Tudor inns and the entertainments offered in their yards.[25] But even before Malvolio enters and interrupts the singing, the space of the theater has been connected to the gastronomic space of an inn. When Feste greets Sir Andrew and Sir Toby with the words, "Did you never see the picture of We Three?" (*TN*, 2.3.15–16), the picture he refers to is a well-known pub sign: it shows *two* asses or *two* fools with the caption "We three loggerheads." Whoever wonders where the *third* ass or fool might be has already solved the riddle because the picture includes the beholder. In the words of Elizabeth Freund, "without conceding asshood, the reader cannot unriddle the picture; but if he fails to read the picture, he is palpably an ass."[26] That is to say, in more positive terms, that this picture, like this nightly scene of feasting, fulfills a social function: they both construct communities. As much as the interpreter of the pub sign sees himself or herself included in what is interpreted, so spectators of Shakespeare's comedy find themselves included in the community of drinkers they are watching. As they follow the performance of the kitchen scene, quite possibly themselves eating and drinking, they become participants and potentially enter the theatrical space. Under Sir Toby's prompting, spectators turn into fellow feasters.

It is only by understanding this metatheatrical twist that turns the playhouse into an alehouse and thus *re*turns to the prehistory of the London stage, that we can understand Malvolio's opposition to the spectacle. When Maria calls him "a kind of Puritan" (*TN*, 2.3.129), we need not even understand this in a strict religious sense to realize that Malvolio represents a different and new regime of social, temporal, and spatial economies, quite the opposite of Sir Toby's theatrical transgressions. Malvolio demands respect for "place, persons," and "time" (*TN*, 2.3.85–86), whereas Toby constantly violates these categories (and later makes Malvolio violate them too: it is the particular cruelty of their hoax to make him play a part through which he transgresses his social station, acting out of place and time)—just as the very practice of play-acting must violate them, that is, must constantly transform place, person, and time to do its work. Sir Toby thus emerges as a figure emblematic of the theater, an embodiment not just of enjoyment but of theatrical playing allied to the work of feasting: a figure that upsets the household order, that heeds neither place nor time, that reverses social hierarchies, and that turns spectators into participants, constructing a community realized in performance.

Sir Toby's theatrical transgressiveness is the reason his answer to Malvolio carries so much cultural force: "Dost thou think because thou art virtuous, there shall be no more cakes and ale?" (*TN*, 2.3.106–07) His retort also suggests why the conflict between Sir Toby and Malvolio has long been a favorite foundation for the Bakhtinian readings of the play and its engagement with carnivalesque culture.[27] According to Mikhail Bakhtin's analysis, "eating, drinking, defecation...as well as copulation" combine to construct what he calls the "grotesque body"—the all-devouring, swelling, and excessive physicality—which goes beyond all boundaries and is realized through carnival.[28] From its first lines, *Twelfth Night* surely is a comedy so steeped in discourses of food that the play's central confrontation between Sir Toby and Malvolio fits into traditional patterns such as Brueghel's battle between carnival and Lent—fundamental cultural oppositions between feasting and fasting—which are theatrically revived in the two figures and in the seasonal celebration the play commemorates.

This conflict is historically significant because the comedy thus involves and evokes distinct memories of popular festivities, as if to offer an occasion for late Elizabethans to relive an abandoned aspect of their Catholic past. For under Anglican auspices around 1600, the old calendar of holidays and seasonal feasts was under pressure to reform. Shakespearean theater, it has been argued,[29] may often have been helpful in reminding audiences of such rites and seasons (as with Purgatory in *Hamlet*), which were officially no longer tolerated nor observed but a generation later were recalled and reworked on the stage. Yet, below the level of theology and state church teaching, many old notions lived on, especially the festive calendar that, according to François

Laroque, "still played a role of major importance in Elizabethan England" and constituted, as he puts it, "a veritable matrix of time."[30] In the context of *Twelfth Night*—a threshold play performed just before the new dynastic era, which was also anticipated with religious hope—the presence of Sir Toby recalls this "matrix of time." He operates as a memory figure, a Lord of Misrule, pitted against contemporary adversaries like the "Puritan" Malvolio. Generally speaking, food often serves memorial functions, especially in religious rites, as evidenced in the Eucharist and the debates surrounding it throughout the sixteenth century as well as throughout this play.[31] But even more so in this comedy, where Sir Toby appears as a representative of traditional carnival culture, food preferences restore a sense of cultural continuity for what has otherwise been discontinued in English religious life.

Such memories are also called up through the specific culinary items in Sir Toby's celebrated retort to Malvolio (*TN*, 2.3.106–07). For English audiences around 1600, "cakes and ale" hold particular resonances in reference to the old faith. According to Ken Albala, for instance, there is a confessional divide associated with the difference between real ale, the traditional English drink Sir Toby is defending here, and beer brewed with hops imported to England from the Continent in large quantities throughout the early Tudor period, rather like the Reformation, which some would also regard as a continental product. The connection between gastronomic and religious culture was not lost on stout defenders of the faith. Popular verses celebrated the connection: "Hops, Reformation, Bays and Beer / came all into England in one bad year…heresie & beer came hopping into England both in a yeere."[32] As a matter of fact, beer was brewed and certainly consumed in England long before the break with Rome.[33] As Peter Clark shows (and as is argued at greater length in chapter 1 of this volume), beer was being imported by 1400, and "within a few years hops for brewing were being brought into England in sizeable quantities."[34] Yet the social perception of it as a reformed, urban, and newfangled drink, threatening to replace time-honored English habits, was rather widespread. As late as 1630, a comic dialogue was published, entitled, *Wine, Beer, Ale, and Tobacco: Contending for Superiority* and introducing the various speakers in their social roles, with "Beer" figuring as "A Citizen" and "Ale" as "A Country-man."[35]

Sir Toby's preferred drink, therefore, aligns him clearly with traditional country tastes.

These are just some indications of the many ways in which the new religion followed or produced new dietary regimes, in which "cakes and ale," the old staple of rustic merriments and annual feasts like wakes, no longer had a place.[36] Another relevant example of the changing foodways in Tudor England is the shifting attitude toward fish. As mentioned at the outset, fish had been a widely consumed and economically important food item, yet it was strongly associated with the "Lenten stuff" of the old church year with its fasting periods and ritual cycles, criticized by Protestants but tolerated, in a typically Elizabethan compromise, so as to protect the local fishing industry.[37] Its religious connotations, however, were clearly Catholic. When in *King Lear* the faithful Kent offers his service to the king, he vows "to serve him truly that will put me in trust, to love him that is honest, to converse with him that is wise and says little, to fear judgment, to fight when I cannot choose, and to eat no fish" (*Lr.*, 1.4.12–15), thus giving his Protestant credentials. From this perspective, Sir Toby's noted predilection for fish, and in particular for the "pickle herring" that causes his hiccups (*TN*, 1.5.112), is just as significant as his taste for ale in emphasizing his relation to the old order.

All these examples, then, should serve to show Sir Toby both as a figure of excess and as a devotee of special diets. Excess links him to old carnival traditions, and his dietary preferences link him to the old faith. In both these ways, Sir Toby's presence on the late-Elizabethan stage may have helped to revive an established sense of bygone ritual practice and to recall for theatrical participants—a community of feasters who, as we have seen, potentially include the audience—the old matrix of time. Against the virtuous Malvolios and other modern "time-pleasers" (*TN*, 2.3.136) in early seventeenth century England, Sir Toby recalls a different regime of temporal organization, seasonal celebration, and ritual festivity, provisionally reestablished in the playhouse as a space of cultural memory. And yet, as I said earlier, this is just half his story. I believe we need to question this traditional account and reverse our perspective on this figure to see what kind of function Sir Toby also and primarily performs: the work of cultural forgetting—a function of the theater, I suggest, much in demand in post-Reformation England.

Staging Oblivion

When Hamlet's or Banquo's ghost returns to haunt the living, the Shakespearean stage reminds spectators of the continued presence of the dead. When Hamlet's ghost appears while Claudio and the court engage in noisy celebration or when Banquo's ghost comes back for the occasion of a banquet, claiming his place at the dinner table, the timing of their coming shows that cultural moments such as mealtimes and festive parties used to offer ritual opportunities for the bereaved to remember, and potentially reimagine, their losses. In "Remembering the Dead at Dinner-Time," Sheila Sweetinburgh makes this argument, with reference to medieval Canterbury, for monastic communities whose former members were commemorated by "the placing of a deceased monk's portions of food and drink on the refectory tables at meal times for a set period after his death, the whole given to the poor once the meal had ended."[38] The Reformation, however, programmatically disrupted this sort of social continuity and communion between the living and the dead. With the abolition of Purgatory, the departed were considered beyond human reach, and any ritual forms of mourning or active service for their souls, like prayers or intercessions, were seen as interfering with the divine will of their predestined fate. Shakespeare's festive comedy indeed reflects this fundamental change in attitude toward the dead, perhaps the most powerful impact of the new theology on everyday life.

Sir Toby's first appearance is a case in point. Upon his entrance in act 1, scene 3, he rebukes his niece Olivia for continued mourning: "I am sure care's an enemy to life" (*TN*, 1.3.2). Toby's attitude is entirely in keeping with the way in which Orsino's messenger in the opening scene first introduced and described Olivia: living withdrawn like a nun, constantly weeping and grieving for her brother, whom "she would keep fresh / and lasting in her sad remembrance" (1.1.30–31). Orsino's response to the report emphasizes the physiological nature of affections that he hopes to turn to his advantage "when liver, brain, and heart, / These sovereign thrones, are all supplied, and filled / Her sweet perfections with one self king" (1.1.36–38). He thus also evokes the economy of body fluids by which love and grief and all other human passions work. In this way, even before the countess makes an actual appearance, she has been identified on the basis of her humoral constitution as a persistent mourner. So it comes as no surprise when we actually meet her that the legitimacy of mourning is the issue of her celebrated little dialogue with Feste, who keeps calling her "madonna":

> Feste: Good madonna, why mourn'st thou?
> Olivia: Good fool, for my brother's death.
> Feste: I think his soul is in hell, madonna.
> Olivia: I know his soul is in heaven, fool.
> Feste: The more fool, madonna, to mourn for your brother's soul
> being in heaven.   (1.5.59–64)

Not unlike Claudius's rebuke to Hamlet in front of the court at Elsinore where he, as Greenblatt remarks, usurps the language of Reformed theology to put an end to Hamlet's mourning, the fool's point to Olivia echoes well-known Protestant polemics against Catholic funeral rites and their constitutive acts of memory.[39] This critique was made in many treatises, such as Thomas Becon's *The Sick Mans Salue* of 1560, an immensely popular and frequently reprinted text arguing against the need for any charitable deeds or memorial practice for the dead, unless we doubt their gift of grace: "Let the Infidels mourne for their dead: the Christian ought to reioyce when any of the faythfull be called from this vale of misery vnto the kingdome of God."[40] That is to say, Olivia's ostentatious mourning in the first part of the play aligns her with pre-Reformation memory rites outlawed in Shakespeare's England a generation earlier.

This diagnosis is confirmed by a crucial detail later, when the countess goes to marry her new love and asks the bridegroom, "go with me and with this holy man / Into the *chantry* by" (*TN*, 4.3.23–24; emphasis mine). A chantry is a chapel specially dedicated to the singing of daily Mass for the souls of the dead, an institution of and for the old religion where now her wedding is to be performed.[41] True, her household is run by a time-keeping steward and indeed governed by the sound of the clock — "*Clock strikes*" (*TN*, 3.1.121) is the only stage direction of this sort in the entire Shakespeare canon, the signature of modern temporal regimes — but the various other indications show that Olivia's Illyrian property is evidently built on Catholic ground.

So it is entirely appropriate that her fool invokes the saints only in his curses ("By'r lady" [*TN*, 2.3.61], "by Saint Anne" [*TN*, 2.3.108]), while otherwise speaking the language of the Reformation and singing about the new Protestant eschatology ("What's to come is still unsure" [*TN*, 2.3.47]). In this perspective, we see how the theatrical performance offers an occasion to remember, or review, specific rites and doctrines of the old religion and how the figure of Olivia functions to evoke such cultural memories. If the early modern playhouse, according to Yates's classic study, is a structure for the art of memory, this art includes religion and may even give provisional compensation for some ritual practices, like mourning, which in Elizabethan England were placed under strict injunctions.[42]

Conversely, the early modern playhouse is a multivalent cultural space and may also work along quite different lines than memory and mourning. We should therefore reverse this established view of Shakespearean theater and consider the ways in which it contributes also to the work of cultural forgetting. Indeed, it is the figure of Sir Toby with his constant gluttony who must prompt such reconsideration. However, to give this argument a broader basis, I need to make a short digression to reflect on the possibility of cultural forgetting, a notion that may well seem paradoxical because it counters our fundamental understanding of memory.

The art of memory, or *ars memoria*, is part of the Renaissance heritage of classical rhetoric. In the course of training orators, rhetoric offers students certain techniques — the famous topoi or commonplaces — to help them memorize all the elements of their well-wrought speeches, which they would otherwise, eventually and naturally, forget. In this traditional view, memory is to forgetting as culture is to nature: a special method of conscious preservation in an intentional effort to combat natural processes of change and decay, generally beyond human activity or volition.[43] Against this background, a cultural method for oblivion is strictly inconceivable because forgetting could never be an art in the sense of an intentional, controlled, and specific technique. Any conscious act that tries to make someone forget something must, inevitably, call the very thing again to mind: a performative contradiction. This paradox led thinkers like Umberto Eco principally to reject the notion: Eco entitled an article "An Ars Oblivionalis?" in the 1980s, only to give his answer at once: "Forget it!" All art operates by signs and by representation; oblivion demands an erasure of signs; therefore, on semiotic grounds, an art of oblivion is a contradiction in terms.[44]

And yet, the term occurs in early modern writing, most prominently in Willis's *Mnemonica*. Here, in the context of remembering without writing, Willis defines the term as follows: "*Deposition* is when we recollect things committed to memory; and having transcribed or transacted them, discharge our memories of them, which is always to be practised at the first opportunity.... *Deposition, or discharging things committed to mind, is not unlike expunging writing out of Table-Books: If therefore there be any Art of *Oblivion* (as some affirm) it may be properly referred hither."[45] This is a remarkable description—reminding us perhaps of Hamlet's table books of memory (*Ham.*, 1.5.107)—especially for a historical period such as the long English Reformation, in which the need to discharge the official cultural memory of so many rites and saints and holy signs was rather pressing. An art of deposition—that is, cultural forgetting—must therefore have been rather useful and much in demand. In fact, the social dimensions and political uses of this art were clearly seen already in the sixteenth century: in the second book of his *Discorsi*, Niccolò Machiavelli remarks that natural catastrophes like plagues or famines are so useful for the purpose of introducing a new religion because they help to erase memories of the old religion quite efficiently, making people forget and thus purging the body politic of unwanted remains and lingering recollections.[46]

Machiavelli's reference to Galenic physiology and the economy of body fluids is revealing: it acknowledges that the activities of eating and digestion can work as a counterforce or counterexercise to memory, especially when food consumption is taken to excess. The same point is indeed made by Willis: "*Food* hurteth the *Memory*,...too much *Repletion dulleth wit*, and is a great enemy to the *Memorative faculty*." As he explains in his treatise, "Variety of dishes, diversity even of wholesome meats is evil, of Sauces worst of all, distracting the stomack by concocting food of several qualities." For this reason, Willis advises all students who would like to keep and train their faculty of memory to strict moderation: "Fly therefore *Drunkennesse* and *Gluttony*, as the mortallest enemies of a good *Memory*."[47] It is precisely on the basis of these dietary rules that we see why anyone who may have reason to promote forgetting as a cultural force can best do so by promoting eating, feasting, drunkenness, and gluttony—which brings us back to Shakespeare's Sir Toby and the cultural function of his constant feasting.

When Sir Toby meets Olivia for the first time in the play—belching, reeking of herring, evidently drunk, and in top spirits—she rebukes him: "Cousin, cousin, how have you come so early by this lethargy?" (*TN*, 1.5.114–15). Her remark registers his state of drunkenness so early in the day as a special immorality, yet the crucial term of her critique is "lethargy": this keyword designates his lack of body discipline, his gluttonous enjoyment beyond all moderation, and his self-forgetting. Etymologically, the word "lethargy" derives from the river Lethe, the underworld river of forgetfulness, which links the pathology of excessive body fluids to the lack, or loss, of memory. As Garrett Sullivan argues on the basis of contemporary medical writing, "the operations of animal spirits in the brain are impeded by the preponderance of phlegm."[48] The glutton and drunkard is lethargic because he is fully focused on his physicality and, hence, unable to perform any cultural work—except, we should add, cultural forgetting. For we need not see the work of cultural forgetting entirely in negative terms, as suggested by Olivia, who is after all a determined mourner, a figure fixated on memory. Unlike her, we should also see the opportunity and bliss provided by the Lethean waters, the stream of forgetting, to those who would like to renew, perhaps even reform, themselves or indeed society:

> What relish is in this? How runs the stream?
> Or I am mad, or else this is a dream.
> Let fancy still my sense in Lethe steep.
> If it be thus to dream, still let me sleep.   (*TN*, 4.1.55–58)

This is how Sebastian, Olivia's lover, describes the curious transformation that has come over him: with reference to the lure of Lethe as a blissful state in which one bathes in the waters of forgetting. As formulated, for instance, in Puck's epilogue to *Midsummer Night's Dream* ("Think...That you have but slumbered here"), dreaming and sleeping are the favored self-descriptions of the early modern theater, a cultural practice that is linked in this way to the workings of oblivion. At the same time, Sebastian's reference to "relish"—the physical pleasure of the palate—links Lethe also to culinary acts, as celebrated in the scenes of merrymaking and carnivalesque feasting in the play. With this speech, Olivia's future husband thus reveals that he has joined the tribe of Toby.

Two points, then, emerge from this analysis: first, we must realize that forgetting involves productive and inventive aspects that are crucial in enabling reformations and establishing something new; second, we must realize that the theater is a particular place where just such aspects are effective—that is, where practices of eating, feasting, and digesting perform continuous transformations of given elements and persistent memories. If Sir Toby, as I have argued, embodies the theatrical and at the same time presents theater as a physical art of the body, then his lethargy must have an impact also on spectators, who turn into participants and, like Sebastian, themselves partake of all these lures of Lethe. In his reversed perspective, Sir Toby's work becomes an agent of forgetting. He is the stage embodiment of culinary consumption and excess—the glutton, drinker, and lethargic artist of forgetfulness, lover of pickle herring, and, as such, a metatheatrical figure of the festive comedy tradition physically countering the culture of commemoration. "Pickleherring" was indeed the emblematic name by which, since the early seventeenth century, the clown was known in the English playing companies who toured the Continent and popularized Shakespeare's plays;[49] alternative names of this comic figure, such as Hanswurst, Potage, Knapkäse, or Stockfisch, all refer to food and thus confirm the close connection of comedy to physicality and of laughter to the body.[50] In this sense, clowns may principally operate as figures of corporality and, at the same time, of cultural forgetting. At any rate, Sir Toby's taste for fish and feasting marks his central function in contemporary processes of social transformation—cultural and religious changes shaped and crucially promoted also by the work of theater, especially the gastronomic art of oblivion practiced through it.

THEATRICAL BELCHING

Thomas Nashe's red herring, with which we began, is certainly
not an isolated case in early modern English culture of making
Shakespeare's contemporaries remember "Lenten stuff" and festive
times. Contemporary cookbooks regularly include instructions as to
what foods are best to buy in certain seasons and are best prepared
during particular periods of the year. *The good Huswifes Handmaide
for the Kitchin,* for example, tells readers on its opening page how "to
knowe the due seasons for the vse of al maner of meats throughout
the yeare":

> Brawn is best from holy Rood day til Lent, and at no other time com-
> monlie vsed for seruice. Bacon, Beefe and Mutton, is good at all tymes,
> but the worst tyme for Mutton is from Easter to Midsommer....
> A Goose is worst at Midsommer, & best in stubble tyme, but
> they be best of all when they be young green Geese. Veale is all
> tymes good, but best in Januarie and Februarie. Kidde and young
> Lambe is best between Christmasse & Lent, & good from Easter to
> Whitsontide.[51]

In this way, kitchen work takes place according to the annual festive
cycle, and the practical advice for cooking, as set down and printed
here, unambiguously evokes the various feast days of the traditional
church year—the old matrix of time that Elizabethan England, as
argued earlier, was under pressure to reform. Yet practical considerations of the market, including the natural availability of certain foods
at certain times, gave seasonal festivities a form of cultural survival,
as a temporal reference system in annual eating habits. Whatever the
official demands for different temporal organization in the Reformation era with its new regime of the clock, there clearly was a level of
everyday practice on which the old order of cyclical ritual experience
continued to exist throughout the early modern period. The theater,
too, was a seasonal business, as comedies like *Twelfth Night* so insistently remind us. Even as commercial entertainments in an industry
of mirth, the plays still evoke specific festive practices and so remind
spectators "to knowe the due seasons." Thus, social change may not
be staged just *in* such plays but also *with* such plays, not least with
their religious implications.

According to Richard Wilson's reading of *Twelfth Night,* "Shakespeare's Illyria maps the religious politics of Elizabethan London."[52] Indeed, as we have seen even from the few points cited, the text offers rich allusions to confessional divides, and especially rich reminders of Catholic rites or doctrines, officially long suppressed. Also, the names of many characters—Maria, Sebastian, Fabian, Andrew, Valentine—echo names of the traditional saints, several of whom could no longer be commemorated by late-Elizabethan worshippers, except by proxy of the stage. So the saints' theatrical return might well have helped to offer compensation for a seasonal practice now officially suppressed. And yet, early modern audiences may find even more occasion to experience the playhouse as a space of cultural forgetting, a space in which the names of saints, for instance, are absorbed, erased, or emptied out of former holiness. In this view, the main point about the various traces of the old religion in this comedy—traces evident, above all, in the play's staged culinary obsessions—neither recalls nor resists Catholicism, but performs, transforms, digests, and *out*-performs it on the stage, so as to be able to consign it to oblivion.

Crucial for this function of the theater is the culinary figure of Sir Toby. Yet, as I have shown, the play offers two quite different views on him, so that he works rather as a twinned or double figure, as if seen through the kind of "natural perspective," which Orsino mentions at the end of the play (*TN*, 5.1.207). When we see Sir Toby in opposition to Malvolio, he appears to be a figure of memory, recalling the traditional rites of festive cycles increasingly suppressed in Protestant society, to survive mainly on the festive stage. But when we see him in opposition to Olivia, Sir Toby appears instead as a figure of purgation, transformation, and forgetting; that is to say, of getting rid of all such ritual memories in and by theatrical enactment. If Olivia, the persistent mourner, works as a figure of Catholic commemoration, Sir Toby functions not just to criticize her old beliefs but to help people forget them. Short of the natural catastrophes envisaged by Machiavelli, such may be the best way to clear the cultural memory: eating and drinking promote lethargy and thereby produce forgetfulness, letting people steep in river Lethe.

This kind of strategic clearing is what I propose to regard as the cultural work of the playhouse, an early modern institution, after all, that was routinely criticized by virtuous believers such as Phillip Stubbes or William Rankins for inducing oblivion, "drinking the wine of forgetfulness," as Rankins put it in 1587 in *A Mirrour of Monsters*.[53] The playhouse was functionally associated with culinary practices and gastronomic acts precisely *because* of all the dangerous, incalculable physical forces that theater involves. Following such critics of the stage we realize how feasting is allied to forgetting, and how both are allied to the playhouse where these arts find their appropriate place. Thus, when people enter such a space of pleasure and consumption, they may well encounter Catholic signs or rites, but these traditional reminders of an old religion mainly recur here so as to be reconsidered and, eventually, consigned to oblivion. When a visitor comes to Illyria, for instance, and has some time to kill before dinner at the local inn, he is likely to go sightseeing: "What's to do? / Shall we go see the relics of this town?" (*TN*, 3.3.18–19), Sebastian asks. There must be quite some notable relics around: "let us satisfy our eyes / With the memorials and the things of fame / That do renown this city" (3.3.22–24). Such memorials and monuments clearly would have been once the central place of ritual practice and commemoration; now they merely figure as tourist sights, local attractions, or diversions for a stranded stranger to "satisfy" his eyes in passing. This change of status may be symptomatic for the relics of the old religion when reencountered on the stage. They now feature as one part among many in some popular entertainment, among other stage attractions and distractions, and even if they were once sacred, their theatrical return helps to empty them of previous significance and so deposition them from cultural memory. They reappear, to use the appropriate metaphor, just like a hiccup, as a physical release.

Of course this is Sir Toby's cultural function, hence his surname, Belch. Belching is a form of discharge, purifying us from unaccommodating elements that have been troubling or disturbing our system, so that we may feel more at ease. For there is no doubt that memory and commemoration are unsettling. When Hamlet makes his promise of remembrance to the ghost, he immediately appeals to his "sinews" to bear him "swiftly up" (*Ham.*, 1.5.94)—that is, to his own physical constitution to hold him and contain the mighty motion of his passions. But when he goes on to claim that "memory holds a seat / In this distracted globe" (1.5.96–97), as quoted at the outset, we should now give his claim a different reading: instead of "memory," we should emphasize "*distracted* globe," so as to stress the nature of theatrical performance as a mode of cultural forgetting, a powerful method of transforming and releasing given cultural meanings simply by staging so many distractions, attractions, and diversions that memory no longer holds a settled seat in anybody's globe: "And duller shouldst thou be than the fat weed / That roots itself in ease on Lethe wharf" (1.5.32–33). The "weed" that Hamlet's ghost, another figure of persistent memory, evoked here as a horrible monstrosity, returns a season later on the London stage with Sir Toby Belch, but with the valuation turned around: for this grotesque glutton, this lethargic, lazy drinker, lover of pickle herring, friend of Falstaff's,[54] and fat weed is evidently quite at ease, and he indeed invites us all to feel at ease, just like Sebastian, to steep our sense in Lethe and to relish our reformation. According to a sixteenth century Italian tale recounted by Piero Camporesi, the journey to the land of Cockaigne leads across the River of Forgetting.[55] Shakespeare's culinary trajectory in these two plays seems to retrace such a trip. *Twelfth Night* thus appears to offer us a twin drama to *Hamlet*, reworking the same issues of memory and mourning, but in another key. Its functional connection of feasting and forgetting, in conclusion, may suggest that the early modern playhouse, too, was built in ease at Lethe wharf.

Chapter 9

Shakespeare's Messmates

JULIAN YATES

> In my experience, when people hear the term *companion species,* they tend to start talking about "companion animals," such as dogs, cats, horses, miniature donkeys, tropical fish, fancy bunnies, dying baby turtles, ant farms, parrots, tarantulas in harness, and Vietnamese potbellied pigs... [but] the category "companion species" is less shapely and more rambunctious than that...less a category than a pointer to an ongoing "becoming with."
>
> —Donna Haraway, *When Species Meet* (2008)

> King: Now, Hamlet, where's Polonius?
> Hamlet: At supper.
> King: At supper! Where?
> Hamlet: Not where he eats but where 'a is eaten. A certain convocation of politic worms are e'en at him. Your worm is your only emperor for diet. We fat all creatures else to fat us, and we fat ourselves for maggots. Your fat king and your lean beggar is but variable service, two dishes at one table. That's the end.
>
> —William Shakespeare, *Hamlet* (1600)

In *When Species Meet,* Donna Haraway uses the word "messmate" to bring home the transformative effects of modeling our world as a set of relations between what she calls a "companion," or "multi-species." The word "companion," as Haraway reminds us, "comes from the Latin *cum panis,* 'with bread.' Mess-mates at table are companions."[1] Beyond questions of those nonhuman animals said to belong to households today under the rubric of the companion animal or pet, or those dogs, sheep, cows, pigs, and goats that had names in early modern households, Haraway's model of the messmate extends beyond anthropic or anthropomorphic models of belonging, of economy, of culture, cooking, and cuisine.[2] For her the human genome serves as a material-semiotic archive of our shared historical association or co-evolution with plant and animal actors of all kinds. In its noncommunitarian or nonintegrative because noncognizable modes, "messmate" includes the polities of bacteria to which our bodies play host and which, in the event of our deaths, will flower and feast upon us, as well as all the very many viral actors for whom our bodies serve as "kitchens." At its most extreme, the figure of the messmate provincializes communal and culinary practices as keyed to somatic and psychic regimens, rendering them shelters from a generalized nonanthropic cooking to which we will all, one day, find ourselves subject.[3]

From the perspective of such a general ecology, human foodways describe an interface between the boundaries of the household or collective (writ large or small) and the world, the kitchen a portal through which streams of animals, plants, and fungus are transformed into what is said to be that most human of *things*, a cuisine.[4] The kitchen waste bin or compost heap, the toilet or privy, mark those places where, having eaten said other beings, and used all those parts of them that we may or that we choose, we return what remains to the world at large. The grave, likewise, suggests our own exit from one food stream and entrance to another by our own becoming compost or soil. "Supper," as the Polonius-stowing Hamlet of act 4, scene 3 remarks to King Claudius, might be the word that worms use for a freshly filled grave. "Your worm is your only emperor for diet," Hamlet opines, "Your fat king and your lean beggar is but variable service—two dishes, but one table."[5] The world is just one great dinner (meaning, in this case, lunch) or kitchen. The "raw," so it turns out, requires the real-time nonanthropic cooking we name death and decay. Your ending, your death, does not mark the elision of questions of relation so much as the moment that your presence becomes that of an uncertainly available and cognizant object. You are gone. And by the manner of your going, you stick around, even as you do not—food for worms, the elements, as you enter into becoming soil.

My aim in this essay is to host or entertain "Shakespeare" from the vantage point offered by this deterritorialized, nonanthropic kitchen. In what follows, I shall try to "kitchen" Shakespeare in a use of the term that sounds strange to our ears, but which would have sounded perfectly normal to those in the sixteenth century, for which the word served as both noun and verb, meaning to host or entertain in or from the kitchen[6]—emphatically not Shakespeare's kitchen or the function of kitchens in Shakespeare's plays, though such a default anthropocentrism remains important and useful. I remain interested in asking what the kitchen's role as interface, with its social routines, ephemeral forms of writing (recipes, chalkboards, reckonings, account books of items purchased and their costs), and its ongoing negotiation of rawness, ripeness, rottenness, its efforts to arrest or foster decay (aging, cooking, preserving, distilling), may tell us about Shakespeare's theatrical and poetic practice. But this essay is driven more by a sense that the plays, already invested heavily in a variety of codes and forms of hospitality, have much to offer about the limits or lessons to be learned from Haraway's figure of the "messmate"—a word that, she hopes, augurs for modes of association that retard an instrumentalization of the world with which we come into being, and which resonates in terms of a collective belonging, if not quite citizenship.

For Haraway, the word "messmate" and its associated modalities of companion or multispecies gesture toward a putative universalism that is concretized by an empirical reckoning or inventorying of particulars, of multiplied differences and samenesses. But the word, even as it augurs in a familiar fashion, does not require any necessary integration of actors into some social or communal unit. It does not in and of itself require the recognition of individual presences. Instead, it designates merely a scene or moment of association, an association that not all of its players may be able to recognize or access. "Messmate" refers, for example, to those with whom we eat at table; to those we eat; and to those who, in the event of our demise or by dint of our continued breathing, eat us. The word comes primed with a hefty rhetorical and political freighting, but that freighting sits strangely with the neutrality of the relations it describes. "Messmate" might best be described, then, as an orientation. It offers no generalizable program of action. It designates merely the vast number of differently animated beings who "share" our tables and with whom we might be said, therefore, to "eat" even as we and/or they may lack the awareness (cognitive, perceptual, ideological) to perceive ourselves as doing so.

In what follows, I begin by tracing out what *Hamlet* may have to teach us about Haraway's project, using the play to parse the biopolitical quotient to the figure of the messmate and the allied terms "companion" and "multispecies." *The Comedy of Errors* (1592–94) serves as my point of entry to the way "messmate" figures a time-bound mode of association, and to the way its functioning might be keyed to a hospitable order of narcissism. *The Tempest* (1611) offers me a conclusion or end point—a scene of estranged eating that takes the form of an episode of taste testing that appears to answer all. For everything, as the romance phrasing of cooking shows goes, was prepared earlier in Prospero's test kitchen.

OF MESSMATES AND MASSES

If what Haraway calls the "rambunctious" word, "messmate," figures some order of horizontal or merely parallel association, a collectivity generated by coming into being with others, by the fact of eating *with* ("eating" generalized to designate any encoding of information), then the modes of association so imagined no longer match up exactly with all those anthropologically charged scenes of eating and speaking together that we have been taught to understand as the archetypal figures of the table.[7] At bottom, the term indicates little more than a positional vector—an eating next to which might be impossible to differentiate from the action of eating another or finding oneself eaten, an eating of and by one's neighbor.[8] Conjugating the word "companion" as noun, adjective, and verb, "'to consort, to keep company,'" Haraway seeks to render the word mobile, transitive, transactional, and thereby to allow it to accommodate a general question concerning hospitality, an ongoing "becoming with" a world that may not be reduced.[9] But the terms hold and promise more than this purely proximal relation. They continue to come primed with a set of humanist desires that offer the hope of more inclusive modes of citizenship, less lethal ways of being. This promise haunts such tables that Haraway frequents in the form of a queasiness to which both individual and collective bodies are prone. How, then, to reckon with words that generalize hospitality beyond the confines of the human or the social even as their ability to refer to an unreduced series of beings remains limited, partial?

When faced with such a problem of description—what do you name the worms that feast now on the man you have killed? What indeed, where indeed, is that man now?—Hamlet, naughtily, winkingly, names them a "convocation," "a certain convocation of politic worms," called into being or configured merely by the occasion of consuming Polonius's flesh. The eucharistic import to these lines and their potential parody of contemporary debates over transubstantiation have been plotted, but their import, for me, lies in the way Hamlet's lines register the presence of still other polities than those that we process as "human," polities that may or may not recognize themselves in such terms.[10] His lines condense also the potential of a spontaneously generated or immanent polity that merely awaits or is brought into being by a change of state and status in its host. The worms simply wait. Polonius dies and so becomes their dinner. Hamlet's act of murder renders him, if you like, a butcher to and for the worms, the vector by which they now eat. Polonius becomes their meat or "mete" (food). But, beyond a rhetorical antianthropocentrism, Hamlet's eucharistic reference gestures toward the successive transformations of flesh (back) into soil that describe an unreduced or general ecology. He extends the fact of cooking to beings other than humans and so convokes worm and worms as cook and kitchen. His logic posits tables other than those at which we eat, tables that are set for and so convoke worms and still other creatures by whose actions we are successively consumed and so transformed.

Of course, Hamlet's dry mass, predicated upon the absence of Polonius's corpse that endures a wet death, serves also as the setup for a put-down of Claudius:

> HAMLET: A man may fish with the worm that hath eat of a king and eat of the fish that fed of that worm.
> KING: What dost thou mean by this?
> HAMLET: Nothing but to show you how a king may go a progress through the guts of a beggar
> CLAUDIUS: Where is Polonius?
> HAMLET: In heaven. Send thither to see. If your messenger find him not there, seek him i'th'other place.   (3.6.26–32)

This associative logic, which replays Protestant refusals to understand the both/and, essence/accidence of transubstantiation, enables Hamlet to posit sitting down to a dinner in which the guests eat the monarch by way of the fish that ate the worm that ate the king. "Where is Polonius?" (3.6.31), replies Claudius, sticking fast to the question. Heaven or the unmoored "other place," replies Hamlet, not naming death, and taunting Claudius to send a messenger there to inquire as to Polonius's new haunt. Claudius gets the point only too well and might even be said to take Hamlet up on the offer, sending him to England, which, as we discover, is to make him his own messenger to death if not necessarily to hell. The eucharistic or sacramental play of these lines speaks to the configuring of relations at table beyond or beneath what we have termed the social. Indeed, by subjecting human-centered or even sovereign modes of relation—see, your majesty, dead kings go on progresses through the "anuses" of worms, fish, and so their subjects—to a nonanthropic cooking, Hamlet makes plain the way, by their repetition, the routines of eating together (and so of configuring our tables) maintain a built world of discourse and matter.[11]

The interchangeability of bodies here, as flesh mingles through its successive transformations, does more than assert some sovereign parasitic logic. By its scandalous inversion, Hamlet's nonanthropic cooking of Polonius signals the way the performative, convoking function of eating together relies on the time-bound consumption of a third thing or being (here, Polonius). And this third thing or being, the he or she or it that is eaten, inhabits a position that oscillates between states, shifting back and forth across assumed divides of species or kind, animate and inanimate, living and dead, organic and machinic. It also implies that there is nothing particularly or even precisely human about figures of "politic convocation," or whatever name we shall give to the social form that results. They represent less an achieved and repeatable because self-identical relation to which we can refer, still less a stable, self-perpetuating entity than a structure that continually calls into being or convokes some *thing*, a gathering of beings that eats *this*. This politic convocation must, in other words, continually be convoked—it exists or endures only by the repetition of certain acts of eating (together). It shall change depending on the guest list and who or what gets eaten. Strictly speaking, the word "companion" (*com-panis*) designates not two but three entities or may be said to configure a relation between two that derives from the sharing and eating of a *this* by which the two come into being by and through a historically particular relation to *this* thing (bread) as well as all the actors (human and not) that make up the infrastructure that underwrites *this* relay. We are convoked by the "thisness" of this bread just as are the worms by the historicity of Polonius's corpse.

Haraway is not explicit regarding the necessary convoking presence of a third thing or entity to her companion species. Such a presence is instead frequently assumed or taken as read. For example, the positive iteration of the companion species she most valorizes, the dog/human relation, comes into being only through a sustained relation to a third thing—not food, but the sport called Agility. Agility actively trains both dog and human to work together and to constitute a collective entity in relation to a third thing, the obstacle course, that they must co-navigate. The sport bears some relation to the order of communication and cooperation that forms between shepherd and sheepdog in relation to a flock of sheep but, in this case, the course or the obstacle takes the place of the recalcitrant sheep.[12] We might say accordingly that the companion species requires an included third, the entity taken and apprehended as food/activity and which therefore is very precisely not convoked but serves as the occasion or ground for the convocation. Companions share in the sustaining function of what is taken as food, in the care and concern showed at table, but also in the guilt/responsibility for what has been eaten. Haraway's figure of the "messmate" hovers in relation to a generalized convoking of what we might call "mass-mates," those entities or ingredients necessary to the convocation of certain entities as subjects, citizens, as those who "eat." The term "messmate" designates and comprehends, therefore, the constitutive power that eating holds as a literal and metaphorical process for making worlds. It conserves and replays a sacramental poetics but does so with the caveat or caution that the entity or thing that convokes or hosts and so is consumed is a messmate also even as it is not so processed or perceived.[13] For not all mass-mates are welcomed as messmates.

While Haraway tends toward a rapturous, positive rendering of the human body as a symphony of differently animated actors, the model itself, the figure of the messmate, remains obstinately and obliquely neutral, nonanthropic, and inhuman. The actors may, on occasion, join in symphonic unity, but the cacophonous warring of overlapping polities or mere ignorance of each other taxes the "love" Haraway says she feels "that when 'I' die, all these benign and dangerous symbionts will take over and use whatever is left of 'my' body."[14] The key, perhaps, and to which, as I shall argue, *The Comedy of Errors* tunes its finale, lies in the final clauses that complete (and undercut) the thought: "if only for a while, since 'we' are necessary to one another in real time." The constitution and dissolution of the first-person plural occurs—may only occur—in real time. It cannot be generalized; it is fragile, bounded. To what does this "we," a defunct human body and its bacteria, refer? It seems to designate nothing more than a discontinuous, multiplied, or merely serial polity. Relations pertain. Yes. But they authorize no statement whatsoever as to matters of sociality. How, then, should we name this "we"? An asociality or nonsociality, perhaps, a putative, terminal future in the mind's eye, that endures even as it does not obey the demarcating boundaries of the table and its companions, and that resides or arrives by the sharing or porting, merely, of some order of relation in "real [though not necessarily 'quality'] time."[15] Here, the historical particularity of the convoking *this* of the Eucharist remains but has been decoupled from a predictable object choice, unmooring the routines that we have for making worlds and persons, rendering the infrastructures so produced mobile and subject to change in successive *nows*. Retain the relation but lose the substance. Renegotiate the boundaries of the table and the list of messmates or mass-mates at every meal. Make new lists of actors at each and every meal. Learn to tolerate the static even as you yourself might get reduced to "noise."[16]

Such a mode of nonintegrative association proves risky and potentially lethal. It might be the matter of an accidental or biological vector. It might be visible only from very particular vantage points. It might be merely another mode of an immanent and so sublated multitude, the potential subject of a nonmystified democracy still to come, or it may endure, flickering in and out of view, according to the working or (un)working of an errant gene or genie with a sense of comedy.[17] Let's venture now into the kitchen and environs of *The Comedy of*

Errors to see what Shakespeare has to teach us about the time-bound convoking of an asocial "we."

On Kitchen Avoidance

The kitchen rarely appears as such in a play by Shakespeare. Literal cauldrons bubble away in the lair of the true heroes of *Macbeth* (1606); Tamora's corpse may be transformed into a figural onstage kitchen-grave-catastrophe-machine as she ingests her sons in *Titus Andronicus* (1590–93) in a perverse reverse pregnancy that rolls back the past; there's all that pie making and some 20 cooks running around in act 4 of *Romeo and Juliet* (1595–97), licking their fingers as they get the Capulets ready for Juliet's second marriage *cum* funeral; but, largely, the plays steer clear of the kitchen, veer away from it, or walk right up to it as a place of metamorphosis or transformation.[18] Of course, kitchens mark the texts as both noun and verb, manifesting in a variety of guises or as a mode of association as in the verbal entertaining of someone in a kitchen, as happens in *The Comedy of Errors* (by play's end, though, an audience has been taught to hear in the verb "to kitchen," as well as in the word "dinner," a flexible (auto)erotic valence that conjoins eating and sex as dual intimacies of the flesh with metamorphic or zoomorphic pleasures and consequences).[19]

Come the end of the play, following the deus ex machina efficacy of Lady Abbess's sorting out of errors and the duke's somewhat surprising suspension of the law (given his earlier mood), Dromio of Syracuse finally meets Dromio of Ephesus. We don't know whether these Dromios recall their earlier encounter, mediated as it was by the door to Antipholus of Ephesus's house, when Dromio of Syracuse played the porter (act 3, scene 1), backed up by the kitchen maid Luce (Nell); but the first words out of his mouth when alone inform his brother of an implied transgression, a moment when the physical identity the two share led to errant substitutions and, in this case, to a near-marriage experience. The trauma, it seems, took place in a kitchen. And even as everyone else in the play happily goes into the "gossip's [godparents'] feast," having apparently recovered from the "Circe's cup" from which the duke thinks they have all drunk (*Err.*, 5.1.271),

Dromio still needs to abreact the episode with his newly found identical twin brother:

> DROMIO S.: There is a fat friend at your master's house
> That kitchened me for you today at dinner.
> She now shall be my sister, not my wife.
> DROMIO E.: Methinks you are my glass, and not my brother.
> I see by you I am a sweet-faced youth.
> Will you walk in to see their gossiping?
> DROMIO S.: Not I, sir. You are my elder.
> DROMIO E.: That's a question. How shall we try it?
> DROMIO S.: We'll draw cuts for the senior. Till then, lead thou first.
> DROMIO E.: Nay then thus:
> We came into the world like brother and brother,
> And now let's go hand in hand, not one before the
> other.   (5.1.414–425)

Apparently, so he told his master, Antipholus of Syracuse, back in act 3, scene 2, sometime around dinner this "fat friend," Nell, the "kitchen wench," became overfamiliar with him. She "laid claim" to him, he says, calling him by his own true name, and "swear[ing he] was assured to her" (3.2.125–26). Not recalling ever having met the woman, let alone their betrothal, Dromio is understandably a bit put off by the fact that Nell seems to have an intimate knowledge of his body. Nell is able to tell him "what privy marks [he] had about [him]," including "the mark of [his] shoulder, the mole in [his] neck, the great wart on [his] left arm" (3.2.126–28). At which point, "amazed" by her words, and suspecting, so he says, that she is a witch, he makes a run for it, interrupting thereby her inventory of his body and her graduation, so we might expect, to yet more intimate personal details or demands.

What actually occurred in the kitchen is hard to discern. Luce (Nell) appears only briefly in act 3, scene 1, brought to the door by her master's furious knocking. What she looks like remains equally uncertain, since Dromio's famously misogynistic after-the-fact description of her as a "very beastly creature" (3.2.82), "all grease" (3.2.89), making her of the kitchen, plays as comical overcompensation for the intimate physical knowledge that she apparently has had of him. Finding himself unnerved by Nell's knowledge of his body, Dromio prefaces his disclosures with a mock poetic blazoning and chorographical description of Nell's body that reverses her claims. All we have to go on, then, is the manner of Dromio's entrance like a man driven—"Why, how now, Dromio. Where run'st thou so fast?" (3.2.71). "I am an ass, I am a woman's man, and besides myself" (3.2.72), he confesses, going on to elaborate that "besides myself I am due to a woman, one that claims me, one that haunts me, one that will have me" (3.2.76–77). The nature of this claim is explicated in reference to his master, for it is "such a claim as you [Antipholus] would lay to your horse" (3.2.80). Dromio finds it all very confusing, and he can't keep things straight, for we learn that "she would have me as a beast—not that, I being a beast, she would have me, but that she, being a very beastly creature, lays claim to me" (3.2.81–82). However, his syntax cannot help but arrive at still other possibilities. Indeed, Dromio's syntactical slippage testifies, perhaps, to a desire he is not prepared to take cognizance of other than in the form of a mobile series of zoomorphic transformations. His position oscillates, and he names himself "besides [him] self," becomes "beast" and then "horse."

Back in the more predictable, homosocial hierarchy of master and servant, Dromio tells Antipholus that he has avoided, so he hopes, a "wondrous fat marriage" (3.2.87). And egging himself on further to higher and higher orders of metaphor, Dromio proclaims that to find a sufficient "measure" for Nell's hips (3.2.101), he shall "find countries in her" (3.2.104). In actuality, he derives whole continents from Nell, moving in short order from Ireland, Scotland, France, and England to America and the Indies. Having experienced his own spot of marital trauma in act 2 when Adrianna, wife to his own identical twin brother, Antipholus of Ephesus, claims that he's her husband and has a go at him for not coming home for dinner, Antipholus proves a very sympathetic listener and sends Dromio to the "mart" to see if any ships are sailing (3.2.168). The two are done, so they think, with Ephesus; done with such Medea-like or siren "witches"—all of Ephesus become some kind of cauldron or kitchen that whips up uncanny effects. It comes as no small relief to both men, then, when they discover that Nell and Adrianna are, in fact, betrothed or married to their identical twin brothers, Dromio and Antipholus of Ephesus. The revelation of this species of likeness explains the hyperspecificity of the errors that each has endured. So, phew! As near-marriage or near-kitchen experiences go, that was close. And such pleasures that remain derive from talking or narrating aloud the putative actions, uses, and labors to which one might have been put.

What's key, I think, about the near-kitchen experiences that haunt Dromio, as he redacts them for his master, is the way the kitchen is presented in the play as a zone of uncertainly human transformation and metamorphosis. Kitchening ceases to be a form of relationality that pertains to self-identical or stable individuals so much as a co-constitutive process in which all are transformed or cooked. The kitchen becomes knowable as a zone of zoo/biopolitical processing—a place of uncertainly pleasurable or painful acts that line up terms across different registers. Nell will use Dromio as his master would use a horse. Cooking or kitchening accordingly goes mobile, a metaphoric extension to other modes of association or encounter. The general ecology Hamlet posits when his worms "kitchen" Polonius exists in the play but encrypted or boxed up in Dromio's attempts to name what might have but did *not* happen.

Beyond staging a comic taming of what Dromio assumes will be a tragic expenditure of his resources (however ironically that plays), the play offers something more durable. As the stage clears in act 5, and the players exit to the offstage feast, we pause with the two Dromios as they reckon with their dual existence. Dromio of Ephesus confesses *somewhat* elliptically to his "kitchening" by "a fat friend" in the place of his brother. Perhaps something did "happen" in the kitchen after all, but if so, the embarrassment will be regularized by the syntax that renders Nell "my sister, and not my wife." Dromio has become all passive once again, waiting on his brother's response, a brother whose sexual property has sought to "kitchen him," to render him her prop as well as property. All this occurs in stark contrast to the hyperactive blazoner of act 3, scene 2 in which Dromio's words reassert a masculine primacy he appeared to lose in the kitchen, where the castrating Nell, he fears, or fears he might like, might have "transformed [him] into a curtal dog," a dog with a docked tail, that is, "and made him turn i'the wheel" (3.2.129–30), reducing him to the motive force that turns the spit for roasting meat. Such it is, he claims, to be claimed as another's horse or like a horse—though the force and the motive might have and may prove different or differently pleasurable.

But Dromio of Ephesus finds that there is nothing to explain. He looks at his brother and sees his own reflection, taking his face for a "glass" or mirror, registering thereby the serial sameness from which the play's very many errors derive: "Methinks you are my glass, and not my brother. / I see by you I am a sweet-faced youth" (5.1.417–18). Fraternal seriality finds itself suspended or folded into a narcissistic identity that proves very inviting or hospitable—"Will you walk in to see their gossiping?" (5.1.419). The first-person plural, this invitation to join in a becoming "we," comes into being in and by a singular "I," finding itself beside itself, to reprise the conjunction Dromio stumbles over as he encrypts his desire to be "kitchened." The narcissism so imagined figures as an extension or self-recognition in and by the other that functions constitutively—an articulation predicated here on a double and a doubling. The two banter a little over which of them was born first. For the elder should, properly, enter first. But they decide, in the end, to suspend such concerns or to decide them at some future date by drawing straws ("cuts"). Leave it to chance to decide the priority. The play ends with the two walking into the feast "hand in hand, not one before the other," "as they came into the world like brother and brother" (5.1.426, 425), an image of nonhierarchical and still anonymous fraternity, a sameness or universality underwritten by the physical interchangeability of these two genetic messmates. But, can the two even be said to have "met," exactly? There is self-recognition, a recognition of the self in the other, but very precisely not recognition of the other per se. Such a radical sameness finds itself circumscribed (of course) by a reconfirmed social hierarchy that the godparents' feast marks.[20] But it supposes a mode of hospitability premised on the particularized sameness of a pair, a species of species that suspends even as it confirms the sovereign importance of the question of belonging, and the drawing down of a boundary.

In having the two Dromios enter a feast we shall not attend and at which the two shall gaze upon, the play offers us the fragile image of a question of priority (which brother comes first and so should enter first), suspending itself into a series that, for the moment, in real time, decides not to know of an organizing syntax or agrees to leave it to chance, to the "cuts" that shall decide such matters and draw down such boundaries.[21] That the play ends here, by this entrance into a feast we shall not attend and which the two shall "see" but perhaps not quite join, marks the moment also at which the stage decouples from the kitchen in a fracture or cut that folds a beginning into an ending: "We came into the world like brother and brother" (*Err.*, 5.1.418); accordingly, for now, let's suspend the issue of priority. Let's posit the indefinite origin or beginning not as a foundation, exactly, or a suspension, but as a "real time," to recall Haraway's phrasing (i.e., temporally bounded), polity of the first-person plural, a polity that endures only by and in a chiastic crossing or splicing of media (kitchen and stage), of pronouns ("we" presences by and in my agreement to say it and to take it as a collective reference), and audiences ("we," the theater audience or "you and I," the readers, look on or encounter a "we" whose coming into being for itself marks its imminent invisibility to us). "*Exeunt*": the audience, the play, this "we," along with the "you" or "I" we were when watching or reading, are gone. Our reality, their reality, this "we," exists only by virtue of this entrance to a place we do not see and may not visit. Its "pastness" is premised on its diegetic and medial futurity—yet to come.

If *The Comedy of Errors* ends by and in a refusal to phenomenalize this feast and this collectivity on stage and so, instead, may be said to archive its possibility, such a withholding figures as more than a failure or refusal. It speaks, perhaps, to the status of plays themselves as, at once, projective and post hoc remainders, and to play-texts therefore as some order of recipe or receipt for generating certain kinds of affects and effects. No need to put the kitchen on stage, then, as the theater is already an analogous space of transformations and tryouts, a space of rehearsal and practice. Figuratively, this withholding speaks also to the difficulty of archiving hospitality, of preserving what seems like an achieved goal, to the bugbear of practice (or the failure of relation between theory and praxis). And so the play insists on the nonimmanent or botched immanence of hospitality as an infinite obligation. These errors worked this time, but they offer no recipe for reactivating the same feelings or results next time. It all could have worked out so very differently. Comedy there shall be, the play seems to suggest, but it defies us to see in that outcome anything more durable than a series of errors, even as those errors might be of a piece, the repetition of patterns that derive from the play's parade of twins and doubles, of conversations that repeat or host differing orders of sense available to differently placed listeners. No eating, then, on stage. No food value even as there may be value had from the way the experience of playgoing invites us to entertain nonintegrative communities premised on a sharing in the event of the performance itself.

Dromio looks at Dromio and decides that he sees himself. He finds himself convoked, takes his likeness as a messmate. But such a modality, the play offers, exists only in real time and may not therefore translate into terms and moves we can routinize as a program that does more than inquire into what might function as a constitutive "thisness" *this* time. The two enter and exit in one movement. Their future remains entirely their own affair. Theater only takes us that far. You have to go into the kitchen yourself.

Taste Test (A Studio Kitchen)

This deferred feast might be said to arrive in *The Tempest*. The kitchen merges with the island stage. But Prospero's island is not exactly a happy place—riven by labor disputes and supply problems as Prospero, Miranda, Ariel, and Caliban cohabit but do not acknowledge one another as messmates. The same goes for the ship that wrecks as the play begins, revealing itself to be wrecked beforehand, a compromised figure of government. If the production leaves Prospero offstage in act 1, scene 1, then we will learn the news that the shipwreck was a magically arranged nonevent or other event only after the fact when Miranda asks whether "by your art, my dearest father, you have / Put the wild waters in this roar," and begs him, if it be so, to "allay them."[22] Disinterested spectator that she is, stranded on the shore watching the wreck, Miranda derives no equanimity or neutrality from the experience.[23] She remains keyed to the sights and sounds of the event, emoting as the experience passes through her like some sensory screen, even as she is unsure of the need to feel what she feels, whether or not it is real or reversible. She has "suffered," she says, "with those that [she] saw suffer" (*Tmp.*, 1.2.5–6). And when the "brave vessel" is "dashed all to pieces . . . O, the cry did knock / Against [her] very heart" (1.2.6–9). But Prospero has things to do, memories to install, or memories whose lack he needs to install by reminding Miranda of all she has not known, does not remember. "Be collected," he tells her, "No more amazement. Tell your piteous heart / There's no harm done" (1.2.13–15). Intervene with your senses.

Like Miranda, then, we may not quite be sure of how to react to the first two scenes. Like her, we may want a parent, say, to tell us what and how to feel. Such it is to be the compeer to the food/knowledge-giver in this parent/child "companion species." We must be very attentive—no wandering off, as Miranda does later in act 1, scene 2, even though she maintains that she doesn't. She nods off as Prospero puts her to sleep so that he can talk with Ariel. Ariel disappoints also—doesn't remember Sycorax or the oak, and a lot more besides that goes unsaid even as Prospero demands he or she say it all over again out loud. Or maybe Ariel does remember but did not attend closely enough to remember not to ask Prospero whether he remembers "the worthy service" Ariel has done (*Tmp.*, 1.2.247–63), and the promises made once Ariel has done his bidding.

Eating under such circumstances proves difficult—though the cooking takes no time at all, for it was "all prepared earlier" in the off-stage, extradiegetic, magical time of Prospero's test or studio kitchen. No "real time" cooking for Ariel and Prospero. Things come to a head in act 3, scene 3, though, as a table sets itself. A banquet unfolds, offers itself like some automatic meal to its guests. You shall find yourselves convoked, so it seems. As if by magic (which of course it is), ship-wrecked Alonso and courtiers, grieving for the loss of Ferdinand, are treated to this picnic: "*Solemn and strange music, and Prospero on the top (invisible). Enter several strange shapes bringing in a banquet, and dance about it with gentle actions and salutations; and inviting the King, etc., to eat, they depart*" (3.3.15–20). The music is just lovely. And as Julia Reinhard Lupton's afterword in this volume invites us to consider, the banquet tunes the play into the biotechnical arrangement of foods and environment that goes by the name "dessert," a temporality of attunement that effects the convoking function of the table and the meal that I have explored in this essay. But it is crucial to note that in *The Tempest* this banquet is deferred; it completes itself or packs itself away such that what we watch and listen to instead are the actors on stage narrating their confusion, their affective swings as they seem to be granted sustenance, gifted a meal. Sebastian, Gonzalo, and Antonio offer a running commentary on the "event." They debate the nature of these "shapes" that enter—"a living drollery," a parade of fantastic or mythical creatures (3.3.21–24); "islanders...of monstrous shape," "but gentle-kind" (3.3.28–32); whatever they may be, an "excellent dumb discourse" (3.3.38). "They vanish…strangely," notes Francisco. "No matter," replies Sebastian, "They have left their viands behind; for we have stomachs. / Wil't please you taste of what is here" (3.3.41–42)? But Alonso won't—"Not I"—but then he will, but only because he "feel[s] the best is past" (3.3.50–51) and that this "feed" will be his last: "I will stand to and feed." Alonso and his courtiers recognize that they are stomachs, that they need to eat so that they may live on. And so Alonso "stand[s] to," but he will not try or test or "taste" the "viands" to see if they are edible, to see if they are food for human persons. He merely will eat. He will take the "viands" as if they were food, no matter how they taste, no matter what the taste test tells them. This will be no banquet, no feast, nothing will be convoked—just men "feeding," akin to beasts.[24]

Alonso and his courtiers "stand to"—they come forward and begin the task of "feeding." He asks the others to "stand to and do as we" (*Tmp.*, 3.3.52), enfolding them within his royal person by the use of the first-person plural that is a sovereign prerogative. They shall feed. The instant they do, however, Ariel reenters as harpy and the banquet disappears by a "*quaint trick.*" In place of food stands the accusing Ariel, and when Ariel is done the shapes return to remove the banquet table "with mocks and mows." Ariel shuts mouths and opens ears, reminding them of a story of usurpation, of abandonment at sea. Alonso and his courtiers have broken with their prince, and that broken contract manifests here as the interruption of a meal, the removal of food as a threat to survival, to living on, to continuing to live—even if the banquet were greeted with what amounts to a metaphysical shrug from the grieving Alonso. Theater trumps the kitchen, offering up its own routines, its spectacles, as an art that enfolds the kitchen and its modes of culinary *poiesis*. The whole island is Prospero's kitchen, even if no one has thus far suggested exactly that his fabled book or books were cookbooks. Nevertheless, his kitchening of Alonso and courtiers carries with it the power to remove hunger, induce sleep, to make them have passion, weep, and pray.

It takes a lot to be Prospero's "messmate." No wonder Caliban just wants to be left to eat alone: get your own wood; "I must eat my dinner" (*Tmp.*, 1.2.331). The once-upon-a-shipwreck companion who

found them and then co-evolved with Prospero and Miranda, learning their language as they learned his island, prefers the undirected,
dogged Stoicism of dining alone to eating with others. Backing off from
Prospero's table with its import-export licenses and collateral dam-
ages, Caliban goes emphatically local, entering into a convoking relationship with the island itself at a level that excludes Prospero's more
elaborate routines. Such a closed, singular circuit in which you grow,
cook, and eat your own food must seem very attractive under such
circumstances, circumstances in which you find yourself reminded
(daily?) of the drawing down of a biopolitical boundary become an
accusation of rape (1.2.345–49).[25] Caliban may end the play gaining
some kind of "acknowledgment," but within the play he roundly
rejects his status as one of Prospero's messmates. They tried him out
at table, so it seems, and found him wanting, so now he eats alone. It's
only Caliban who cooks, then, even if he takes his food in a manner
that Prospero might consider "raw" or marked by the moral philo-
sophically empty calories of Trinculo and Stephano's "butt" of sack as
the three collectively "kiss the book" (2.2.128–30).[26] The three of them
convoke their alternate, stunted polity by their marching exit to the
tune of "Ban' ban' Ca-Caliban" (2.2.179)—an exit that reads like some
pseudoidolatrous parody of the presentation of the Bible to Elizabeth I
at her coronation, a Bible that she kissed, writing thereby her own sovereign claims into the text of biblical authority in quasi-sacramental
fashion and/or as the carrying of "the monstrance at Corpus Christi."[27]

By its end, *The Tempest* may be about forgiveness, about getting
home, going back, and managing to do so in a way that forgets or integrates the residues of the past, but for its duration we remain on an
island, within the contours of Prospero's will. The play's tuning of hospitality remains entirely oriented to the future—to Prospero's putative surrender of a risk managed and managing of persons and feasts.
Caliban may be left to it and enabled thereby to embark on some yet
to be imagined majority on the island, convoking still other communities to come, but for now he and we remain caught within what seems
like a botched set of companion species relations that have devolved
to enslavement or stewardship—neither quite mess nor mass mates.[28]

Still there is hunger. Still there is cooking, even if what Caliban eats
defies the norms of the "raw" and the "cooked" as far as Prospero is

concerned. The island offers a world or a time of estranged physiology and sensory confusion that Miranda, tuned as she is, describes as "wonder," an uncertainty as to the limits and boundaries between things. *The Tempest* stages the "kitchen" as an entirely abstract process, a set of routines that constitutes the differences between humans and other animals, between sovereign and subjects, as they are lived, felt, and eaten. The lines it draws between theater and kitchen constitute no lines at all, disclosing the way the metaphysics of both disassociate the time of making and rehearsal from the moment of performance and presentation. Utopian visions of social revolution, tanked up by Stephano and Trinculo's "butt of sack" (*Tmp.*, 2.2.128–30) along with Gonzalo's nostalgic plantation of the isle (2.1.145–56), register the pull that dreams of other modes of social organization, of other "cuisines" and "kitchens," have upon us. But the play seems to say that they are impossible or impassable convocations—even as it recalls them still. Likewise, the play leaves open the possibility that Caliban's "dinner" might one day represent another kitchen or cuisine—leaving open a purchase on culture to beings rejected as messmates, and not yet or not at all regarded as human. A general ecology of the kitchen remains thinkable by *The Tempest* even as we recognize that Prospero alone decides its limits.

As Haraway might here opine, on her way to an Agility class with Cheyenne, the dog for whom she serves as "person," the table that shall accommodate all such creatures as might be said to "cook" remains an elusive design. The point of a general ecology is that it subsumes the human, empties out a specificity to our hold on the social, demotes us from a seat at the table to serving as food on that table for others. And as I have tried to show in this essay, such an awareness of an unreduced cuisine or ecology marks Shakespeare's plays in several ways, sporting figures of association such as Hamlet's "politic convocation," the Dromios' time-bound "we," and Caliban's closed-circuit cuisine in which he convokes his sovereignty by entering into a solo relation to the island. These figures may not endure beyond the plays that generate them. They do not offer a mimetic politics or practice that delivers on all that Haraway desires, but they signal the way the activity of making, of cooking and playing, the kitchen and the theater, in which cook and player serve as hosts for processes that convoke, opens a window onto the relays and routines we have for making worlds, for constituting ourselves and others.

Who or what decides the limits of *your* kitchen? Do you even know its boundaries? *Who* and *what* are you cooking, have you cooked? Who or what cooks you?

Chapter 10

Room for Dessert:
Sugared Shakespeare and the
Dramaturgy of Dwelling

JULIA REINHARD LUPTON

A 2012 exhibit at the Minneapolis Institute of Art, "Supper with Shakespeare," features the Renaissance "banqueting" or dessert course, famous for its edible fantasias. In the comestible tableau recreated by artisanal food historian Ivan Day, a gleaming tower of sugar based on Elizabethan garden follies oversees knot gardens crafted out of marchpane (marzipan). Such fabulous sugar works, combining the talents of a sculptor and goldsmith with those of a cook, form the spectacular core of a tradition linking dessert to architecture that stretches from the exploding pies of the Middle Ages to Renaissance sugar works to the bridezilla wedding cakes, reality show bake-offs, and designer cupcake wars of the twenty-first century. Rather different is the overtly political sculpture of Kara Walker, who displayed a huge sugar sphinx at the Domino Sugar Factory in Williamsburg, Brooklyn, under the Renaissance title "A Subtlety"; whereas Ivan Day celebrates an ancient craft, Walker's work calls attention to the historical link between sugar cultivation, slavery, and the survival of racist archetypes in contemporary food and art regimes.[1]

The great nineteenth century chef Marie-Antoine Carême famously called confectionary the "main branch of architecture" in order to give an intellectual rationale for his elaborate pastry and sugar fabrications based on ancient building types. I am interested in the deep connection between architecture and dessert. What engages me, however, are not castles of sugar but, rather, the way that dessert constitutes a final act in the sequence of the meal, opening a space where renewed forms of social, gustatory, and environmental encounters can take place. Although I am interested in the politics of sugar, my focus is not on sugar's racial and imperial history but, rather, on the role of dessert in crafting spaces of disclosure, encounter, and digestive reflection. Dessert in its modern sense as a final course of sweet foods, often though not necessarily shared with company for a festive occasion, is defined by an act of clearing that precedes and affords the acts of sumptuary display that are sometimes exercised in its name; it is this dynamic between clearing and appearing, moreover, that affiliates dessert with theater.

In his extraordinary study *Arranging the Meal*, the great food historian Jean-Louis Flandrin argues that dessert emerged as a sweet course separate from the rest of the meal in the period stretching from the sixteenth to the eighteenth century. "Dessert," he notes, comes from *desservi*, the act of clearing the table; dessert in its first uses refers

> not to a collection of dishes...but to the course that came after the table was cleared (*desservi*) for the first time since the start of the meal. Up to that point, dishes from the preceding course were simply removed (*relevé*), that is, replaced one at a time by the dishes of the next course, the table never being left bare. For this last stage, all dishes were cleared from the previous course. It was long the practice even to take away the top tablecloth as well, the dessert dishes then being set on the second tablecloth beneath.[2]

The analogy with drama is immediate and compelling. Whereas scenes are lightly marked by the fluid exit and entrance of actors on the stage, often without an implied change of location, acts imply a more fundamental resetting of setting, mood, time, or even worlds. If the main courses in the classical meal constitute a series of scenes that flow imperceptibly into one another, dessert is dinner's final act and its epilogue, a demarcated episode that both reasserts and reflects on the meal's dramatic character as an unfolding sequence of offerings that allows certain forms of appearing to take place. These forms of disclosure include the appearing of *food* in its capacity to delight as well as to nourish; the appearing of *guests* in the risky performance of personhood; the appearing of *labor* in its capacity to confect, present, support, and inhabit worlds; the appearing of *things* as haptic bearers of multiple affordances; and the appearing of *ambience* as an intangible feature of setting that includes sound, aroma, and the effects of reflected light. Through its always-incipient pastoralism, which casts architecture as landscape architecture, dessert also brings into visibility the networked relationship of these diverse actors to one another that is implicit in every scene of commensality.

The interplay of these forms of appearing in the drama of the meal gather and mingle under the conceptual canopy formed by "dwelling," those routines of living associated especially with our creaturely needs for shelter, sustenance, and sociability and organized around architectural concerns with setting, place, and locale.[3] The dessert course, from the time it came into existence in the Renaissance and early modern period, contributes to the arts of dwelling by curating moments of digestive reflection that link space, time, labor, leisure, and seasonality in potent bundles of fruit, sugar, nuts, dairy, pastry, and spice; bursts of flavor, color, and texture that stimulate conversation, manifest connectedness, and anchor memory. Dessert as *desservi* provides the occasion for an environmental and phenomenological engagement with food as part of a larger scene composed of biotechnical confabulations and affordances; it is precisely dessert's invitations to affiliation and acknowledgment, moreover, that have been largely occluded in our era of industrial sweets. What I am calling "room for dessert"—the act of clearing that precedes and solicits appearing—reveals the intimate affiliation of the confectionary arts with the spatial and environmental as well as affective and spectacular work of theater. In a range of Shakespearean dramas, from the urban settings of *The Taming of the Shrew* and *Romeo and Juliet* to the romance landscapes of *The Tempest* and *The Winter's Tale*, Shakespeare periodically identifies this room for dessert with the space of the stage, borrowing the forms of curation, attention, display, and manifestation cultivated by dessert for the purposes of dramatic action and subjective and worldly acknowledgment.

COOKING, DWELLING, THINKING:
RENAISSANCE DESSERT SCENOGRAPHY

In the European cookbook tradition, architecture emerges in relation to cooking and eating as both setting for and metaphor of the meal. One of the very first cookbooks to appear in print was Platina's *On Right Pleasure and Good Health;* written by the first librarian for the new Vatican Library, this book reflects Platina's interests, which stem from his vast knowledge of classical texts rather than from hands-on experience in the kitchen. Early in the book, drawing on a classical topos, he presents the proper siting and building of one's estate as a condition of eating well: "A civilized and intelligent man should choose, in the city as well as in the country, the place most advantageous for the time of year, pleasant, delightful, charming where he may build, where he may devote his efforts to farming, where he may relax with his artistic interests, where he may, in sum, commune with the gods themselves."[4] This humanist ideal, explored by Douglas Lanier in his contribution to this volume, defines the man who dwells well as a creature who lives in harmony with the elements, especially air and earth; as a landowner who enjoys some proximity to the labors of husbandry; and as a scholar-poet whose environmental attunements imply an immanent theology: "he may, in sum, commune with the gods themselves."

Platina's account of dwelling as both a world-building and a world-attentive act anticipates Heidegger's location of *Wohnen* (dwelling) in the fourfold relationship formed by earth, sky, mortals, and gods:

> "On the earth" already means "under the sky." Both of these *also* mean "remaining before the divinities" and include a "belonging to men's being with one another." By a *primal* oneness the four—earth and sky, divinities and mortals—belong together in one.... This simple oneness of the four we call *the fourfold.* Mortals *are* in the fourfold by *dwelling.* But the basic character of dwelling is to spare, to preserve. Mortals dwell in the way they preserve the fourfold in its essential being, its presencing. Accordingly, the preserving that dwells is fourfold.... In saving the earth, in receiving the sky, in awaiting the divinities, in initiating mortals, dwelling occurs as the fourfold preservation of the fourfold. To spare and preserve means: to take under our care, to look after the fourfold in its presencing.... Dwelling itself is always a staying with things.

Dwelling, as preserving, keeps the fourfold in that with which mortals stay: in things.[5]

The very figure of the fourfold suggests the outline of a rudimentary house, one crafted not out of straw, wood, or brick but out of those habits and routines that nest architecture in a cat's cradle of social and environmental metabolisms. Platina anticipates Heidegger's sense that architecture can and should draw together horizontal and vertical dimensions of being within supple and resonating structures composed in response to and as an expression of landscape (earth), climate (air), sociability (mortals), and a receptiveness to higher or prior forms of order and accountability (the gods). Both Platina and Heidegger, moreover, consider building (*Bauen*, the hardscape composed by architecture proper) in dynamic relationship with dwelling (*Wohnen*, the softscape woven by the repertoires of living). Architecture responsively conceived and sited supports and solicits thoughtful habitation by incorporating the qualities of place, the interdependence of persons, and the routines of living into the way that settlements and dwellings are organized.

Thus, Platina's brief humanist sketch on building well (*Bauen*) frames a much longer tract on eating well (which belongs to *Wohnen*). Although Platina has much to say about sweet dishes of various kinds, which appeared throughout the medieval and Renaissance meal, he has only one paragraph on the "third," or fruit, course:

> If it happens that you have eaten meat, either roasted or boiled according to the time of year, eat either apples or sour pears. Some, among whom is Nicander, in an amazing way approve the radish, derived from *radices* [roots], because, taken after food, it helps digestion, reduces phlegm by penetrating to the depths of the stomach, holds down the vapors from rising to the head, and purges the kidney and bladder....A bit of very hard cheese is thought to seal the stomach and stop vapors from seeking the head and brain. Also it easily takes away squeamishness arising from too fat or sweet a meal. The more refined tables eat anise and coriander rolled in sugar as a remedy for mouth and head; the common people, fennel; all, chestnuts, whose force is cold and dry.... Taken with sugar or honey, they are thought to reduce phlegm. In addition, the eating of quince, pomegranate, especially the sour, and of all things that are astringent, like pulse and pistachios, is not frowned upon. Either almonds or hazelnuts or

other nuts ought to be eaten after fish because they are thought to repress the cold and damp force of fish with their dryness.[6]

Platina's third course includes fruits, nuts, and cheese as well as candied seeds and spices. The service was not exclusively sweet (just try serving radishes for dessert!).[7] Focusing on the digestive properties of foods, Platina presents this course as part of a sequence, with some types of fruit more appropriately following certain types of meat. Digestion is understood primarily as a physiological property, but the separation of these foods into a third and final course demarcates a space-time for digestion in its more reflective and ruminative senses. Finally, Platina's vision of the third course at once differentiates the social classes and is modest and inclusive in its dietary aims: the wealthy eat candied spices, "the common people" take their anise in the form of fennel, and everyone eats chestnuts. Although Platina writes from a position of educated privilege, the foodscape implied by his third course encompasses a comprehensive social and biotechnical scene composed of a range of foods and eaters.

Sugar cultivation began in India, where sweet dishes were bound up with creation myths, votive offerings, and festival observances.[8] Arab cuisine both borrowed sugar from India and added key ingredients to the Indian repertoire, a marriage that in turn had an immense impact on medieval European cookery; Platina's "anise and coriander rolled in sugar" manifests the Hindu-Arab-European exchange of flavors and ingredients, like the candied anise served in Indian restaurants today. (Wherever sugar, rice, saffron, almonds, jellies, rosewater, and ices as well as artichokes, spinach, and eggplants appear on European tables, the Indo-Muslim influence is in evidence.)[9] Sugar, however, does not dominate Platina's table, which is given over, rather, to a mix of fresh and preserved fruits and nuts. Candying and conserving allows perishable foods to be eaten later in the year; rather than being *un*-seasonal, however, such densely flavored essences seem to capture and transfer seasonality as such, along with the human art and effort required to transmit it. The jellies and marmalades of the Renaissance pantry are culinary memory banks that store and display both flavor and labor in their luminous liquefactions.[10] Heidegger converges with housekeeping in Platina's third course, which participates in acts of "keeping" and "preserving" that acknowledge rather than deny the fact of our habitation between air and earth.

Whereas Platina's *On Right Pleasure and Good Health* is a humanist tract written by a scholar-librarian, Bartolomeo Scappi's *L'arte et prudenza d'un maestro cuoco* (The art and craft of a master cook) (1570) formalizes the experience of a master chef who ran the kitchens for three cardinals and two popes. He begins his massive study of food and food practices by comparing his craft to that of the architect:

> It is necessary, therefore, insofar as my many years of experience have taught me, that a skilled and competent Master Cook, wishing to have a good beginning, a better middle, and a best ending, and always to derive honour from his work, should do as a wise Architect, who, following his careful design, lays out a firm foundation and on it presents to the world useful and marvelous buildings. The design of the Master Cook must be the fine and dependable method produced by experience, of which he should have acquired such knowledge that he could serve rather in the Office of the Steward than the Steward should serve as Cook. And he should strive to satisfy unusual, diverse tastes with delicate dishes. Not least, the dishes should be tasty and agreeable to the palate as well as pleasant and delightful to the eye with their pretty colours and appetizing appearance. The first foundation upon which he will set his main base must be his understanding of and experience with various kinds of foodstuffs.[11]

Scappi's comparison of cooking with architecture parallels the bids for professional acknowledgment made by many artisans striving to enhance their crafts with the prestige of design. Architecture is more than an analogy for Scappi, however: his book is distinguished by its detailed engravings of kitchen spaces and kitchen implements, images that document the architectural conditions of cooking, including cooking in the field for a household constantly on the diplomatic move. Design enters Scappi's text both as an intellectual discourse furthering a planner's attitude toward the overall structure of the meal and as the comportment of an artisan-technician responding more immediately to the environments or taskscapes of work and labor.[12] Contemporary designers and environmental psychologists would speak here of affordances, the array of actions that objects and settings communicate to those who use them, whether through shape, color, size, or more explicit semiotic signals such as words. Buttons, handles, and levers combine physical shape with learned associations, manifesting affordances as intermediaries between object and subject and between physical and sociocultural attributes.[13] Affordances inhere in the implements and locations of dwelling, presenting tactile cues to action that are themselves the product of social and environmental interactions and adjustments.

Like Platina, Scappi is attentive to the mise-en-scène of the meal, understood spatially and environmentally:

> You should be aware of the seasons of the year, for you have seen quite well how felicitously Reverend Don Francisco has had [the table] set in springtime in cheerful locations that are sheltered from the breeze, in summer in airy, shaded places where there is lots of bubbling water, in the fall in a temperate location with an eastern exposure rather than northern, and in winter in rooms decorated with a variety of tapestries, sculptures, and paintings to please guests; and always has the table of a length proportionate to its width, so that the attendants can set out and remove courses easily and those who are serving food or drink can move around freely and without inconvenience to their lords.[14]

Scappi treats meals as mobile events that accommodate and acknowledge seasonal shifts in order to enhance the comfort, pleasures, and meanings of mealtime. The affordances of the setting include temperature and ambience ("airy, shaded place," "bubbling water"). Scappi also pays attention to the affordances of furniture: a properly proportioned table facilitates the effortless movement of domestic labor, a service choreography conceived for the benefit of the assembled aristocrats but calculated from the perspective of a *maestro cuoco* aware of the workings of a large household staff. Design functions in Scappi's text as both a template for professionalization (the master chef as architect of dinner) and as a more embedded and implicit ecology of tacit knowledge and local uses (the cook as responsive stage manager of objects and settings). The title of Scappi's book *L'arte et prudenza d'un maestro cuoco* captures these two senses, with *arte* evoking the formal discourses of *disegno*, and *prudenza* naming the more vernacular competencies of dwelling.

Writing 100 years after Platina, Scappi gives more detail than his forbearer regarding the rhythms of the emerging dessert course. The Italian service alternated between *cucina* and *credenza*, between the warm meals overseen by the cook and the cold dishes supervised by the pantler or steward. The steward or *scalco*, as Scappi makes clear with some irritation in his opening remarks on architecture, super-vised the cook and the whole household staff. Because the preserved fruits and candied spices of the *credenza* course belonged to the pan-try and not the kitchen, dessert recipes were largely neglected in the great Renaissance cookbooks of France and Italy, which focused on the products of the *cucina*. In the Italian service, a *credenza* course always ended the meal, although there were cold courses throughout; the *cre-denza* that began the meal was called the *antipasto*, and the *credenza* at the end was the *postpasto*. A *collazione* was a meal consisting exclusively of *credenza* dishes, both sweet and savory, and could be enjoyed in different parts of the house or estate; sometimes the *col-lazione* included a dramatic performance or entertainment.[15] Scappi records a "collation at the end of August in a vineyard after Vespers" and another *collazione* "arranged at the end of May on a Friday in Trastavere in a garden." At the latter party, the table was adorned with "diverse flowers and foliage" and *la credenza*—referring to the side-board that held the dishes as well as to the food arrayed upon it—was furnished with silver, gold, glass, and majolica vessels, along with a suite of sugar statues depicting Diana with nymphs. In Scappi's text, the *postpasto* is marked by standing up from the table, washing hands with water and white napkins, and then enjoying a final service of "sweet fresh fennel," candied fruits, seeds, and spices (perhaps in a separate room).[16] The action of *desservi* resonates in these gestures of rising, cleansing, and removing as well as in the pastoral character of the *credenza* course as a portable offering that could be eaten in a range of settings. *Postpasto* is Renaissance Italian for dessert.

Scappi's papal spreads far outspend Platina's frugal humanist dietary, but both texts radiate a sense of pastoral and dramaturgical responsiveness to time and locale. In Platina and Scappi's environmen-tally attuned works, dessert erects its own fourfold; as such, dessert is indeed a branch of architecture, understood not mimetically (desserts look like buildings) but existentially (dessert participates in the work of dwelling by bidding the conditions of habitation to appear). Both Platina's third course and Scappi's *postpasto, credenza,* and *collazione* stage occasions that permit participants in the feast to reengage with setting: the table, the room, and the company but also the season, the region, and the cosmos, through digestive-reflective processes that manifest the wonder and scandal of their linkages.

Neither Platina nor Scappi's architectural musings specifically concern dessert, which was still emerging as a separate course in the Renaissance; indeed it is the tempo of that emergence that concerns me here. The French word *dessert* was used infrequently in England (and never by Shakespeare) until the later seventeenth century. Instead, the word "banquet" or "bankett" often referred to a festive course of cold or sweet dishes eaten in a separate location, after the clearing of the main hall, equivalent to the Italian *collazione*. Under Elizabeth, the banqueting course was often eaten in a "withdrawing room" (the root of "drawing room"), or in separate structures that were architecturally distinct from the main house.[17] Sometimes banqueting houses—dessert rooms—were built on the roof, like the "little domed banqueting turrets" at Longleat, each housing six guests at most.[18] Banqueting houses could also be garden pavilions located a short walk from the great house, perhaps connected by a gallery. The temporary character and pastoral decor of Renaissance banqueting houses associated dessert with acts of retreat with the power to test social and environmental relationships in a place apart.

Prior to the Restoration, English cookbooks were far more workmanlike than the splendid productions of Platina and Scappi. Figure 1 shows the frontispiece of what we might identify as an English dessert cookbook from 1653.[19] The book promises to teach the art of candying and preserving and the creation of "Sugar-works," the kinds of fanciful sculptures that Scappi served up on his *credenza*. The author also offers recipes for baked goods (pies, biscuits, cakes, tarts, fritters), the wetter desserts still favored by the English (puddings, syrups, leaches,[20] broths, snow), and banqueting confections like marzipan. Throughout the book, food and medicinal recipes lie side by side; a few items are designated as "banqueting stuff," such as marigolds preserved "in Spanish Candy."[21] Hugh Platt's 1602 *Delights for Ladies, to Adorn Their Persons, Tables, Closets and Distillatories* is also a proto-dessert cookbook, thanks to its emphasis on the conservation of fruits and flowers and its concomitant focus on the arts of the pantry rather than the kitchen (in Scappi's terms, the *credenza* rather than the *cucina*). Addressing a range of concoctions and activities that are both more and less than dessert in the modern sense, these compilations reveal the multiple scenes of life—from the culinary to the medicinal to the cosmetic—to which fruited foods contributed their various properties.

Robert May's *The Accomplish't Cook*, published in the wake of the civil war and its disruptions to traditional elite hospitality, famously begins with a loving description of a piece of extravagant food theater that culminates in a banqueting course. Under the heading "Triumphs and Trophies in Cookery, to be used at Festival Times, as Twelfth Day, &c.," this representative anecdote, not a recipe but rather a memorial reconstruction, includes a ship made out of pasteboard loaded with gunpowder, pies pulsing with live frogs and birds, a pastry stag that bleeds claret when an arrow is removed from his side, and eggshells filled with rosewater for the ladies to throw at one another ("to sweeten the stinck of the [gun]powder"). As the spectacle comes to a conclusion, "candles are lighted, and a Banquet brought in, the musick sounds, and every one with much delight and content rehearses their actions in the former passages. These were formerly the delights of the Nobility, before good House-keeping had left *England*, and the Sword really acted that which was only counterfeited in such honest and laudable Exercises as these."[22] The banquet enters here as a separate service that crowns and reflects upon the food folly that has preceded it; dedicated to "rehearsing" the actions of the triumph, the banqueting course comes with its own ambience, provided by candles and music that diffuse, extend, and deepen the mood of levity released by the pastry pyrotechnics.

May's dessert tableau is a nostalgic homage to the Caroline court; the goal of his book, however, is not to recreate that world but, rather, to translate royalist skills and values into postwar cooking projects for smaller householders living "some distance from Towns or Villages."[23] Given its aspirational character, May's recipes are more elaborate and decorative than those that appear in many English cookbooks, including patterns for cut crusts that release steam and reveal the fruited fillings beneath. Although May's pastry templates take us further than other cookbooks of the period into the design of dessert, he does not reveal the architectural secrets lauded in the prefatory poem by James Parry, who praises May as one "Who can in Paste erect, of finest

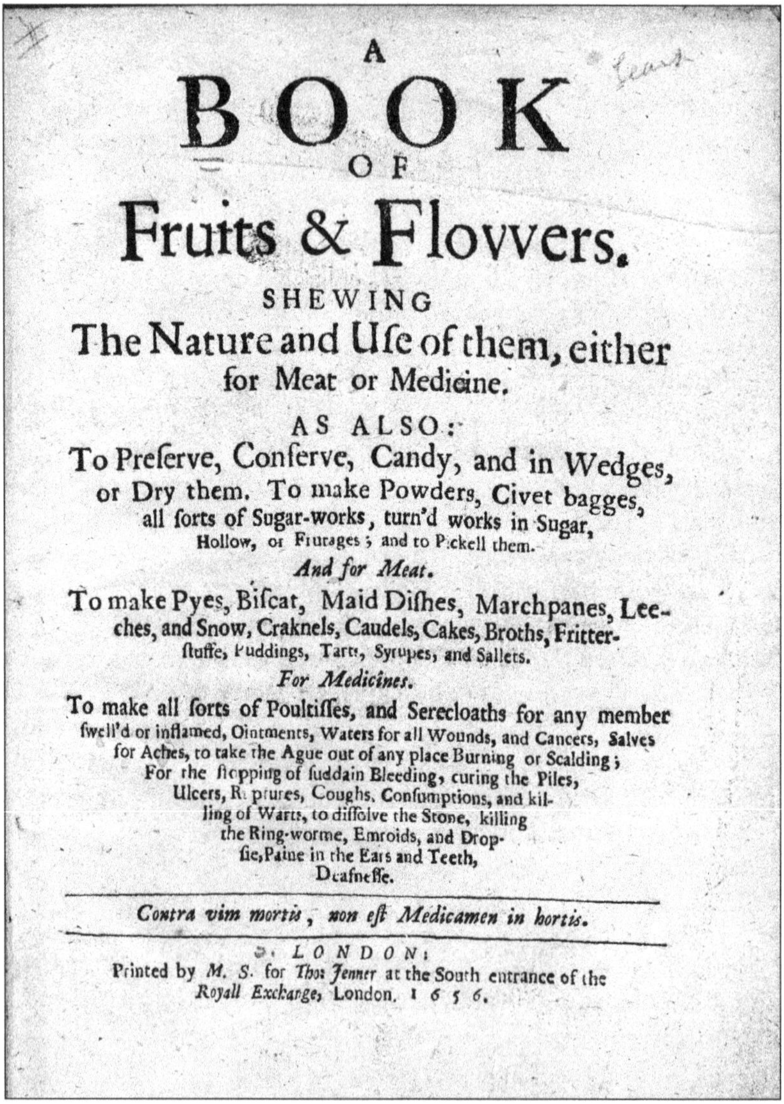

A
BOOK
OF
Fruits & Flovvers.

SHEWING

The Nature and Use of them, either
for Meat or Medicine.

AS ALSO:

To Preferve, Conferve, Candy, and in Wedges,
or Dry them. To make Powders, Civet bagges,
all forts of Sugar-works, turn'd works in Sugar,
Hollow, or Frutages ; and to Pickell them.

And for Meat.

To make Pyes, Bifcat, Maid Difhes, Marchpanes, Lee-
ches, and Snow, Craknels, Caudels, Cakes, Broths, Fritter-
ftuffe, Puddings, Tarts, Syrupes, and Sallets.

For Medicines.

To make all forts of Poultiffes, and Serecloaths for any member
fwell'd or inflamed, Ointments, Waters for all Wounds, and Cancers, Salves
for Aches, to take the Ague out of any place Burning or Scalding ;
For the ftopping of fuddain Bleeding, curing the Piles,
Ulcers, Ruptures, Coughs, Confumptions, and killing of Warts, to diffolve the Stone, killing
the Ring-worme, Emroids, and Drop-
fie, Paine in the Ears and Teeth,
Deafneffe.

Contra vim mortis, non eft Medicamen in hortis.

LONDON:
Printed by *M. S.* for *Thos Jenner* at the South entrance of the
Royall Exchange, London, 1 6 5 6.

Fig. 1. Frontispiece of an English dessert cookbook, 1653. Reproduced
courtesy of the Botany Library, Harvard University Library.

flour, / A compleat Fort, a Castle, or a Tower." May's bills of fare, moreover, do not include any specific prescription for a third course or dessert service; his menus are restricted to two courses (which do include some sweet items), perhaps because his book, following the French and Italian cookbook tradition, concerns the kitchen and not the pantry.[24]

Also writing after the English civil war, Hannah Woolley gives us more sense of dessert in modest circumstances, including service and spatial routines. Both widowhood and poor health seem to have led Woolley into writing as a livelihood, and she markets her book as a means of assisting women who have been displaced by the war. Toward the end of *The Queen-Like Closet*—the title and frontispiece themselves an architectural rendition of culinary knowledge—Woolley instructs her readers in the art of serving sweets to guests: "Serve three or four small dishes also with Sweet-meats, such are most in season, with Vine Leaves and Flowers between the Dishes and the Plates, two wet Sweet-meats, and two dry, two of one colour, and two of another, or all of several colours. Also a Dish of Jellies of several colours in one Dish, if such be required."[25] Woolley brightens her table with loose leaves and flowers from the garden, and the sweet offerings themselves compose a still life arranged with a painterly attention to color, texture, and contrast. In her seasonal menus, Woolley does not use the word "dessert," but as illustrated in figure 2, she presents the traditional third course in a manner similar to Platina and in a rhythm clearly linked to the action of *desservi*.

Woolley's dessert service is typographically and choreographically distinct from the main menu, a separation marked by the act of clearing: "After these are *taken away*, then *serve in* your Cheese and Fruit."[26] Platina's modesty as to the kinds of foods served converges here with Woolley's English sense of thrift.[27] At the end of the *Closet*, however, Woolley gives her imagination over to a sugar-work fantasia, a garden of candied fruits and marzipan animals arranged in a basket as a portable landscape suitable for presentation as a gift. This nested scene, with its scenic sensibility and gift character, is Woolley's more modest counteroffer to May's "Triumphs and Trophies."

All of these authors, in different ways and to varying degrees, treat dessert as a kind of culinary landscape architecture. The clearing

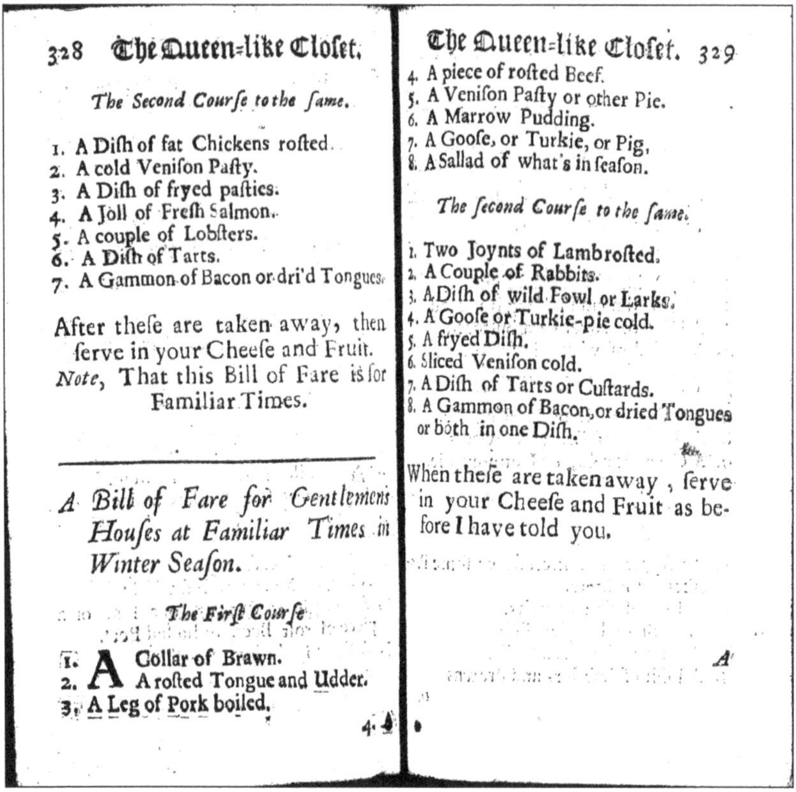

328 The Queen-like Cloſet.

The Second Courſe to the ſame.

1. A Diſh of fat Chickens roſted.
2. A cold Veniſon Paſty.
3. A Diſh of fryed paſties.
4. A Joll of Freſh Salmon.
5. A couple of Lobſters.
6. A Diſh of Tarts.
7. A Gammon of Bacon or dri'd Tongues.

After theſe are taken away, then ſerve in your Cheeſe and Fruit.
Note, That this Bill of Fare is for Familiar Times.

A Bill of Fare for Gentlemens Houſes at Familiar Times in Winter Seaſon.

The First Courſe

1. A Collar of Brawn.
2. A roſted Tongue and Udder.
3. A Leg of Pork boiled.

4. A

The Queen-like Cloſet. 329

4. A piece of roſted Beef.
5. A Veniſon Paſty or other Pie.
6. A Marrow Pudding.
7. A Gooſe, or Turkie, or Pig,
8. A Sallad of what's in ſeaſon.

The ſecond Courſe to the ſame.

1. Two Joynts of Lamb roſted.
2. A Couple of Rabbits.
3. A Diſh of wild Fowl or Larks.
4. A Gooſe or Turkie-pie cold.
5. A fryed Diſh.
6. Sliced Veniſon cold.
7. A Diſh of Tarts or Cuſtards.
8. A Gammon of Bacon, or dried Tongues or both in one Diſh.

When theſe are taken away, ſerve in your Cheeſe and Fruit as before I have told you.

A

Fig. 2. Hannah Woolley, *The Queen-Like Closet*. Courtesy of the Huntington Library.

marked by the simple presentation of fruits and cheeses harbors within its horticultural parameters the promise of more spectacular forms of appearing: confections that transport the pastoral theme into a key that showcases the cook's artifice and ingenuity. Its ingredients gathered from the orchard, the dairy, and the pantry, dessert is kissing cousin to the picnic, each dedicated to indoor-outdoor continua defined by portable foods arranged on moving fields of fabric. From Platina to Woolley, the Renaissance dessert course manifests a commensal flow between clearing and appearing, between the minimalist pastoral of simple foods presented in conjunction with the earth that bore them and the virtuoso pastoral of the higher confectionary arts. At once nature preserve and theme park, dessert as a form of dwelling insistently folds human inventiveness into the genius loci that hosts it.[28]

To clear the table completely is to reset the evening, to allow for a new beginning. (There is still time to land a flirtation or retract an insult.) Dessert is the "beginning of the end," but it is a beginning nonetheless; as such, dessert participates in what Giorgio Agamben calls the messianic "time that remains."[29] Sweet foods are associated in many traditions with divine favor and a taste of heaven; the gradual exclusion of meat and the increasing celebration of fruit associate the landscape of the dessert table with the garden of Eden. If Woolley's elaborate dessert basket is a representation of paradise, her modest sharing of foliage and jellies is Edenic in its own way. The most minimalist dessert is also the most messianic: the *afikomen* (derived from the Greek word for dessert), the piece of matzoh that is split in half at the beginning of the Passover seder and then reconstituted at its end as an image of redemption. Even the melding of Christian, Muslim, Hindu, and Greco-Roman traditions in the heady spices and soft comfort zones of dessert seems messianic, an unexpected ingathering of peoples, flavors, and culinary languages around a common table set up outdoors.

DESSERT AS *DESSERVI*:
SHAKESPEAREAN RENDITIONS FROM CITY TO COURT

Throughout his plays, Shakespeare taps the sumptuary rhythms, service routines, fantastic yearnings, and locational sensibility of dessert. I focus here on two early dramas, *The Taming of the Shrew* and *Romeo and Juliet*, in which dessert belongs to urban performance ecologies, and then I turn to *The Tempest* and *The Winter's Tale*, which engage the courtly spectacle of dessert transmitted by Robert May. These plays reflect different theatrical orientations—the two earlier dramas geared more to the open air architecture of the public theater and the latter plays more cognizant of the indoor private spaces of Blackfriars and Whitehall. In all these plays, however, the event of dessert collates and sets forth the environmental interdependencies of work, labor, and action in the scene of hospitable eating.

At the end of *The Taming of the Shrew*, Lucentio hosts an after-supper party that brings the bridal celebrations to a close:

> Feast with the best, and welcome to my house.
> My banquet is to close our stomachs up
> After our great good cheer. Pray you, sit down,
> For now we sit to chat as well as eat.[30]

While "our great good cheer" refers to the major meal hosted by the brides' father, Baptista, the "banquet" course, composed of portable pantry foods, could be hosted in Lucentio's more modest lodgings. Tranio performs the office of the steward or *scalco*, the household stage manager who assures that the banqueting stuff arrives at its destination. In *Taming of the Shrew*, dessert takes place in, and connects the spaces among, an urban setting that includes the kind of wealthy bourgeois establishment that we attribute to Baptista, "a rich gentleman of Padua," and the temporary students' quarters occupied by young Lucentio, come from Pisa to study the humanities. The stage directions indicate some onstage showing of food, or at least of the serving dishes, while the directions also demonstrate that workers are required to bring the offerings onstage: "*the servingmen with Tranio bringing in a banquet.*"[31] The entry presents objects and persons in conjunction with one another, not only indicating the choreography of labor that supports dessert but also linking that choreography to the work of the theater: the servingmen within the diegesis of the play world are stagehands in the theater, so that both dinner and drama manifest themselves as collaborative enterprises engaging multiple forms of labor within a physical space defined by the possibility of exit and entrance.

The postprandial procession of the guests to another location taps the scene-changing invitation of dessert as *desservi*. The banquet's dietary function, "to close our stomachs up," could come right out of Platina, who avers that "the third course should be briefly described as a seal to the stomach, as if in conclusion."[32] In his first speech in the play, Lucentio had already declared his humanist commitments to what Tranio calls "suck[ing] the sweets of sweet philosophy" (*Shr.*, 1.1.28); here culinary humanism returns the "sweet" metaphor to the table from which it stems. The conclusion to the wedding feast is also the conclusion to the play as a whole: the room cleared by and for dessert constitutes the space of appearing in which the new brides variously perform or refuse to perform their virtues for their husbands and for the audience gathered to witness this marital symposium. Dessert is also a space of conversation, in the humanist tradition of the symposium (often translated as "banquet"): "For now we sit to chat as well as eat."[33] Petruchio immediately establishes himself as hostile to the kinds of discourse associated with dessert and with humanist conviviality more generally, as described by Douglas Lanier in chapter 7 of this volume; a man of action, Petruchio answers Lucentio's welcome with churlish impatience: "Nothing but sit and sit, and eat and eat!" (*Shr.*, 5.2.12). If Petruchio, as bad a guest as he is a host, ensures that the proceedings are primarily coercive, the theatrical and imaginative lining that cushions and illuminates the room for dessert occasions the chance for wit, irony, and play. Can we imagine Kate's tart performance as a culinary-theatrical triumph or trophy (as Robert May would have it) that allows her to reserve a convivial space for herself in the marriage to come?[34] In this volume, Lanier writes that conversation was "the most conspicuous sign of a temporary suspension of social differences and the creation of commensality." The small wooden trenchers or *rondels* on which dessert foods were served often featured on their decorated bottom side little poesies satirizing married life; the poems would be read out loud after the banqueting stuff had been enjoyed in a "roundelay" of postprandial entertainment afforded by the trenchers themselves.[35] Although Kate's rhetorical sprezzatura appears to conform to Petruchio's normative guidelines for wifely behavior, her speech *as speech* reaffirms the humanist ideals that he discounts and boldly places her as a participant within its symposial zone. The meal for Sly may also be a dessert course, since it is served in the bedroom, consists of "sack" and "conserves," and includes an entertainment; if so, the whole play unfolds under the sign of banqueting stuff.

In *Romeo and Juliet,* also set in urban Italy, dessert occurs early in the play, setting the stage for first encounters rather than final reflections. The bustle of servants at the vibrant edge of act 1, scene 5, dramatizes the act of clearing as an orchestration of laboring persons, mobile objects, and pleasant confections in preparation for the forms of appearing to come:

> FIRST SER.: Where's Potpan that he helps not to take away? He shift a trencher! He scrape a trencher!
> SECOND SER.: When good manners shall lie all in one or two men's hands, and they unwashed too, 'tis a foul thing.
> FIRST SER.: Away with the joint-stools, remove the court-cupboard, look to the plate. Good thou, save me a piece of marchpane, and as thou loves me, let the porter let in Susan Grindstone and Nell—Anthony and Potpan![36]

The men are engaged in the act of *desservi,* of clearing the hall of its furniture and its dinnerware in order to make room for the approaching festivities. The court cupboard affords the same serve-and-display functions as the Italian *credenza.* They refer in passing to one of the most beloved creations on the banqueting table, the marchpane or marzipan that was often formed into imaginative shapes and colored or gilded for festive effect.[37] The servingmen are saving the leftovers for their own after-hours party in the messianic "time that remains," a dessert-after-the-dessert in which the workers plan for their own pleasure and rest. The rooms cleared for dessert emerge here as part of an open floor plan dedicated to and served by different streams of labor and leisure. This evening the guests will include not only those formally invited, but also the cruising party crashers Romeo, Mercutio, and Benvolio, and, for the after-party, Susan Grindstone and Nell, servingwomen from down the street.[38] This brief scene places dessert in a networked urban *oikos* that houses both production and consumption for its proprietors, their servants, and a mixed company of invited and uninvited visitors. If *The Taming of the Shrew* emphasizes the flow among urban palaces and rented quarters tracked by the ritual progress of the bridal party, *Romeo and Juliet* dramatizes the back entrances that connect different households and classes in the collaborative production of dessert. Although the servingmen belong to Platina's "fennel" class and the Capulets to the "candied anise" club, the servants' ingenious and thrifty collection of leftovers creates a social continuum of dessert enjoyment.

Romeo and his band never get to sample the marchpane. As they depart, Capulet tells them, "Nay, gentlemen, prepare not to be gone: / We have a trifling foolish banquet towards" (*Rom.*, 1.4.234–35). The Oxford Shakespeare editor Jill Levenson comments, "Capulet disparages the dessert course just coming—sweetmeats, fruit, wine—as silly and without value, probably to enhance the effect of its sumptuous arrival."[39] In his staging of dessert as a form of theatrical work, Shakespeare has placed the emphasis on the *clearing* that precedes and enables *appearing*, substituting the sumptuary display of banqueting stuff with the mutual discovery of Romeo and Juliet. In 1598, Francis Meres famously referred to Shakespeare's "sugared sonnets." Supplemented by other ambient and symbolic effects of hospitality, such as Romeo's torch-bearing office, the sweet space of the sonnet (soft and sonic, mobile and mellifluous) takes shape in the opening for encounter and acknowledgment first cleared by the servingmen as they make room for dancing and dessert.[40]

Later, the Nurse plays the role of pantler when she is told to "take these keys and fetch more spices," since "they call for dates and quinces in the pastry" (*Rom.*, 4.4.1–2). She stewards a "broken banquet" (in the larger sense of the interrupted feast developed by Lanier in this volume), since "our wedding cheer" will be changed to "a sad burial feast" (4.5.87). Reversing the order of leftovers in *Hamlet*, the cotquean Capulet's "baked meats" (4.4.5) (glossed as "pastries, pies" by Arden editor René Weis) will coldly furnish forth the funeral table.[41] Now the thrift of the servingmen as they commandeer their dessert of leftovers takes on the aspect of a carnival inversion conducted in the tragic mode.[42] The play's final banqueting scene occurs in the mausoleum: "A grave—O, no, a lantern, slaughtered youth, / For here lies Juliet, and her beauty makes / This vault a feasting presence full of light" (5.4.84–86). Romeo declares that Juliet's beauty transforms the dark and earthbound grave into a "lantern" that rezones the vault for feasting. A lantern was the cupola within domes that allowed light into the space below; many banqueting houses in the sixteenth century were situated within the lanterns of small domed turrets, chosen

for their elevation above the landscape, their openness to the elements, and their convivial intimacy.[43] The image construes the built
environment as a kind of phenomenological machine, a frame for the
production and disclosure of aesthetic effects achieved through cho-
reographed acts of dwelling that include the routines of hospitality
and conviviality. Romeo's "lantern" and "feasting presence" share
haptic and architectural commitments with the dessert course.

In *The Tempest*, spectacle and *desservi* coincide: the shipwrecked
Italians, famished and disoriented, are treated to a spectacular aural
and visual display:

> Gonzalo: Marvelous sweet music!
> *Enter several strange shapes bringing in a banquet, and dance about
> it with gentle actions of salutation; and inviting the King, etc., to
> eat, they depart.*[44]

Whereas *The Taming of the Shrew* and *Romeo and Juliet* momentarily acknowledge and celebrate the dramaturgical labor involved in
making dessert, *The Tempest* renders the work of cooking and service
more automatic and fantastic through the conceit of spirits as agents
of technical wonders. In all three plays those who steward dessert are
also simultaneously stagehands engaged in dramaturgical work and
labor. The earlier plays, however, embedded in the institution and
architecture of the London public theater, emphasize the traffic patterns of the urban *oikos*, whereas the latter play, flirting with the technology and aesthetics of the court masque, effaces the laboring aspects
shared by culinary and theatrical work in the very moment of drawing those processes into visibility on the stage's space of ostension
and acknowledgment. As Lanier notes, the masque, often performed
in banqueting houses, was "an extension of royal culinary entertainment," and he reads the scene in *The Tempest* as a demonstration of
the violation of humanist convivial ideals in courtly culture.

Ariel's banquet itself, of course, appears only to disappear: "*Thunder
and lightening. Enter Ariel, like a harpy, claps his wings upon the
table, and with a quaint device the banquet vanishes*" (*Tmp.*, 3.3.51,
s.d.). The precipitous removal of the banquet before anyone can
partake of it collapses the *desservi* that defines the entrance of dessert with the removal of dishes that signals its exodus. The action

also suggests that the foods appearing before us (likely glued in place for security of transport) are pure illusion, confected of wax, wood, or glass rather than sugar, paste, and fruit—designed only for display, like Scappi's tableau of Diana and nymphs or May's triumphs and trophies. The "sweetness" of the music noted by Gonzalo ("Marvelous sweet music!") names a pure transfer, a haptic affect and aura that floats among gustatory, auditory, erotic, and visual receptors in order to distill and release an aesthetic penumbra.[45]

If the accent is on artifice (courtly, culinary, and theatrical), the scene as a whole nonetheless devolves into one of Shakespeare's most conspicuous environmental settings, an island marked by its exposure to competing forms of cultivation and habitation as well as differing comportments of apprehension and appreciation. Naming the existential function of clearing, Ariel declares the island "most desolate" (*Tmp.*, 3.3.80), equating the empty table with the austere place in which the Italians find themselves. Then, completing the *desservi*, Ariel himself "vanishes" and the table is borne away by dancing "shapes": "*He vanishes in thunder. Then, to soft music, enter the shapes again, and dance with mocks and mows, and carrying out the table [they depart].*" (3.3.82, s.d.). The island of "desserts" (of confection and spectacle, abundance and automation) is reduced and remanifested as a "desert island" (a region of creaturely exposure and forced labor, including the affective labor extracted from Ariel himself).[46] *The Tempest*'s banquet course flows between gestures of clearing and appearing in order to reveal the essence of dessert as a biotechnical engagement with the spatial disposition and environmental conditions of commensality as well as the forms of deprivation, exclusion and employment that commensality usually requires.

In act 4, scene 3 of *The Winter's Tale*, the young shepherd enters with a shopping list from his stepsister Perdita larded with sweet foods:

> Let me see, what am I to buy for our sheep-shearing feast? *(He takes out a paper)* Three pounds of sugar, five pound of currants, rice—what will that sister of mine do with rice? But my father hath made her mistress of the feast, and she lays it on....I must have saffron to colour the warden pies; mace; dates none, that's out of my note; nutmegs, seven; a race or two of ginger, but that I may beg; four pound of prunes, and as many raisins o'th'sun.[47]

The young man knows that Perdita will make warden pie (a pastry of pears), but he is not sure about the rice: "What will that sister of mine do with rice?" The inclusion of the more costly rice (the young shepherd is confused by its appearance) may signal the wealth of Perdita's adoptive family and their willingness to share their surplus and reward the labor of their workers in the sheep-shearing celebration. Joan Fitzpatrick observes that the feast appears to be vegetarian and that many of the items on the shopping list, including rice, are imported luxury items.[48]

Given the ingredients on her list, a pudding seems to be in order: the sugar, raisins, and spices on the shepherd's list show up frequently in Renaissance recipes for whitpot, a dried fruit and dairy pudding featured in country diets in the western parts of England. Perdita's appellation as the "queen of curds and cream" (*WT*, 4.4.161) identifies her as the "Whitpot queen" of those Whitsun pastorals that she uses to mark her reticent retreat from her own festive exuberance: "Methinks I play as I have seen them do / In Whitsun pastorals—sure this robe of mine / Does change my disposition" (4.4.133–35, p. 177n). Blended together in a soft junket of associations, the young shepherd's shopping list and Perdita's Whitsun reference release a fragrant cloud of ingredients, practices, and controversies, including the dairy menus and holiday actions of Pentecostal celebration; the binding of Jewish, Christian, and agrarian calendars around the postpaschal feast; and the debate within Christendom about the propriety of Whitsuntide.[49] Perdita's pudding, with its Levantine rice, ginger, mace, ginger, nutmeg, and saffron and its eager indulgence in curds and cream, melds Jewish, Christian, Muslim, Hindu, and Hellenistic traditions in a homely dish to be shared by laborers, small landowners, disguised royalty, and an itinerant urbanite.

The statue scene at the end of *The Winter's Tale* evokes the banqueting houses of higher Renaissance dessert practice. Announcing the existence of Hermione's statue "in the keeping of Paulina," the Third Gentleman confides that the royal party "with all greediness of affection" has gone to Paulina's lodgings, where "they intend to sup" (5.2.100–01), "sup" implying a lighter meal or *collazione*. Paulina keeps the statue in a "removed house," an outbuilding whose function as a chapel-gallery affiliates it with the Renaissance banqueting house. *The Winter's Tale* was performed at the Banqueting House at

Whitehall in 1611, a setting that would on that occasion have associated the play as a whole with the specialized space-time of dessert and its environments of entertainment. If the statue scene is marked by a sense of courtly spectacle, Shakespeare's emphasis on the rhythm of withdrawal keeps in play the existential function of clearing that gives dessert its dramatic character. Thus, Leontes speaks of a journey through spaces of removal:

> Your gallery
> Have we passed through, not without much content
> In many singularities; but we saw not
> That which my daughter came to look upon,
> The statue of her mother. (*WT*, 5.3.10–14)

The wandering syntax of his plea enacts the effortful action of *desservi* as retreat to a space apart in search of a final occasion for refreshment and recognition as well as purgation and digestion.

When Leontes finally sees Hermione, his language shimmers with the haptic offerings of dessert: "this affliction hath a taste / As sweet as any cordial comfort" (*WT*, 5.3.76–77). Cordials—distilled beverages often combining fruits, spices, sugar, or honey with bitter herbs like wormwood and rue—were a key liquid component of the dessert course thanks to their restorative as well as aromatic qualities.[50] The revelatory flow of grace in this scene is "cordial" in the intoxicating, convivial, affective, and gustatory resonances of the word, even to the point of retaining a rueful edge of bitterness in the hesitations and remembrances of the play's final recognitions.[51] He exclaims upon touching Hermione, "Oh, she's warm! / If this be magic, let it be an art / As lawful as eating" (5.3.109–11). Leontes's enigmatic phrase distills the several properties of the dessert course, including its ritual dimensions, its healing promise, and its aesthetic effects. Dessert is "an art / As lawful as eating," combining technicity, decorum, and display with an openness to the seasons and the potentialities and constraints of creaturely life.

The play's final "cordial comfort" is the blessing that Hermione pours out for Perdita. Her prayer speaks twice of preservation:

> Tell me, mine own,
> Where has thou been *preserved*...
> ...For thou shalt hear that I,

>Knowing by Paulina that the oracle
>Gave hope thou wast in being, have *preserved*
>Myself to see the issue.   (*WT*, 5.3.123–28)

Gillian Woods links preservation in this passage to techniques of embalming.[52] A little differently, I smell the whiff of a connection with the kitchen arts of preserving, a word featured in the titles of many recipe collections of the period.[53] The attitude inculcated by blessing acknowledges vulnerability in order to encourage resilience, the virtue of preservation, insofar as it reminds us of the contingent nature of human flourishing. What Hermione asks the gods to "pour out"—for Perdita but also for us—is an aqua vitae distilled from the first fruits of a childbirth lost, the sweetness of the present restoration tempered with the rosemary and rue of grace and remembrance (*WT*, 4.4.74–76). Hermione's blessing allows us to digest the folly of the play (its fantastic improbabilities) with the virtues of a custom—the affordances of blessing—without making us swallow more than is palatable (a forced forgiveness). Hermione's blessing is sweet, but not too sweet. The statue scene recapitulates the magic of the banquet in a powerfully human way—what looks like a "triumph and trophy" instead descends into a scene of achingly beautiful intimacy.

In *Romeo and Juliet, The Taming of the Shrew, The Tempest,* and *The Winter's Tale,* Shakespeare reveals *clearing as the truth of dessert,* insofar as the dessert course takes shape through a defining gesture of withdrawal, separation, and semiautonomous development within its own sector of household work and culinary knowledge. If the rooms made by and for dessert appear elitist and exclusive in their cultivation of courtly attitude and luxury ingredients, the environmental decor, seasonal attunement, and increasingly lacto-fruititarian menu of dinner's final act suggest forms of encounter, attention, and enjoyment premised on acknowledging the conditions and commonalities of creaturely life within a pacific-pastoral ambience.[54] A dessert worthy of the name renders its ground newly visible and tangible. Dessert emerges against the *earthen ground* that brings forth fruit, nuts, and cereals but also against the *white ground* of the second tablecloth revealed beneath the first. The ground also includes the social institutions and workflows that produce dessert as a form of domestic theater and collective enjoyment. In all four plays, though under theatrical regimens that range from open-air urbanism to courtly entertainment, those who manage the spaces of mealtime pass across the stage, their labors momentarily manifested and accounted for in the room created by the act of *desservi*.

"Room for dessert" designates the dynamic between clearing and appearing that shapes the moment between dishes and valediction as a *kairos* that affords enjoyment, reflection, and revelation. Dessert contributes to the work of dwelling by bringing voiding or clearing into relationship with presentation, fullness, and satiety as well as with image, semblance, and play. To eat cake is to refuse to live by bread alone. In Heideggerian fashion, dessert brings earth and sky into relationship with human conviviality and the community of the gods, whether through the open architecture of the great Elizabethan banqueting houses, or through the simple but deliberate scattering of leaves and blossoms on the frugal housewife's table. In an age in which sugar threatens to saturate every meal in a neo-medieval influx of massively deterritorialized sweetness, I proffer this "room for dessert" as an ethical commons or ongoing design resource for thinking about our collective relationships to cooking and eating and to the spaces and places dedicated to sustenance and commensality. Certainly there is an aesthetic dimension, an interest in "appearing" that can be tracked in the do-it-yourself food styling boom on Pinterest and other sites. But the room for dessert also presents an internal logic of bounding, waiting, and separating, built out of expectation and acknowledgment rather than fear and loathing that might be invited back into the commensal rhythms destroyed by our eat-while-you-drive culture. Dessert's original ties to seasonality, in the form of both fresh and preserved fruits, obviously resonate with elements of the slow food, locavore, urban farming, and community-supported agriculture movements. It is worth pointing out that post-Fordist platforms of affective labor, digital communication, and virtuoso performance play a role not only in destroying the room for dessert through the saturation of food products with sugar and corn syrup but also in creating alternate destinies for dessert, whether in the form of food porn cooked up by Photoshop and brought to you by Instagram; the websites that connect consumers with local farms; the new food writing published in venues like *Lucky Peach, Sated,* and *Gather;* or the thousands of online sites that promote food preparation, food politics, and food writing.

"Room for dessert" might also offer a model for the humanities. It is something of a cliché to speak of the arts and humanities as "icing on the cake," as lovely but superfluous add-ons in a period of limited resources.[55] Rather than simply defending humanities as meat and potatoes, however, which would mean emphasizing the instrumental benefits of our fields at the expense of the reflective and aesthetic capacities that we have historically cultivated, we might also link the proverbial "icing on the cake" to the social, digestive, and renewing function of dessert considered in its full rhythmic and spatial unfolding. The humanities permit a clearing—the establishment of spaces for free discussion and for the bringing into visibility of overlooked or unconsidered phenomena from everyday experience, from past periods of history, and from unfamiliar cultures and comportments. These clearings allow for rumination and reflection; they can also gather us for future action and make us attentive to the environments in which action occurs. In other words, the humanities can help us learn how to "make room for dessert": how to rezone spaces, reorganize scripts and services, and reoccupy forgotten forms of life so that our settings for work and for dwelling afford more opportunities for acknowledgment, for creativity, and for action.

Notes

Notes to Introduction

1. William Shakespeare, *The Tempest*, in *The Complete Pelican Shakespeare*, ed. Stephen Orgel and A. R. Braunmuller (New York: Penguin Classics, 2002), 3.3.19. Citations of Shakespeare's plays are from this edition and are hereafter cited in the text by act, scene, and line number.

2. Plato, "Phaedo," in *The Collected Dialogues of Plato*, ed. Edith Hamilton and Huntington Cairns, trans. Hugh Tredennick (Princeton, N.J.: Princeton University Press, 1961), 47, 64d. For useful summaries of the denigration of food in Western philosophy, see Deane W. Curtin and Lisa M. Heldke, *Cooking, Eating, Thinking: Transformative Philosophies of Food* (Bloomington: Indiana University Press, 1992), 5, 209–11; Carolyn Korsmeyer, *Making Sense of Taste: Food and Philosophy* (Ithaca, N.Y.: Cornell University Press, 1999), 11–37; Michiel Korthals, "The Birth of Philosophy and Contempt for Food," *Gastronomica* 8, no. 3 (Summer 2008): 62; Steven Shapin, "The Philosopher and the Chicken: On the Dietetics of Disembodied Knowledge," in *Science Incarnate: Historical Embodiments of Natural Knowledge*, ed. Christopher Lawrence and Steven Shapin (Chicago: University of Chicago Press, 1998), 21–50; Elizabeth Telfer, *Food for Thought: Philosophy and Food* (London: Routledge, 1996), 24–37.

3. Michel de Montaigne, "On the Vanity of Words," book 1, essay 51; our translation. Donald M. Frame renders the phrase as "the science of guzzling," while Rebhorn settles on "the art of the gullet." Florio, Montaigne's first English translator, covers all the bases: "the science of skill of epicurisme and gluttonie." This is not to say that Montaigne himself did not value cuisine but, rather, that he was quick to make fun of those who valued it in the wrong ways, or to the exclusion of the life of the mind. Michel de Montaigne, *The Complete Essays of Montaigne*, trans. Donald M. Frame (Stanford, Calif.: Stanford University Press, 1958), 222; Wayne Rebhorn, *Renaissance Debates on Rhetoric* (Ithaca, N.Y.: Cornell University Press, 2000), 220; Michel de Montaigne, *The Essayes of Montaigne*, trans. John Florio (London, 1603), 166.

4. We take this formulation from Jordan Rosenblum, *Food and Identity in Early Rabbinic Judaism* (Cambridge: Cambridge University Press, 2010), 3. The term "commensal" is first developed in William Robertson Smith, *Lectures on the Religion of the Semites* (London: A. and C. Black, 1907), 274.

5. Emmanuel Levinas, *Nine Talmudic Readings*, trans. Annette Aronowicz (Bloomington: Indiana University Press, 1990), 97.

6. For classic work on the subject, see Mary Douglas, *In the Active Voice* (London: Routledge and Kegan Paul, 1982); Mary Douglas, ed., "Standard Social Uses of Food: Introduction," in *Food in the Social Order: Studies of Food and Festivities in Three American Communities* (New York: Russell Sage Foundation, 1984), 1–39; Claude Lévi-Strauss, *Structural Anthropology* (New York: Basic Books, 1963); Claude Lévi-Strauss, *The Raw and the Cooked* (New York: Harper and Row, 1969); Anna Meigs, "Food as a Cultural Construction," in *Food and Culture: A Reader*, ed. Carole Counihan and Penny Van Esterik (New York: Routledge, 1997). For recent research, see, among many others, Claude Grignon, "Commensality and Social Morphology: An Essay of Typology," in *Food, Drink and Identity: Cooking, Eating and Drinking in Europe since the Middle Ages*, ed. Peter Scholliers (Oxford: Berg Publishers, 2001), 23–33; Martin Jones, *Feast: Why Humans Share Food* (Oxford: Oxford University Press, 2007); Stephen Mennell, Anne Murcott, and Anneke H. van Otterloo, *The Sociology of Food: Eating, Diet, and Culture* (London: Sage, 1992); Stephen Mennell, *All Manners of Food* (Chicago: University of Illinois Press, 1996); Emiko Ohnuki-Tierney, *Rice as Self: Japanese Identities through Time* (Princeton, N.J.: Princeton University Press, 1993); Michael Pollan, *Cooked: A Natural History of Transformation* (London: Penguin, 2013); Rosenblum, *Food and Identity*; Richard W. Wrangham, *Catching Fire: How Cooking Made Us Human* (New York: Basic Books, 2009). In the early modern period, see especially Bruce Thomas Boehrer, *The Fury of Men's Gullets: Ben Jonson and the Digestive Canal* (Philadelphia: University of Pennsylvania Press, 1997); Ilana Krausman Ben-Amos, *The Culture of Giving: Informal Support and Gift-Exchange in Early Modern England* (Cambridge: Cambridge University Press, 2011); Michel Jeanneret, *A Feast of Words: Banquet and Table Talk in the Renaissance*, trans. Jeremy Whiteley and Emma Hughes (Chicago: University of Chicago Press, 1991); Maggie Kilgour, *From Communion to Cannibalism: An Anatomy of Metaphors of Incorporation* (Princeton, N.J.: Princeton University Press, 1990); Craig Muldrew, *Food, Energy and the Creation of Industriousness: Work and Material Culture in Agrarian England, 1550–1780* (Cambridge: Cambridge University Press, 2011); Keith Wrightson, "Mutualities and Obligations: Changing Social Relationships in Early Modern England," *Proceedings of the British Academy* 139 (2006): 157–94. For a fuller analysis of the subject, see David B. Goldstein, *Eating*

and Ethics in Shakespeare's England (Cambridge: Cambridge University Press, 2013), 1–26.

7. See, for example, Allison Carruth, *Global Appetites: American Power and the Literature of Food* (Cambridge: Cambridge University Press, 2013); Denise Gigante, *Taste: A Literary History* (New Haven, Conn.: Yale University Press, 2005); Timothy Morton, ed., *Cultures of Taste / Theories of Appetite: Eating Romanticism* (New York: Palgrave Macmillan, 2004); Kyla Wazana Tompkins, *Racial Indigestion: Eating Bodies in the Nineteenth Century* (New York: New York University Press, 2012).

8. A brief list of the important work on the subject includes Robert Appelbaum, *Aguecheek's Beef, Belch's Hiccup, and Other Gastronomic Interjections: Literature, Culture, and Food among the Early Moderns* (Chicago: University of Chicago Press, 2006); Joseph Candido, "Dining out in Ephesus: Food in The Comedy of Errors," in *The Comedy of Errors: Critical Essays*, ed. Robert S. Miola (New York: Garland, 1997), 199–225; Stanley Cavell, "'Who Does the Wolf Love?': Coriolanus and the Interpretations of Politics," in *Shakespeare and the Question of Theory*, ed. Patricia Parker and Geoffrey Hartman (New York: Methuen, 1985); Joan Fitzpatrick, *Food in Shakespeare: Early Modern Dietaries and the Plays* (Aldershot, U.K.: Ashgate, 2007); Goldstein, *Eating and Ethics*; Kim Hall, "Guess Who's Coming to Dinner?: Colonization and Miscegenation in The Merchant of Venice," *Renaissance Drama* 23 (1992): 87–111; David Hillman, *Shakespeare's Entrails: Belief, Scepticism, and the Interior of the Body* (Basingstoke, U.K.: Palgrave Macmillan, 2007); Hillary Nunn, "Playing with Appetite in Early Modern Comedy," in *Shakespearean Sensations: Experiencing Literature in Early Modern England*, ed. Katharine A. Craik and Tanya Pollard (Cambridge: Cambridge University Press, 2013), 101–17; Peter A. Parolin, "'Cloyless Sauce:' The Pleasurable Politics of Food in Antony and Cleopatra," in *Antony and Cleopatra: New Critical Essays*, ed. Sara Munson Deats (New York: Routledge, 2005), 213–29; Kristen Poole, *Radical Religion from Shakespeare to Milton: Figures of Nonconformity in Early Modern England* (Cambridge: Cambridge University Press, 2000); Caroline Frances Eleanor Spurgeon, *Shakespeare's Imagery and What It Tells Us* (Cambridge: Cambridge University Press, 1935); Wendy Wall, *Staging Domesticity: Household Work and English Identity in Early Modern Drama* (Cambridge: Cambridge University Press, 2002). See also the many fine contributions in the three special issues on Shakespeare and food to date: *Shakespeare Jahrbuch* 145 (2009), *Early Modern Studies Journal* vol. 2 (2013), and *Shakespeare Studies* vol. 42 (2014).

9. William Shakespeare, *Hamlet*, ed. Ann Thompson and Neil Taylor, The Arden Shakespeare, 3rd ser. (London: Thomson Learning, 2006), 4.3.29–30.

10. A limited amount of work has been done on food and Shakespeare's poetry; see Wendy Wall, "Distillation: Transformations In and Out of the Kitchen," in *Renaissance Food from Rabelais to Shakespeare: Culinary Readings and Culinary Histories,* ed. Joan Fitzpatrick (Farnham, U.K.: Ashgate, 2010), 89–106.

11. Drinking alone, like eating alone, constitutes its own complex phenomenon. As Adam Smyth writes, "the solitary drinker was (and is) a powerfully transgressive figure." Adam Smyth, ed., *A Pleasing Sinne* (Suffolk, U.K.: D. S. Brewer, 2004), xv.

12. Ibid., xvi.

13. See Michel Serres, *The Five Senses: A Philosophy of Mingled Bodies* (London: Continuum, 2008), 152–235, for an analysis of taste and digestion that considers food and drink simultaneously, as aspects of a whole.

14. Our model is a marvelous essay collection of which the current editors were lucky to be a part: Jennifer Munroe and Rebecca Laroche, eds., *Ecofeminist Approaches to Early Modernity* (Basingstoke, U.K.: Palgrave Macmillan, 2011).

15. Alfred W. Crosby, *The Columbian Exchange: Biological and Cultural Consequences of 1492,* 30th Anniversary Edition (New York: Greenwood, 2003); Kim Hall, "Culinary Spaces, Colonial Spaces: The Gendering of Sugar in the Seventeenth Century," in *Feminist Readings of Early Modern Culture,* ed. Valerie Traub, M. Lindsay Kaplan, and Dympna Callaghan (Cambridge: Cambridge University Press, 1996); Sidney W. Mintz, *Sweetness and Power: The Place of Sugar in Modern History* (1985; repr., New York: Penguin Books, 1986).

16. See, respectively, Richard Wilson, "'Like the Old Robin Hood': 'As You Like It' and the Enclosure Riots," *Shakespeare Quarterly* 43, no. 1 (Apr. 1, 1992): 1–19; Chris Fitter, "'The Quarrel Is between Our Masters and Us Their Men': Romeo and Juliet, Dearth, and the London Riots," *English Literary Renaissance* 30, no. 2 (2000): 154–83; E. C. Pettet, "*Coriolanus* and the Midlands Insurrection of 1607," *Shakespeare Survey* 3 (1950): 34–42; Annabel Patterson, "'*Speak, Speak!*' The Popular Voice and the Jacobean State," in *Shakespeare and the Popular Voice* (Cambridge, Mass.: Basil Blackwell, 1989), 120–53; David George, "Plutarch, Insurrection, and Dearth in *Coriolanus,*" in *Shakespeare and Politics,* ed. Catherine M. S. Alexander (Cambridge: Cambridge University Press, 2004), 110–24.

17. Ken Albala, *The Banquet: Dining in the Great Courts of Late Renaissance Europe* (Urbana: University of Illinois Press, 2007), 4.

Notes to Chapter 1 / Parolin

1. Jean Howard, "Introduction to *Henry IV, Part 2,*" in *The Norton Shakespeare,* ed. Stephen Greenblatt, Walter Cohen, Jean E. Howard, and Katherine Eisamann Maus (New York: Norton, 2008), 1323.

2. William Shakespeare, *Henry IV, Part One*, in *The Norton Shakespeare*, 2nd ed., ed. Stephen Greenblatt, Walter Cohen, Jean E. Howard, and Katharine Eisaman Maus, 1177–1254 (New York: W. W. Norton, 2008), 1.1.84–85. All references to *1 Henry IV* are taken from this edition, hereafter cited in the text by act, scene, and line number.

3. William Shakespeare, *The Second Part of King Henry IV*, ed. Giorgio Melchiori, The New Cambridge Shakespeare (Cambridge: Cambridge University Press, 1989), 5.5.43. All references to *2 Henry IV* are taken from this edition, hereafter cited in the text by act, scene, and line number.

4. In chapter 4 of this volume, Karen Raber notes the links between foreignness and danger to England's national health in the *Henry IV* plays; she stresses, for example, that Falstaff's reliance on imported drink marks him as a problem. This link between foreignness and danger requires a degree of finesse in masking the foreign components that inform the Englishness of both small beer and the ascendant prince.

5. Accounting for memory in Shakespeare's histories, Jonathan Baldo, *Memory in Shakespeare's Histories: Stages of Forgetting in Early Modern England* (London: Routledge, 2012), 100, argues that for Hal "there is something princely about forgetfulness" in that forgetfulness allows a prince to work with a blank political slate by avoiding the messiness of history. My essay is about the crisis provoked when princely forgetfulness fails.

6. Diane Purkiss, "Crammed with Distressful Bread? Bakers and the Poor in Early Modern England," in *Renaissance Food from Rabelais to Shakespeare: Culinary Readings and Culinary Histories*, ed. Joan Fitzpatrick (Farnham, U.K.: Ashgate, 2010), makes a comment about the implications of eating that helpfully can be applied to drinking in *2 Henry IV*: "If each act of eating is social, it follows that everything which can be eaten can also become a way of experiencing identity and enmeshment" (12).

7. *Oxford English Dictionary*, 3rd ed., s.v. "creature," http://www.oed.com.libproxy.uwyo.edu/view/Entry/44082?redirectedFrom=creature#eid (accessed Feb. 1, 2014).

8. The *OED* also provides the following definition (1d) of "creature," which is specifically relevant to small beer in *2 Henry IV*: "*humorous.* Usu. with *the.* Alcoholic drink, *esp.* whisky." While this definition applies to the play, the sense of "created thing or being" is still primary — small beer, like whisky and other alcohol, is a social product that carries social implications.

9. My sense of the animation of the creature parallels Julian Yates's reading of the "messmate" in chapter 9 of this volume, in which he argues that vitality and agency extend beyond the human subject to the level of the microbial. Acted upon by messmates, the ostensibly human subject is susceptible at any moment to becoming the object, as I argue is the case with Hal.

10. Iain Gately, *Drink: A Cultural History of Alcohol* (New York: Gotham Books, 2008), 111.

11. Barbara Sebek notes in chapter 2 of this volume that the references to Spanish wines in *The Merry Wives of Windsor* are also anachronistic, and that they thereby force that play to engage with the global economic system of the late sixteenth century.

12. Judith M. Bennett, *Ale, Beer and Brewsters in England: Women's Work in a Changing World, 1300–1600* (New York: Oxford University Press, 1996), 17.

13. Peter Clark, *The English Alehouse: A Social History, 1200–1830* (London: Longman, 1983), 97.

14. Ibid., 31.

15. Ibid., 31.

16. Andrew Boorde, *Dyetary of Helth* (1542), F2r–v.

17. Reginald Scot, *A Perfite platforme of a Hoppe Garden* (1576), B2r–v.

18. Ibid., 5–6.

19. William Harrison, *The Description of England* (1577), 135.

20. Fynes Moryson, *An Itinerary*, vol. 4 (Glasgow: James MacLehose and Sons, 1908), 62.

21. *Wine, Beer, Ale, and Tobacco: Contending for Superiority* (1629), B2r.

22. Bennett (*Ale, Beer, and Brewsters*, 80) cites John Taylor's ongoing nationalistic championing of ale over beer as late as 1651, but historians agree that by the mid-seventeenth century, beer dominated the market.

23. Ibid., 85, 88–92, 78.

24. Ibid., 7.

25. This reference is to *The Merry Wives of Windsor*, ed. Walter Cohen, in *The Norton Shakespeare*, 1265–1320.

26. For an excellent account of women's essential but often hidden work outside the mainstream economy, see Natasha Korda, *Labours Lost: Women's Work and the Early Modern English Stage* (Philadelphia: University of Pennsylvania Press, 2011). In chapter 2 of this volume, see Barbara Sebek's discussion of how Mistress Quickly's references to Spanish wine inject the global marketplace into the domestic world of *The Merry Wives of Windsor*.

27. Cedric C. Brown notes Robert Herrick's inclusion of strong beer in his catalogue of delicacies served at Christmas: "Drink now the strong Beere, / Cut the white loafe here, / The while the meat is a shredding / For the rare Mince-Pie." Cedric C. Brown, "Sons of Beer and Sons of Ben: Drink as a Social Marker in Seventeenth-Century England," in *A Pleasing Sinne: Drink and Conviviality in Seventeenth-Century England*, ed. Adam Smyth (Cambridge: D. S. Brewer, 2004), 6.

28. Gervase Markham, *The English Housewife*, ed. Michael R. Best (Kingston, Ontario: McGill-Queen's University Press, 1986), 205.

29. Ibid., 288n11.

30. Clark, *English Alehouse*, 97–98.

31. Rebecca Bach, "Manliness before Individualism: Masculinity, Effeminacy, and Homoerotics in Shakespeare's History Plays," in *A Companion to Shakespeare's Works, Vol. II: The Histories*, ed. Richard Dutton and Jean E. Howard (Malden, Mass.: Blackwell, 2006), 220.

32. As Raber notes in chapter 4 of this volume, the global wine trade was seen to weaken England economically and morally through the influx of foreign goods.

33. Christine Hoffmann, "Biting More than 'We' Can Chew: The Royal Appetite in *Richard II* and *1 and 2 Henry IV*," *Papers on Language and Literature: A Journal for Scholars and Critics of Language and Literature* 45, no. 4 (2009): 358.

34. In a similar vein, Karen Raber, in "Animal Bodies" (paper presented at the Shakespeare Association of America, Toronto, Mar. 2013), notes the prince's dissociation from the world in *1 Henry IV* and compares the prince's horsemanship to Hotspur's: "where we saw Hotspur's thighs kissing/tasting/touching his mount, what we are being given here is a completely antithetical relationship — Hal's thighs are clearly divided from his horse, his body encased in metal, his cuisses providing an important division that prevents him from becoming an actual centaur like Musidorus, and rather structures his relationship with his horse as one of abstract, mythic god to machine-like conveyance."

35. Bach notes, "To be unequivocally affirmed as men in the history plays, male characters must speak and behave as subjects of their superiors and kings must subject themselves to God" ("Manliness before Individualism," 229).

36. Bourdieu would seem to endorse such an application because he stresses the importance of taste not just as an idea but as a physical experience: "one cannot fully understand cultural practices unless 'culture,' in the restricted, normative sense of ordinary usage, is brought back into 'culture' in the anthropological sense, and the elaborated taste for the most refined object is reconnected with the elementary taste for the flavors of food." Pierre Bourdieu and Richard Nice, *Distinction: A Social Critique of the Judgement of Taste* (Cambridge, Mass.: Harvard University Press, 1984), 1.

37. Ibid., 1.

38. Ibid., 6.

39. As Phyllis Rackin points out in *Stages of History: Shakespeare's English Chronicles* (Ithaca, N.Y.: Cornell University Press, 1990), "the royal authority that Henry V finally represents is an achievement, not an inheritance" (79).

40. William Shakespeare, *Henry V*, ed. Katharine Eisaman Maus, in *The Norton Shakespeare*, 2nd ed., ed. Stephen Greenblatt, Walter Cohen,

Jean E. Howard, and Katharine Eisaman Maus, 1471–1548 (New York: W. W. Norton, 2008), 2.1.114.

41. Jean Howard and Phyllis Rackin argue in *Engendering a Nation: A Feminist Account of Shakespeare's English Histories* (London: Routledge, 1997), that, "From a feminist standpoint, one of the most striking features of the second tetralogy is the restriction of women's roles" (137).

42. Ovid, *The xv bookes of P. Ouidius Naso, entytuled Metamorphosis, translated oute of Latin into English meeter, by Arthur Golding Gentleman, a worke very pleasaunt and delectable,* trans. Arthur Golding (London: Willyam Seres, 1567), 30r.

43. Analyzing *1 Henry IV*, Raber sees the freedom from physical limitations as essential to the Prince's political success: "what Hal achieves could be considered a variation of distributed cognition, in which his bodily dissociation from a specific form of interanimality makes possible his more complete participation in a system of human cognition spread across a wider array of social structures and groups" ("Animal Bodies," 8).

44. Ibid., 29r, 28v.

45. Purkiss reveals that one of the pantler's central tasks was to "chip" or remove the crust from the bread to "keep it soft" ("Crammed with Distressful Bread," 17).

46. *The Brewer's Plea; or, A Vindication of Strong-Beere and Ale* (London: I. C., 1647), 3.

Notes to Chapter 2 / Sebek

This essay benefited immeasurably from Amy Tigner's and David Goldstein's astute and stimulating suggestions. I am grateful to the providers of supportive venues in which I presented versions of this work: Jyotsna Singh's collection on the global Renaissance, Mary Ellen Lamb's and Adam Zucker's seminar at the Shakespeare Association in Washington D.C., the Shakespeare Association of America Open Submission competition for the 2010 conference in Chicago, and the Houston Distinguished Visiting Scholar program at the University of Houston. Thanks to Ann Christensen for collegial hospitality in Houston. The Colorado State English Department (especially then chair Bruce Ronda) and the College of Liberal Arts supported a sabbatical leave and professional development funds to attend conferences and work at the Folger Shakespeare Library. Dan Vitkus, Roze Hentschell, Rebecca Laroche, Lynne Magnusson, and Susan Frye offered tantalizing research leads and helpful feedback at various stages. Affectionate thanks to John Gerlach for everything.

1. William Shakespeare, *The Merry Wives of Windsor,* in *The Norton Shakespeare,* 2nd ed., ed. Stephen Greenblatt, Walter Cohen, Jean E. Howard, and Katharine Eisaman Maus (New York: W. W. Norton, 2008),

3.5.17–19, 24–27. Unless otherwise noted, all references to Shakespeare's plays are from this edition. On eggs as an aphrodisiac, see William Shakespeare, *The Merry Wives of Windsor*, ed. T. W. Craik (Oxford: Clarendon Press, 1989), 172n29. On eggs as one of the ingredients used to remedy "changed" wines and to treat storage vessels, see William Philips, *A Book of Secrets* (London, 1596), sigs. E3–E3ᵛ.

2. This is true of all of the Falstaff plays. The first quartos of *1 Henry IV*, *2 Henry IV*, and *Merry Wives* appeared in 1598, 1600, and 1602, respectively. The official ban on Anglo-Spanish trade extended from May 1585 to the Treaty of London ratified in August 1604.

3. Describing the play as Shakespeare's "only thoroughly English comedy" in his introduction to the *The Merry Wives of Windsor*, Arden Shakespeare, ed. Giorgio Melchiori (London: Cengage Learning, 2000), 1, Melchiori addresses the complex ways that "English" can be construed in the play. He notes that Jeanne Addison Roberts offers the most sustained study of the play's Englishness in her *Shakespeare's English Comedy: The Merry Wives of Windsor in Context* (Lincoln: University of Nebraska Press, 1979). Richard Helgerson considers the play's engagement with linguistic colonialism and postcolonialism in "Language Lessons: Linguistic Colonialism, Linguistic Postcolonialism, and the Early Modern English Nation," *Yale Journal of Criticism* 11, no. 1 (1998): 289–99. Remarking on the play's topographical precision, Anne Barton, "The London Scene: City and Court," in *The Cambridge Companion to Shakespeare*, ed. Margreta de Grazia and Stanley Wells (Cambridge: Cambridge University Press, 2001), 115–16, claims that "in this and almost all other respects," *The Merry Wives of Windsor* is "a special case." The question of the play's topicality and locatedness, especially when attending to the great differences between the 1602 quarto and the first folio, is a central concern in Leah Marcus, *Puzzling Shakespeare: Local Reading and Its Discontents* (Berkeley: University of California Press, 1988), and Barbara Freedman, "Shakespearean Chronology, Ideological Complicity, and Floating Texts: Something Is Rotten in Windsor," *Shakespeare Quarterly* 45, no. 2 (Summer 1994): 190–210.

4. Feminist accounts of this neglect of the play can be found in Elizabeth Pittenger, "Dispatch Quickly: The Mechanical Reproduction of Pages," *Shakespeare Quarterly* 42, no. 4 (1991): 389–408; and Phyllis Rackin, *Shakespeare and Women* (Oxford: Oxford University Press, 2005), 48–71.

5. Pamela Allen Brown offers a sustained study of neighborhood as a framework in "Near Neighbors, Women's Wars and Merry Wives," in her *Better a Shrew than a Sheep: Women, Drama, and the Culture of Jest in Early Modern England* (Ithaca, N.Y.: Cornell University Press, 2003). Wendy Wall, "Unhusbanding Desires in Windsor," in *A Companion to Shakespeare's Works*, vol. 3, ed. Richard Dutton and Jean Howard

(Malden, Mass.: Blackwell, 2003), shows how the play represents a "national community protected by a constant patrol of linguistic, social, and sexual improprieties" so that "the village constructs a domestic home front relentlessly claimed by citizens" (378, 380). Mario Di Gangi, "The Social Relations of Shakespeare's Comic Households," also in Dutton and Howard, *A Companion*, notes that social relations of the household are "fully inscribed within those of the neighborhood and even the nation" and that the citizen households of the play are "remarkably open to various outsiders" (101, 104).

6. Wendy Wall, *Staging Domesticity: Household Work and English Identity in Early Modern Drama* (Cambridge: Cambridge University Press, 2002), 90, 112. Critical interest in domesticity, gender, and sexuality also informs the discussions by Heather Dubrow, *Shakespeare and Domestic Loss: Forms of Deprivation, Mourning, and Recuperation* (Cambridge: Cambridge University Press, 1999); Natasha Korda, "'Judicious oeillades': Supervising Marital Property in *The Merry Wives of Windsor*," in *Marxist Shakespeares*, ed. Jean Howard and Scott Shershow (London: Routledge, 2001), 82–103; Mary Ellen Lamb, *The Popular Culture of Shakespeare, Jonson, and Spenser* (New York: Routledge, 2006); and Carol Thomas Neely, "Confining Madmen and Transgressing Boundaries: *The Comedy of Errors, The Merry Wives of Windsor*, and *Twelfth Night*," in her *Distracted Subjects: Madness and Gender in Shakespeare and Early Modern Culture* (Ithaca, N.Y.: Cornell University Press, 2004), 136–66. I hope to add to critical interest in the discourses of gender and sexuality by insisting on setting them alongside a global perspective.

7. One exception is Richard Helgerson, who points out how "The local and domestic...are also engaged in a series of actions that involve a much broader national and even international community," in "The Buck Basket, the Witch and the Queen of Fairies: The Women's World of Shakespeare's Windsor," in *Renaissance Culture and the Everyday*, ed. Patricia Fumerton and Simon Hunt (Philadelphia: University of Pennsylvania Press, 1999), 167.

8. Walter Cohen, introduction to *Merry Wives of Windsor*, in *The Norton Shakespeare*, 1256; Ania Loomba, "Outsiders in Shakespeare's England," in *The Cambridge Companion to Shakespeare*, ed. Margreta de Grazia and Stanley Wells (Cambridge: Cambridge University Press, 2001), 153; Jonathan Gil Harris, *Shakespeare and Literary Theory* (Oxford: Oxford University Press, 2010), 192–93.

9. On London as a world city, see Crystal Bartolovich, "'Baseless Fabric': London as a 'World City,'" in *The Tempest and Its Travels*, ed. Peter Hulme and William H. Sherman (Philadelphia: University of Pennsylvania Press, 2000), 13–26.

10. On these competing interest groups, see Robert Brenner, *Merchants and Revolution: Commercial Change, Political Conflict, and London's*

Overseas Traders, 1550–1653 (Princeton, N.J.: Princeton University Press, 1993). On the Spanish Company and its history, see discussion in text below and Pauline Croft's introduction to her collection of documents in *The Spanish Company* (Chatham: London Record Society, 1973), vii–xxix.

11. Berkshire Record Office, Doc ref D/EX1130/4/1. Thanks to Lisa Spurrier, BRO archivist, who found this record and who reports in an e-mail exchange of September 25, 2009, that all of the Windsor borough quarter session records before 1657 — which would contain the actual licenses for innkeepers to sell wine — are lost.

12. For a detailed look at the extensive presence of English traders in the islands, see my "Canary, Bristoles, Londres, Ingleses: English Traders in the Canaries in the Sixteenth and Seventeenth Centuries," in *A Companion to the Global Renaissance*, ed. Jyotsna Singh (Malden, Mass.: Wiley-Blackwell, 2009), 279–93. I draw on that essay in the current chapter, which can be read as the companion piece to this one. William Harrison's "Of the Nauie of England," a chapter on the English navy in *An Historicall Description of the Iland of Britaine, An Electronic Edition*, ed. Henry Ellis, notes that ships bound for "Hispaniola or New Spain" touched at the Canaries. http://www.perseus.tufts.edu/hopper/text?doc= Perseus%3Atext%3A1999.03.0083%3Abook%3D2%3Achapter%3D17 (accessed Dec. 28, 2015).

13. I borrow from Claire Jowitt's study of the "pirate meme" in *The Culture of Piracy: English Literature and Seaborne Crime* (Burlington, Vt.: Ashgate, 2010), thus characterizing the imaginative uses of Spanish wines in literary texts. A foundational study of the emergence of a world economy is Immanuel Wallerstein, *The Modern World-System* (New York: Academic Press, 1974). See also Alan K. Smith, *Creating a World Economy: Merchant Capital, Colonialism, and World Trade, 1400–1825* (Boulder, Colo.: Westview Press, 1991).

14. Joan Fitzpatrick, *Food in Shakespeare: Early Modern Dietaries and the Plays* (Burlington, Vt.: Ashgate, 2007), 19, notes that Falstaff's culinary choices in *1 Henry IV* render him familiar, and she lists sack among the items that most playgoers would know and consume. Fitzpatrick here glosses over the foreign origins of sack, perhaps attesting to the extent of its domestication in the play.

15. William D. Phillips Jr., "The Frustrated Unity of Atlantic Europe: The Roles of Spain and England," in *Material and Symbolic Exchange between Spain and England, 1554–1604*, ed. Anne Cruz (Burlington, Vt.: Ashgate, 2008), 5–6. The most comprehensive source on England's wine trade in the Middle Ages, our period, and beyond is André Simon's *The History of the Wine Trade in England*, 3 vols. (London: Wyman and Sons, 1907).

16. Pauline Croft, "English Commerce with Spain and the Armada War, 1558–1603," in *England, Spain, and the Gran Armada, 1585–1604*,

ed. M. J. Rodriguez-Salgado and Simon Adams (Edinburgh: John Donald, 1991), 245, 250. *Oxford English Dictionary*, 3rd ed., Nov. 2010, online version June 2012, s.v. "vintage," n., def. 2a and 2b, http://www.oed.com.libproxy.usc.edu/view/Entry/2176 (accessed June 28, 2012).

17. L. Alberti and and A. B. Wallis Chapman, *English Merchants and the Spanish Inquisition in the Canaries: Extracts from the Archives in Possession of the Most Hon. the Marquess of Bute* (London: Royal Historical Society, 1912). Pauline Croft, "Trading with the Enemy, 1586–1604," *Historical Journal* 32 (1989): 281–302.

18. Croft, "Trading with the Enemy," 283–84.

19. Croft, "English Commerce with Spain," 242–43, 258.

20. See Alberti and Chapman, *English Merchants*, for a fascinating account of these traders. For their Spanish counterparts in the fifteenth century—Castilians and Basques who traded with England even when the Castilian crown forbade it—see Phillips, "Frustrated Unity," 10.

21. Thomas Nichols, *A Pleasant Description of the Fortunate Ilands, Called the Ilands of Canaria, with Their Straunge Fruits and Commodities, Composed by the Poore Pilgrim* (London, 1583). Nichols's text is the first in any language to be devoted exclusively to the Canary Islands.

22. Jason Eldred offers a succinct and thorough overview of the various strains of English policy on Spain and how the more hawkish factions violated merchant interests in "'The Just will pay for the sinners': English Merchants, the Trade with Spain, and Elizabethan Foreign Policy, 1563–1585," *Journal for Early Modern Cultural Studies* 10, no. 1 (2010): 5–28. The standard study is Kenneth R. Andrews, *Elizabethan Privateering: English Privateering during the Spanish War, 1585–1603* (Cambridge: Cambridge University Press, 1964). See also Croft, "Trading with the Enemy," and "English Commerce with Spain." See Jowitt, *The Culture of Piracy, 48–78*, for a discussion of the variable receptions of Drake's exploits. In addition to Barbara Fuchs's introduction to the special issue of the *Journal for Early Modern Cultural Studies* 10, no. 1 (2010), two recent collections reconsider "black legend" discourse and other assumptions about Anglo-Spanish relations: Cruz, *Material and Symbolic Circulation;* and *Rereading the Black Legend: the Discourses of Religious and Racial Difference in the Renaissance Empires*, ed. Margaret Greer, Walter D. Mignolo, and Maureen Quilligan (Chicago: University of Chicago Press, 2007).

23. Bernardo J. García García, "The Peace with England, from Convenience to Necessity, 1596–1604," in Cruz, *Material and Symbolic Circulation*, 140.

24. The Company charter was originally created in 1577 but had been defunct since the outbreak of hostilities in 1585. A precursor to the Spanish Company existed during Henry VIII's reign in the form of the Andalusian Company, but it was largely an attempt to codify privileges

that the Spanish had already granted to English merchants in Seville. See Croft's introduction to *The Spanish Company*.

25. Brenner, *Merchants and Revolution*, 86.

26. Gervase Markham, *The English Housewife*, ed. Michael R. Best (Kingston, Ontario: McGill-Queen's University Press, 1986), 137, 142. Seres is Jerez, from which the names sherry and sherry-sack originate.

27. James Howell, *Familiar Letters, or Epistolae Ho-Elianae*, vol. 2 (London: J. M. Dent, 1903), 201–02.

28. Conflicted representations of sack thread through broader six-teenth and seventeenth century discourses about drink. Sack serves both as shorthand for self-indulgence and moral laxity *and* as the celebrated source of health and agent of consolation, conviviality, and merry-making. But because of the important place of the Canary Islands in global trade networks and their place as a testing ground and launchpad for voyages between the Old World and the New, sack and Canary bear a special symbolic and literal burden in Shakespeare and a wide range of other early modern texts. On conflicting discourses of drink, see Adam Smyth's introduction and the essays in *A Pleasing Sinne: Drink and Conviviality in Seventeenth-Century England*, ed. Adam Smyth (Martlesham, U.K.: Boydell and Brewer, 2004). The sharpened class, national, and political codings of drink are addressed by several writers in that volume. On a culture of drinking as competitive, structured play, see Gina Bloom, "Manly Drunkenness: Binge Drinking as Disciplined Play," in *Masculinity and the Metropolis of Vice*, ed. Roze Hentschell and Amanda Bailey (New York: Palgrave, 2010), 21–44. In the same volume, Laurie Ellinghausen discusses the complex socioeconomic dynamics of university drinking culture in "University of Vice: Drink, Gentility, and Masculinity in Oxford, Cambridge, and London" (45–65). Howell's nod to theological contro-versy, *Familiar Letters*, points to how intensely the wine-versus-beer-or-ale debates heat up as we move further into the seventeenth century and the civil war period. I address these topics in "'More natural to the nation': Situating Shakespeare in the 'Querelle de Canary,'" *Shakespeare Studies* 42 (2014): 106–21. For an excellent broad history of wine from its origins to the present, see John Varriano, *Wine: A Cultural History* (London: Reaktion Books, 2010).

29. George Steckley, "The Wine Economy of Tenerife in the Seventeenth Century: Anglo-Spanish Partnership in a Luxury Trade," *Economic History Review*, n.s. 33, no. 3 (Aug. 1980): 342–43. At the peak of the trade in 1681, London customs officials taxed enough Canary to fill 4.5 million quart bottles. I cite these numbers and contextualize them in the broader debates about sack, ale, and questions of national identity in "'More natural to the nation.'"

30. Miles Ogborn, *Global Lives: Britain and the World, 1550–1800* (Cambridge: Cambridge University Press, 2008), 232–37. On the centuries

of conquest of the islands and their sixteenth century aftermath, see David Abulafia, *The Discovery of Mankind: Atlantic Encounters in the Age of Columbus* (New Haven, Conn.: Yale University Press, 2008), and Felipe Fernandez-Armesto, *The Canary Islands after the Conquest: The Making of a Colonial Society in the Early Sixteenth Century* (Oxford: Oxford University Press, 1982).

31. Alberto Vieira, "The Sugar Economy of Madeira and the Canaries, 1450–1650," in *Tropical Babylons: Sugar and the Making of the Atlantic World, 1450–1680*, ed. Stuart B. Schwartz (Chapel Hill, N.C.: University of North Carolina Press, 2004), 72.

32. Joan Thirsk, *Food in Early Modern England: Phases, Fads, Fashions, 1500–1760* (London: Continuum, 2007), 49, 56. Thirsk notes that there was probably regional variation in whether sugar or honey was more used in cooking, with the use of sugar more prominent in southern England; yet sugar use penetrated to the north as well.

33. Vieira, "Sugar Economy of Madeira," 61–63.

34. Not to mention colonial processes and modes of exploitation. On the relations between the transport of botanicals, the slave trade, and the transformation of English gardens, see Amy Tigner, "The Flowers of Paradise: Botanical Trade in Sixteenth- and Seventeenth-Century England," in *Global Traffic: Discourses and Practices of Trade in English Literature and Culture from 1550 to 1700*, ed. Barbara Sebek and Stephen Deng (New York: Palgrave Macmillan, 2008), 137–56. In the same volume, Ann Christensen discusses a dramatized version of the vexed interplay between English housewives and East India Company ventures in "'Absent, Weak, or Unserviceable': The East India Company and the Domestic Economy in *The Launching of the Mary, or The Seaman's Honest Wife*," 117–36.

35. Citing this very line, the *OED* defines "burnt" as "made hot" (adj., def. 5), but notes that the precise early sense is doubtful. A quotation from 1876 suggests that "burnt" wines were preparations that included spices and sugar, further enhancing the sack/sugar conjunction that runs through the play and early modern culinary practices.

36. In addition to "good cheer," Ford's invitation includes entertainment for his fellows: "besides your cheer, you shall have sport: I will show you a monster" (3.2.67–68). The "monster" he refers to is the coupling of Falstaff and his wife that he believes they will see when he brings the group home. Interestingly, the Host's refusal of Ford's invitation follows Mr. Page's class-specific explanation of why he rejects Fenton for his daughter: Page (somewhat accurately) reads Fenton as a broke, profligate aristocrat trying to strengthen his fortunes with Page's "substance" (3.2.63). For critics who have debated the play's treatment of class conflict, see note 39 below.

37. Wellcome MS 213, Mrs. Corlyon's receipt book, 35, http://archives .wellcome.ac.uk/dserve/recipebooks/MS213.pdf. Thanks to Amy Tigner for alerting me to this recipe.

38. See the following editions of *Merry Wives: The Merry Wives of Windsor*, ed. Barbara A. Mowat and Paul Werstine (New York: Washington Square Press, 2004); *The Merry Wives of Windsor*, ed. Russ McDonald (New York: Penguin Books, 2002); *The Merry Wives of Windsor*, in *The Complete Works of Shakespeare*, 4th ed., ed. David M. Bevington (New York: HarperCollins, 1992); and *The Riverside Shakespeare*, 2nd ed., ed. G. Blakemore Evans (Boston: Houghton Mifflin, 1997).

39. Critics who have debated the play's production of courtly ver- sus town values include Peter Erickson, "The Order of the Garter, the Cult of Elizabeth, and Class-Gender Tension in *Merry Wives of Windsor*," in *Shakespeare Reproduced*, ed. Jean Howard and Marion O'Connor (London: Methuen, 1987), 116–42; Freedman, "Shakespearean Chronology"; Maurice Hunt, "'Gentleness' and Social Class in *The Merry Wives of Windsor*," *Comparative Drama* 42, no. 4 (Winter 2008): 409–32; Rosemary Kegl, *The Rhetoric of Concealment: Figuring Gender and Class in Renaissance Literature* (Ithaca, N.Y.: Cornell University Press, 1994); Leah Marcus, *Unediting the Renaissance* (New York: Routledge, 1996); and Wall, "Unhusbanding Desires." Giorgio Melchiori and Walter Cohen also address these concerns in the Arden and Norton editions, respec- tively. More recently, Lamb discusses how the play stages "evolving self- narratives of the middling sort of Windsor in terms of the aristocracy" and a "pattern of appropriation and rejection" of popular culture (*Popular Culture, 146*). Quickly's account of the assaults on Mrs. Ford by "the best courtier of them all" (2.2.59) resonates enticingly with Frederick, Count Mompelgard, the German lord who, along with his envoy Hans Jacob Breuning von Buchenbach, badgered Queen Elizabeth for election to the Order of the Garter with what Quickly calls "letter after letter, gift after gift" (2.2.62). As Freedman shows convincingly—not drawing on Quickly's passage, however—the strategic political considerations sur- rounding Garter election, installation, and investiture were a way for the English to maneuver in geopolitical affairs, including England's place in Iberian-dominated trade ("Shakespearean Chronology," 199–205).

40. Jowitt, *The Culture of Piracy*, offers a thorough study of the flexible treatment of "piracy" in the period, varying according to genre and politi- cal circumstances.

41. Patricia Parker, "Interpreting through Wordplay: Shakespeare's *The Merry Wives of Windsor*," in *Teaching with Shakespeare: The Critics in the Classroom*, ed. Bruce McIver and Ruth Stevenson, 166–204 (Newark: University of Delaware Press, 1994), 176.

42. Howell, *Familiar Letters*, 198.

43. In a similarly pointed set of references, and with rhetoric akin to the Host of the Garter in *Merry Wives,* Thomas Middleton's Host in "The Meeting of Gallants at an Ordinary; or, The Walks in Paul's" (1603) says that his "heart bleeds nothing but alicant" in response to the dismal spectacle he has just recounted of plague-ridden corpses being piled into ditches. He enjoins his tavern companions to shun the sadness that his tales might prompt by drinking sack together: "let not this make you sad, gallants. Sit you merry still. Here, my dainty bullies, I'll put you all in one goblet, and wash all these tales in a cup of sack." *The Complete Works of Thomas Middleton* (Oxford: Oxford University Press, 2007), 194. Considering the possible obscurity of Quickly's Spanish wine references, we might compare Shakespeare's strategy of veiling them here to the survival of Martinist jokes in Mistress Quickly's language in the history plays. See Kristen Poole, "The Puritan in the Alehouse: Falstaff and the Drama of Martin Marprelate," in her *Radical Religion from Shakespeare to Milton: Figures of Nonconformity in Early Modern England* (Cambridge: Cambridge University Press, 2000). Quickly's use of the plural "canaries" resonates in *2 Henry IV* when she says Doll Tearsheet has "drunk too much canaries, and that's a marvellous searching wine" (*2H4*, 2.4.21–22). In that very scene, both Doll and Quickly vehemently repel the aggressive verbal and sexual assaults of Pistol.

44. Lamb, *Popular Culture,* 137.

45. Pistol's lines resonate with the Pistol of *2 Henry IV,* especially the aggressive brawling that takes place in Mistress Quickly's alehouse in act 2, scene 4. The relocation of Quickly's place of employment from alehouse to Caius's house accords with the arguments of critics such as Wall who insist on this play's focus on the domestic realm.

46. Perhaps also, given the Canarian thrust of Quickly's speech, it invokes Drake's failed raids on the Canaries in 1585–87 and 1595, or the successful sacking of Las Palmas, Gran Canaria, by the Dutch pirate Pieter Van der Does in 1599—an anonymous firsthand account of which was translated and published in England soon after it took place. *The conquest of the Grand Canaries made this last summer by threescore and thirteene saile of shippes* (London, 1599).

47. Korda, "'Judicious oeillades,'" 93–95. A wonderful moment in *Twelfth Night* likewise tropes sexual pursuit as nautical or piratical assault, and this imagery is similarly associated with Canary drinking and even (obliquely) the Spanish language. In the midst of a paean to drinking "healths" to his niece—and part of a defense of Andrew Aguecheek's and his own nightly drunkenness—Toby spews a (faux) Spanish phrase: "Castiliano vulgo, for here comes Andrew Agueface" (*TN*, 1.3.35–36). Toby then uses a variety of nautically inflected terms such as "accost," to urge Andrew to approach Maria. When Maria exits, Toby remarks that Andrew "lackest a cup of Canary...when did I see thee so put down?" (41–68).

See Tobias Döring's essay in chapter 8 of this volume, which discusses the relationship between drinking and the erasure of memory in *Twelfth Night*.

Notes to Chapter 3 / Kanelos

1. See Clifford A. Wright, *A Mediterranean Feast* (New York: William Morrow, 1999), esp. 430. The Spanish were particularly associated with the *bigerade*, a bitter orange. As Wright indicates, however, the provenance of Sicilian oranges may be more complex than generally assumed, since the Arabs, who ruled both Spain and Sicily during the centuries before the rise of Aragon, were the conduit for oranges from their point of origin, likely in the provinces of Yunnan and Kwangsi in southeast China (300).

2. For another instance of Spanish influence on Shakespeare's comedies, see Barbara Sebek, chapter 2 in this volume.

3. Geoffrey Bullough, ed., *Narrative and Dramatic Sources of Shakespeare*, vol. 2 (London: Routledge and Kegan Paul, 1963), 112.

4. William Shakespeare, *Much Ado about Nothing*, ed. Peter Kanelos, The New Kittredge Shakespeare (Newburyport, Mass.: Focus, 2010), 2.1.228–29; hereafter cited in the text.

5. "A 'Civil orange' was an orange from Civil, i.e., Seville. It is bittersweet" (ibid., 24n228).

6. *Coriolanus* (2.1) and *The Winter's Tale* (4.4).

7. Bullough, *Narrative*, 113.

8. See Wright, *Mediterranean Feast*, esp. 549–60.

9. Dante, *The Divine Comedy*, vol. 1, *The Inferno*, trans. Mark Musa (London: Penguin Books, 2003), 10.119: "the Second Frederick is here." In his translation, Mark Musa notes, "The Emperor Frederick II (1194–1250) is in the circle of the Heretics because of the commonly held belief that he was an Epicurean" (166).

10. C. L. Barber, *Shakespeare's Festive Comedy* (Princeton, N.J.: Princeton University Press, 1972), 5.

11. Ibid., 121.

12. In William Shakespeare, *Much Ado about Nothing*, ed. Sheldon P. Zitner, The Oxford Shakespeare (Oxford: Oxford University Press, 1993), 16.

13. Northrop Frye, "The Argument of Comedy," in *An Anthology of Shakespeare Criticism and Theory, 1945–2000*, ed. Russ Macdonald (Oxford: Blackwell, 2004), 94.

14. Galen, quoted in Joan Fitzpatrick, *Food in Shakespeare* (London: Ashgate, 2007), 2–3.

15. It is not by chance that "man" and its cognates appear more frequently in *Much Ado* than in any of Shakespeare's other plays; see William Shakespeare, *Much Ado about Nothing*, ed. Claire McEachern, The Arden Shakespeare (London: Thomson Learning, 2006), 59.

16. Fitzpatrick, *Food in Shakespeare*, 3.

17. Ibid., 4.

18. William Shakespeare, *Twelfth Night*, ed. Kier Elam, The Arden Shakespeare (London: Cengage, 2008), 1.3.83–84. Robert Applebaum discusses the perceived deleterious effects of eating beef in *Aguecheeck's Beef, Belch's Hiccup, and Other Gastronomic Interjections: Literature, Culture and Food among the Early Moderns* (Chicago: University of Chicago Press, 2006), esp. chap. 1. See also Tobias Döring, chapter 8 in this volume, for more information about feasting in *Twelfth Night*.

19. Joan Thirsk, *Fooles and Fricassees: Food in Shakespeare's England* (Seattle: University of Washington Press), 21.

20. Ibid., 21.

21. William Harrison, *Description of England* (1577), from *Modern History Sourcebook*, chap. 3, "Of Gardens and Orchards," http://www.fordham.edu/halsall/mod/1577harrison-england.asp#Chapter III (accessed Aug. 23, 2013).

22. Thirsk, *Fooles and Fricassees*, 21.

23. Ibid., 21.

24. McEachern, *Much Ado*, 258n30.

25. Ibid., 258n30.

26. Charles Beauclerk, *Nell Gwyn: Mistress to a King* (London: Grove Press, 2006), 56.

27. William Shakespeare, *King Henry V*, ed. T. W. Clark, The Arden Shakespeare (London: Thomson Learning, 1995).

28. Kanelos, *Much Ado*, 3n23.

29. Harry Berger Jr., "Against the Sink-a-Pace: Sexual and Family Politics in *Much Ado About Nothing*," in *Making Trifles of Terrors: Redistributing Complicities in Shakespeare*, ed. Peter Erickson (Stanford. Calif.: Stanford University Press, 1997), 20.

30. Kittredge, in Kanelos, *Much Ado*, 15n53.

31. McEachern, *Much Ado*, 206n3.

32. *Oxford English Dictionary*, 2nd ed. (Oxford University Press, 1989), s.v. "Beatrician," adj.; *OED Online*, Apr. 30, 2011, http://dictionary.oed.com.

Notes to Chapter 4 / Raber

1. William Shakespeare, *Henry IV, Part 2*, in *The Complete Works of Shakespeare*, 5th ed., ed. David Bevington (New York: Longman, 2003), 4.3.95–115. Unless otherwise noted, all references to Shakespeare's plays are to this edition, hereafter cited in the text.

2. Jonathan Gil Harris, *Sick Economies: Drama, Mercantilism and Disease in Shakespeare's England* (Philadelphia: University of

Pennsylvania Press, 2003). Harris's discussion of "taint"(52–82) includes mention of the German Rhenish wines and the significance of their appearance in *The Merchant of Venice* (75), which originally prompted this essay's topic.

3. Ibid., 5–8.

4. Ibid., 73.

5. Rhenish was white, or "Rhine" wine.

6. It is no accident, I would say, that by 2 *Henry IV* Hal is expressing an appetite for small beer (2.2.12); his rejection of sack (and the extreme represented by Falstaff's love for it) is shortly to be complete. In this moment when he is registering discomfort over his reliance on the tavern dwellers like Poins, he finds even this most English of drinks a possible contamination of his will to remain separate, in control of his convivial desires. For more on small beer and Hal's character, see Peter Parolin's essay in this volume (chapter 1).

7. Benjamin Bertram, "Falstaff's Body, the Body Politic, and the Body of Trade," *Exemplaria* 21, no. 3 (Fall 2009): 296–318.

8. Ibid., 309.

9. James Nicholls, "*Vinum Brittanicum:* The 'Drink Question' in Early Modern England," *Social History of Alcohol and Drugs* (Spring 2008): 191; Gascoigne's quote (sig A5v in the 1576 *A Delicate Diet for Daintiemouthde Droonkards*), appears also in Nicholls (191).

10. Thomas Young, *England's Bane; or, The Description of Drunkenness* (London: William Jones, 1617), D2r.

11. Thomas Heywood, *Philocothonista; or, The Drunkard Opened, Dissected, and Anatomized* (London: Robert Raworth, 1635), 29, 47. On the problem with drinking too many healths, see Nicholls, "*Vinum Brittanicum*," 194–96, especially his discussion of William Prynne.

12. Heywood, *Philocothonista*, 91, 47.

13. Frederick W. Hackwood, *Inns, Ales, and Drinking Customs of Old England* (London: Bracken Books, 1985), 154.

14. Heywood includes the term in his list of drinking cant phrases, but its origins are early in the century. In "Going Dutch in London City Comedy: Economies of Sexual and Sacred Exchange in John Marston's *The Dutch Courtesan* (1605)," *English Literary Renaissance* 40, no. 1 (Winter 2010): 88–112, Marjorie Rubright argues that the relationship between the English and the Dutch depicted on the stage (and presumably elsewhere in the literature) in this period was not necessarily about continental others as much as about "problematically proximate ethnicities," since the Dutch had a significant and long-standing presence in London in particular (90–91). Rebecca Lemon discusses the resistance to drinking healths in "Compulsory Conviviality in Early Modern England," *English Literary Renaissance* 43, no. 3 (2013): 381–414, including its origins as a foreign practice (384–86).

15. Thomas Nashe, *Pierce Penniless's Supplication to the Devil* (London: Shakespeare Society, 1842), 52, 53.

16. Gregory A. Austin, *Alcohol in Western Society from Antiquity to 1800: A Chronological History* (Santa Barbara, Calif.: ABL-Clio, 1985).

17. Susan Doran, *Elizabeth I and Foreign Policy, 1558–1603* (New York: Routledge, 2000), 64.

18. Clarence's death scene in Shakespeare's play seems to come from broadly circulated accounts available at the time but has no absolutely proven basis in historical reality; for a rehearsal of sources, and historians' reactions to the story, see John Webster Spargo, "Clarence in the Malmsey Butt," *Modern Language Notes* 51, no. 3 (Mar. 1936): 166–73.

19. There are all sorts of issues (too many to cover here) invoked in Clarence's reference to "Burgundy," mainly related to English dynastic connections in the region, all of which are present in the first plays of the tetralogy. Clarence is clearly having a dream that reproduces his past flight to France, for which he is branded "false, fleeting," but in so doing he also invokes the ongoing problem of French interference in English politics, whether at the time of Henry VI or in Elizabeth's day. For a complete account of the historical Clarence's life, see M. A. Hicks, *False, Fleeting, Perjur'd Clarence: George, Duke of Clarence, 1449–78* (Gloucester: Allan Sutton, 1980).

20. The distinction between varieties of sweet, highly alcoholic wines in the period can be extremely fuzzy: any sweet white wine could end up being called "sack" or "Canary," whether it was produced in the Canary Islands or not. The origins of the Malvasia grape are Greek, even if the sixteenth century beverage was associated with the island of Madeira. Portuguese Madeira is still made through an unusual process of heating the wine, which concentrates its flavor. The process evolved from the actual fate of barrels of the wine aboard ships bound to and from the major trade port of Madeira — to extend the wine's life for the trip, producers added grape spirits (hence, it's a fortified wine), which blended and heated with the ship's movement and temperature, until a uniquely flavored product emerged. David Hancock writes that in the Atlantic sea trade, malmsey, or Madeira, wine outperformed competitor wines because other wines "did not possess the same capacity as Madeira to benefit from heat, and high temperature was a constant companion on board voyages." David Hancock, *Oceans of Wine: Madeira and the Emergence of American Trade and Taste* (New Haven, Conn.: Yale University Press, 2009), 112. It is thus possible to say that malmsey aided the sea trade, but that trade in turn created malmsey. Hancock also notes, "apart from Port, Sherry, and some Canary, wine degraded long before it arrived in America" (112), confirming the desirability of those wines for long sea trips. The multiple benefits of such wines remained a factor in trade even into the nineteenth century.

21. "The Goode Gossippes Song," in *Songs and Carols,* ed. Thomas Wright (London: Percy Society, 1848), 14.

22. Patrick Forbes, ed., *A Full View of the Transactions in the Reign of Queen Elizabeth,* 2 vols. (1740–41), 1:388.

23. John Aylmer, *An Harborow for Faithful and Trew Subjects* (London: John Day, 1559), L4v, notes at the same time that even Caesar called the French "light and inconstant."

24. Eliot is quoted in David Womersley, "France in Shakespeare's *Henry V,*" *Renaissance Studies* 9, no. 4 (1995): 443.

25. Rowland Cotterill, "The Structural Role of France in Shakespeare's First and Second Historical Tetralogies," *Renaissance Studies* 9, no. 4 (1995): 460–76.

26. Bertram, "Falstaff's Body," 313. Bertram contrasts Hal's larger world with the world that Falstaff is within himself: a more limited, private, physical domain.

27. Spargo, "Clarence," 169. Spargo uses the work of Heinz Goldschmidt, a German historian, to show that Edward IV was familiar with the method from travels in the Netherlands (169–70), and that the addition of stabbing to the drowning in Shakespeare's play also had its historical analogue in some of these cases.

28. As Spargo points out, it isn't clear from Shakespeare's text if there is indeed wine in the butt, or if it now contains water (ibid., 172).

29. *The Drunkard's Prospective* (1656), qtd. in Hackwood, *Inns, Ales, and Drinking,* 161.

30. *The Remains of Sir Walter Raleigh* (London, 1657), 102–03, 104.

31. Young, *Englands Bane,* F2v–F3.

32. Alden T. Vaughan and Virginia Mason Vaughan, *Shakespeare's Caliban: A Cultural History* (New York: Cambridge University Press, 1991), 19.

33. See Karen Britland, "Circe's Cup: Wine and Women in Early Modern Drama," and Adam Smyth, "'It were far better be a *Toad,* or a *Serpent,* then a Drunkard': Writing about Drunkenness," both of which appear in *A Pleasing Sinne: Drink and Conviviality in Seventeenth-Century England,* ed. Adam Smyth (Cambridge: D. S. Brewer, 2004), 109–26 and 193–210, respectively. Britland discusses the nature of the island (114), and Smyth discusses the comparison made between forests, islands, and other wild places to taverns in the contemporary antialcohol diatribes.

34. Marina Warner, "'The foul witch' and Her 'freckled whelp': Circean Mutations in the New World," in *"The Tempest" and Its Travels,* ed. Peter Hulme and William H. Sherman, 97–113 (Philadelphia: University of Pennsylvania Press, 2000), 103.

35. Britland, "Circe's Cup," 111.

36. Qtd. in Thomas G. Olsen, "Ascham's *The Scholemaster,* Italianate Englishmen, and the Protestant Circe," *Reformation* 12 (2007): 125.

37. Gascoigne, *A Delicate Diet*, sig C2r.

38. Heywood, *Philocothonista*, opp. frontispiece.

39. See, for instance, Charles Frey's "*The Tempest* and the New World," in *Shakespeare Quarterly* 30, no. 1 (Winter 1979): 29–41, for this reference, but also for the history of establishing the origins of the Setebos reference, and its aftermath in early criticism.

40. John Gillies, "'The open worlde': The Exotic in Shakespeare," in *New Casebooks: The Tempest*, ed. R. S. White (New York: St. Martin's Press, 1999), 191–203. Pigafetta recounted the tale of the Patagonian Indians of Tierra del Fuego.

41. See, for instance, John C. McCloskey, "Caliban, Savage Clown," *College English* 1 (1940): 354–55, or Kermode's introduction to the Arden edition of the play. William Shakespeare, *The Tempest*, ed. Frank Kermode, The Arden Shakespeare (Cambridge, Mass.: Harvard University Press, 1952), xxxvii.

42. For a full account of mutual misreadings, see Sabine MacCormack, "Demons, Imagination and the Incas," in *New World Encounters*, ed. Stephen Greenblatt (Berkeley: University of California Press, 1993), 101–26.

43. Richard Hakluyt, *Divers Voyages Touching the Discovery of America*, ed. John Winter Jones (Cambridge: Hakluyt Society, 1849), 8.

44. Sir Walter Raleigh, *Discoverie of the Large, Rich, and Bewtiful Empire of Guiana* (London, 1596), 79, 96.

45. Ibid., "Preface to the Reader," 4.

46. Caliban's status as a kind of manufactured hybrid, partially educated by Prospero and seeking more full agency through his experiments with the newcomers' sack, is perhaps best understood in light of Homi Bhabha's arguments about the unstable process of identity formation under colonization in *The Location of Culture* (New York: Routledge, 1994).

47. Qtd. in Anthony Pagden, "*Jus et factum:* Text and Experience in the Writings of Bartholomé de las Casas," in Greenblatt, *New World Encounters*, 87.

48. Raymond A. Urban, "Why Caliban Worships the Man in the Moon," *Shakespeare Quarterly* 27, no. 2 (Spring 1976): 204.

Notes to Chapter 5 / Gerhardt

1. William Shakespeare, *Coriolanus*, in *The Norton Shakespeare: Based on the Oxford Edition*, 2nd ed., ed. Stephen Greenblatt, Walter Cohen, Jean E. Howard, and Katharine Eisaman Maus (New York: Norton, 2008), 1.1.16–17; hereafter cited in the text.

2. Maurice Charney, "The Dramatic Use of Imagery in Shakespeare's *Coriolanus*," *ELH* 23, no. 3 (1956): 183–93; E. C. Pettet, "*Coriolanus* and the Midlands Insurrection of 1607," *Shakespeare Survey* 3 (1950): 34–42; Gail Kern Paster, "To Starve with Feeding: The City in *Coriolanus*," *Shakespeare Studies* 11 (1978); Annabel Patterson, "'Speak, Speak!' The Popular Voice and the Jacobean State," in *Shakespeare and the Popular Voice* (Cambridge, Mass.: Basil Blackwell, 1989), 120–53; Richard Wilson, "Reading against the Grain," *Seventeenth Century* 6, no. 2 (1991): 111–48; Nate Eastman, "The Rumbling Belly Politic: Metaphorical Location and Metaphorical Government in *Coriolanus*," *Early Modern Literary Studies: A Journal of Sixteenth- and Seventeenth-Century English Literature* 13 (2007): 39; David George, "Plutarch, Insurrection, and Dearth in *Coriolanus*," in *Shakespeare and Politics*, ed. Catherine M. S. Alexander (Cambridge: Cambridge University Press, 2004), 110–24; James Kuzner, "Unbuilding the City: 'Coriolanus' and the Birth of Republican Rome," *Shakespeare Quarterly* 58, no. 2 (2007): 174–99; Maurizio Calbi, "States of Exception: Auto-Immunity and the Body Politic in Shakespeare's *Coriolanus*," in *Questioning Bodies in Shakespeare's Rome* (Göttingen, Germany: Vandenhoeck & Ruprecht., 2010), 77–94.

3. Janet Adelman, "'Anger's My Meat': Feeding, Dependency, and Aggression in *Coriolanus*," in *Representing Shakespeare: New Psychoanalytic Essays*, ed. Murray M. Schwartz and Coppélia Kahn (Baltimore: Johns Hopkins University Press, 1980), 129–49.

4. Stanley Cavell, "*Coriolanus* and Interpretations of Politics ('Who Does the Wolf Love?')," in his *Disowning Knowledge in Six Plays of Shakespeare* (New York: Cambridge University Press, 1987), 157.

5. Ibid., 168.

6. James L. Calderwood, "*Coriolanus*: Wordless Meanings and Meaningless Words," *Studies in English Literature, 1500–1900* 6, no. 2 (1966): 211–24; Arthur Riss, "The Belly Politic: Coriolanus and the Revolt of Language," *ELH* 59, no. 1 (1992): 53–75; Zvi Jagendorf, "*Coriolanus*: Body Politic and Private Parts," *Shakespeare Quarterly* 41 (1990): 455–69; Cathy Shrank, "Civility and the City in *Coriolanus*," *Shakespeare Quarterly* 54, no. 4 (2003): 406–23.

7. Riss, "Belly Politic," 53.

8. Cavell, "Interpretations of Politics," 146.

9. Sir Philip Sidney, "The Defence of Poesy," in *Sir Philip Sidney: Selected Prose and Poetry*, 2nd. ed., ed. Robert Kimbrough (Madison: University of Wisconsin Press, 1983), 125.

10. Paster, "To Starve with Feeding," 126; also see Eastman, "Rumbling Belly Politic," para. 8, 14, 37, who understands this imagery as a reference to the "grain-distributing bureaucracy" of English cities and towns, particularly London, during the implementation of grain subsidy programs during dearth.

11. Michael Schoenfeldt, "Fables of the Belly in Early Modern England," in *The Body in Parts: Fantasies of Corporeality in Early Modern Europe*, ed. David Hillman and Carla Mazzio (New York: Routledge, 1997), 249.

12. Thomas Starkey, *A Dialogue between Pole and Lupset*, ed. T. F. Mayer (London: Royal Historical Society, 1989), 39–40. The angled brackets mark interlineated insertions into the main text.

13. On the figure of the plowman and the tradition of complaint literature associated with him through the sixteenth century, see Andrew McRae, *God Speed the Plough: The Representation of Agrarian England, 1500–1660* (New York: Cambridge University Press, 1996), 23–109.

14. Wilson, "Reading against the Grain," argues that Menenius's belly image "naturalise[s] the invisible transactions of commodity circulation" (118); compare with Shrank, "Civility and the City," who argues that the citizens' interruption of Menenius asserts their view of "mutual participation" (415); also see Eastman, "Rumbling Belly Politic," who argues that the play approaches dearth from an urban perspective.

15. Arjun Appadurai, "Introduction: Commodities and the Politics of Value," in *The Social Life of Things: Commodities in Cultural Perspective*, ed. Arjun Appadurai (New York: Cambridge University Press, 1986), argues that such myths typically are "produced by traders and speculators who are largely indifferent to both the production origins and the consumption destination of commodities, except insofar as they affect fluctuations in price" (48).

16. Paster, "To Starve with Feeding," 126; also see similar comments in George, "Plutarch, Insurrection, and Dearth," 122.

17. Paul Slack, "Dearth and Social Policy in Early Modern England," *Social History of Medicine* 5, no. 1 (1992): 6.

18. John Walter and Keith Wrightson, "Dearth and the Social Order in Early Modern England," *Past and Present* 71 (1976): 31–32.

19. Stephen Hipkin, "The Structure, Development, and Politics of the Kent Grain Trade, 1552–1647," *Economic History Review* 61, no. S1 (2008): 133; Walter and Wrightson, "Dearth and the Social Order in Early Modern England," 33; Andrew B. Appleby, *Famine in Tudor and Stuart England* (Stanford, Calif.: Stanford University Press, 1978), 144.

20. Walter and Wrightson, "Dearth and Social Order," 28–34; Slack, "Dearth and Social Policy," 9–12.

21. Staffs RO, Sutherland MSS., D593/S/4/10/3; qtd. in Slack, "Dearth and Social Policy," 6.

22. Steve Hindle, "Imagining Insurrection in Seventeenth-Century England: Representations of the Midland Rising of 1607," *History Workshop Journal* 66, no. 1 (2008): 29.

23. Hugh Plat, *Sundrie Nevv and Artificiall Remedies against Famine. Written by H. P. Esq. Vppon Thoccasion of This Present Dearth* ([London]:

Printed by P[eter] S[hort] dwelling on Breadstreet hill, at the signe of the Starre, 1596), A2r, Early English Books Online (accessed Dec. 29, 2015).

24. Ibid., A3r.

25. Ibid., A3v.

26. Adelman, "'Anger's My Meat,'" 129, notes that Shakespeare "shapes his material from the start in order to exacerbate these fears [from the Midlands rising]"; compare with Wilson, "Reading against the Grain," who argues that the mid-1590s dearth forms the background for the play; Eastman, "Rumbling Belly Politic" also focuses his attention on the mid-1590s but argues that *Coriolanus* reflects anxiety regarding the institutional hoarding necessary for grain subsidy programs.

27. For an account of Shakespeare's consultation of Livy's *Ab urbe condita* as source material, see Anne Barton, "Livy, Machiavelli, and Shakespeare's *Coriolanus*," in *Shakespeare and Politics,* ed. Catherine M. S. Alexander (Cambridge: Cambridge University Press, 2004), 68–69. Barton argues that Shakespeare relied on this text not so much for its ordering of events as for its emphasis on the active political actions of the citizens. As Barton puts it, "the attitudes and interests of *Ab Urbe Condita,* as we understand that work now, live to a striking extent in this last of his Roman plays" (77).

28. Pettet, "Midlands Insurrection of 1607"; George, "Plutarch, Insurrection, and Dearth."

29. Plutarch, *The Lives of the Noble Grecians and Romanes Compared Together by That Graue Learned Philosopher and Historiographer, Plutarke of Chaeronea; Translated out of Greeke into French by Iames Amyot,* trans. Thomas North (London: Thomas Vautroullier and John V. Vight, 1579), 243, Early English Books Online (accessed Dec. 29, 2015).

30. Ibid., 243.

31. Yet Shakespeare does adopt Plutarch's report that the tribunes spread sedition because they perceived "great scarcitie of corne to be within the cittie, and though there had bene plenty enough, yet the common people had no money to buye it" (ibid., 243). As the First Citizen argues of the patricians, "They ne'er cared for us yet: suffer us to famish, and their storehouses crammed with grain" (*Cor.,* 1.1.70–72).

32. Moreover, Plutarch notes that the first elected tribunes, Junius Brutus and Sicinius Vellutus, had "only bene the causers & procurers of this sedition" (*Lives,* 240). In *Coriolanus,* Menenius calls the First Citizen "the great toe of this assembly" (1.1.144), accusing him of seeking advancement by fomenting riot: "Thou rascal, that art worst in blood to run, / Lead'st first to win some vantage" (1.1.148–49). Yet the play remains silent on the origins of the tribunes and, in fact, displays their distinction from the group of citizens by having Sicinius and Brutus appear onstage with the citizens. Menenius is proven incorrect in his accusation of the First Citizen.

33. Adelman, "'Anger's My Meat,'" 137–38.

34. On food marking class distinctions, see Ken Albala, *Eating Right in the Renaissance* (Berkeley: University of California Press, 2002), 187–95; Joan Thirsk, *Food in Early Modern England: Phases, Fads, Fashions, 1500–1760* (London: Hambledon Continuum, 2006), 19, 37; Craig Muldrew, *Food, Energy and the Creation of Industriousness: Work and Material Culture in Agrarian England, 1550–1780* (Cambridge: Cambridge University Press, 2011), 38–39.

35. On this subject, see Peter Parolin's chapter 1 in this volume on Hal's fondness for small beer in *2 Henry IV*.

36. Wilson, "Reading against the Grain," 115, argues that Coriolanus is figured as "the type of improving landlord that was enclosing Midland counties for…convertible husbandry."

37. Cavell, "Interpretations of Politics," 155.

NOTES TO CHAPTER 6 / LEMON

1. William Shakespeare, *The Second Part of Henry the Fourth*, in *The Norton Shakespeare*, 3rd ed., ed. Stephen Greenblatt, Walter Cohen, Suzanne Gossett, Jean E. Howard, Katharine Eisaman Maus, and Gordon McMullan. (New York: Norton, 2016). All quotations from *Henry IV*, parts 1 and 2, as well as from *Henry V* and *Macbeth*, come from this edition. I use *Henry IV* to describe the two plays which are, as Laurie Shannon, *Sovereign Amity: Figures of Friendship in Shakespearean Contexts* (Chicago: University of Chicago Press, 2002), puts it, "one play in two bodies" (166).

2. Barbara Sebek, in chapter 2 of this volume, illuminates the tensions in the Anglo-Spanish wine trade in connection with Falstaff's representation.

3. Joshua B. Fisher, "Digesting Falstaff: Food and Nation in Shakespeare's *Henry IV* Plays," *Early English Studies* 2 (2009): 12–13, offers a fresh reading of Falstaff's ingestion of English foods; the banishment of Falstaff is therefore especially challenging since he is so closely linked to English national identity.

4. Falstaff is one of Shakespeare's most popular characters: "Falstaff has become a kind of god in the mythology of modern man," says Dover Wilson, *The Fortunes of Falstaff* (New York: Cambridge University Press, 1961), 128; "when we are wholly human…we become most like either Hamlet or Falstaff," according to Harold Bloom, *Shakespeare: The Invention of the Human* (New York: Penguin Books, 1998), 745.

5. In its argument on appetitive opposition, this essay contributes to those critical readings on Falstaff's threat to sovereignty. See Shannon, *Sovereign Amity*; Kristen Poole, *Radical Religion from Shakespeare to*

Milton: Figures of Nonconformity in Early Modern England (Cambridge: Cambridge University Press, 2000); David Womersley, "Why Is Falstaff Fat?," *Review of English Studies: A Quarterly Journal of English Literature and the English Language,* 47, no. 185 (1996): 1–22.

6. On Falstaff's gluttony, see Fisher, "Digesting Falstaff," who explores the relationship between culinary consumption and national anxiety; Nina Taunton, "Food, Time and Age: Falstaff's Dietaries and Tropes of Nourishment in *The Comedy of Errors,*" *Shakespeare Jahrbuch* 145 (2009): 91–105. For a medical argument about Falstaff's condition, see Henry Buchwald and Mary E. Knatterud, "Morbid Obesity: Perceptions of Character and Comorbidities in Falstaff," *Obesity Surgery* (2000): 402–08. See also Barbara Everett, "The Fatness of Falstaff: Shakespeare and Character," *Proceedings of the British Academy* 76 (1990): 109–28, who explores how Falstaff's fatness symbolically represents Shakespeare's creative richness.

7. To some, this isolation might be read as a sign of Lent. On the shift from Carnival to Lent in the Henriad, see David Ruiter, *Shakespeare's Festive History: Feasting, Festivity, Fasting and Lent in the Second Henriad* (Farnham, U.K.: Ashgate, 2003); François Laroque, *Shakespeare's "Battle of Carnival and Lent"* (New York: Macmillan, 1998), and *Shakespeare's Festive World: Elizabethan Seasonal Entertainment and the Professional Stage,* trans. Janet Lloyd (Cambridge: Cambridge University Press, 1991); Neil Rhodes, "Shakespearean Grotesque: The Falstaff Plays," in his *Elizabethan Grotesque* (New York: Routledge, 1980). Influential studies of the carnivalesque elements of Falstaff and Shakespearean drama more generally include Michael Bristol, *Carnival and Theater: Plebian Culture and the Structure of Authority in Renaissance England* (New York: Methuen, 1985); Peter Stallybrass and Allon White, *The Politics and Poetics of Transgression* (Ithaca, N.Y.: Cornell University Press, 1986). See also Charles Whitney, "Festivity and Topicality in the Coventry Scene of *I Henry IV,*" *English Literary Renaissance* 24, no. 2 (Spring 1994): 410–48. On the range of Falstaff's roles, see Arthur Kinney, "Shakespeare's Falstaff as Parody," *Connotations* 12, nos. 2–3 (2002–03): 105–25.

8. Numerous critics have argued that Falstaff must be banished because he functions as a Vice figure to be overcome for Hal to rule as king; see Robert Weimann, *Shakespeare and the Popular Tradition in the Theater,* ed. Robert Schwartz (Baltimore: Johns Hopkins University Press, 1978), 128–31.

9. While critics frequently reference Falstaff's sack speech, single studies of it are rare. See Alan D. Isler, "Falstaff's Heroic Sherris," *Shakespeare Quarterly* 22, no. 2 (Spring 1971): 186–88, and Jill L. Levenson, "Shakespeare's Falstaff: 'The Cause that Wit Is in Other Men,'" *University of Toronto Quarterly* 74, no. 2 (2005): 722–28.

10. Louise Hill Curth and Tanya M. Cassidy, "'Health, Strength, and Happiness:' Medical Constructions of Wine and Beer in Early Modern England," in *A Pleasing Sinne: Drink and Conviviality in Seventeenth-Century England*, ed. Adam Smyth (Woodbridge, Suffolk: D. S. Brewer, 2004), 143–60. On Galenic medicine and self-regulation through diet, see Ken Albala, *Eating Right in the Renaissance* (Berkeley: University of California Press, 2002); Joan Fitzpatrick, *Food in Shakespeare: Early Modern Dietaries and the Plays* (Aldershot, U.K.: Ashgate, 2007); Gail Kern Paster, *The Body Embarrassed: Drama and the Disciplines of Shame in Early Modern Europe* (Ithaca, N.Y.: Cornell University Press, 1993); Joan Thirsk, *Food in Early Modern England: Phases, Fads, Fashions, 1500–1760* (London: Hambledon Continuum, 2007).

11. Nicholas Culpepper, "Complete Herbal," in *The Essential Writings of Nicolas Culpepper* (Whitefish, Mont.: Kessinger, 2005), 149; Timothy Bright, *A treatise of melancholie Containing the causes thereof, & reasons of the strange effects it worketh in our minds and bodies: with the physicke cure, and spirituall consolation for such as haue thereto adioyned an afflicted conscience* (London, 1586), 137.

12. John Lyly, *Mother Bombie*, in *Complete Works*, vol. 3, ed. R. W. Bond (Oxford: Clarendon Press, 1902), 2.5.14, p. 52.

13. Michael C. Schoenfeldt, *Bodies and Selves in Early Modern England: Physiology and Inwardness in Spenser, Shakespeare, Herbert, and Milton* (Cambridge: Cambridge University Press, 1999); Gail Kern Paster, *Humoring the Body: Emotions and the Shakespearean Stage* (Chicago: University of Chicago Press, 2004).

14. As with any medicine that is healing in moderate doses and lethal in larger ones, the alcohol Falstaff trumpets forms and erodes communities depending upon the quantities consumed. As Joshua Scodel's *Excess and the Mean in Early Modern English Literature* (Princeton, N.J.: Princeton University Press, 2002) illuminates, a vast literature chronicles this pharmacological phenomenon.

15. Ibid.; Stella Achilleos, "The *Anacreontea* and a Tradition of Refined Male Sociability," in Smyth, *"A Pleasing Sinne,"* 21–36.

16. Michelle O'Callaghan, *The English Wits: Literature and Sociability in Early Modern England* (Cambridge: Cambridge University Press, 2007), and "Tavern Societies, the Inns of Court, and the Culture of Conviviality in Early Seventeenth-Century London," in Smyth, *"A Pleasing Sinne,"* 37–54.

17. Falstaff's call for good fellowship comes precisely at the moment his cowardice at Gadshill has been exposed.

18. On drinking culture, see Anna Bryson, *From Courtesy to Civility: Changing Codes of Conduct in Early Modern England* (Oxford: Clarendon Press, 1998); and Alexandra Shepard, *Meanings of Manhood in Early Modern England* (Oxford: Oxford University Press, 2006).

19. S. E. Sprott, "Sir Edmund Baynham," *Recusant History* 10 (1969): 96. See also Leslie Hotson, "Roaring Boys at the Mermaid," *Atlantic* 152 (1933): 73–84; Burton Milligan, "The Roaring Boy in Tudor and Stuart Literature," *Shakespeare Association Bulletin* 15, no. 3 (1940): 184–90. On "The Damned Crew," see Epigram 22 in Samuel Rowlands, *The Letting of Humors Blood in the Head-Vaine* (London 1611), 84. On Pistol as the play's primary swaggerer, see S. E. Sprott, "The Damned Crew," *PMLA* 84, no. 3 (May 1969): 492–500; and Daniel C. Boughner, "Pistol and the Roaring Boys," *Shakespeare Association Bulletin* 11 (1936): 226–37. Yet Falstaff, too, resonates with these mischief makers, Baynham being described (as one might say of Falstaff) a "very fantastical sponge...that fed upon young landlords, riotous sons and heirs"; cited in Daniel C. Boughner, "*The Drinking Academy* and Contemporary London," *Neophilologus* 19, no. 4 (1934): 274. Further, in the subculture of roisterers and gallants, temperance was depicted as tedious and weak. The play "The Drinking Academy" presents a crew of second sons, all receiving training at this "academy." Here inexperienced men learn to drink and dice. These young profligates, Broughner argues, are only too eager to spend their patrimonies on riotous living. Therefore, "heavy drinking, although formerly despised, was...honorable and even necessary to the gallant" ("Pistol," 278). Thus, excess was built into certain formulations of the honor code.

20. Of course, Falstaff's threat as a roaring boy is humorous, given his incapacity. He is more *miles gloriosus* than threatening man-at-arms. Roman New Comedy's braggart soldier combines with the Elizabethan era's roaring boy to form this lampooned warrior. As Wilson writes in *The Fortunes of Falstaff*, "he is the Old Soldier on the make, or in a state of perpetual repair, and Shakespeare exhibits him busy upon a number of disreputable devices for raising money, which were attributed, in whispers, or even at times in printed books, to old soldiers in Elizabeth's reign" (cited in Kinney, "Shakespeare's Falstaff as Parody," 111). Falstaff is, however, compromised as a roaring boy because his body, as Valerie Traub argues, appears feminine and maternal; Valerie Traub, *Desire and Anxiety: Circulations of Sexuality in Shakespearean Drama* (New York: Routledge, 1992), 56–59.

21. B. Ann Tlusty, "The Public House and Military Culture in Early Modern Germany," in *The World of the Tavern*, ed. Beat Kümin and B. Ann Tlusty (Aldershot, U.K.: Ashgate, 2002), 150, and *Bacchus and Civic Order: The Culture of Drink in Early Modern Germany* (Charlottesville: University of Virginia Press, 2001).

22. Bernard Capp, review of *Meanings of Manhood in Early Modern England*, in *Reviews in History*, review no. 380, http://www.history.ac.uk/reviews/review/380 (accessed Mar. 26, 2012). See also A. Lynn Martin, *Alcohol, Sex, and Gender in Late Medieval and Early Modern Europe* (London: Palgrave Macmillan, 2001); and Alexandra Shepard, *Meanings*

of Manhood in Early Modern England (Oxford: Oxford University Press, 2002).

23. Gina Bloom, "Manly Drunkenness: Binge Drinking as Disciplined Play," in *Masculinity and the Metropolis of Vice, 1550–1650*, ed. Amanda Bailey and Roze Hentschell (New York: Palgrave Macmillan, 2010), 23.

24. Rebecca Lemon, "Compulsory Conviviality in Early Modern England," *English Literary Renaissance* 43, no. 3 (Sept. 2013): 381–414; Adam Smyth, "'It were far better to be a *Toad* or a *Serpant*, then a Drunkard': Writing about Drunkenness," in Smyth, *A Pleasing Sinne*, 193–210.

25. *William Hazlitt*, ed. Alexander Ireland (London: Frederick Warne, 1889), 82.

26. Harold Clarke Goddard, *The Meaning of Shakespeare*, vol. 1 (Chicago: University of Chicago Press, 1960), 185.

27. Albert Harris Tolman, *Falstaff and Other Shakespearean Topics* (Whitefish, Mont.: Kessinger, 2005), 11.

28. Ian Frederick Moulton, "Fat Knight, or What You Will: Inimitable Falstaff," in *A Companion to Shakespeare's Works*, ed. Richard Dutton and Jean Howard (Oxford: Blackwell, 2003), 229. Moulton addresses Falstaff's sexuality, and his impotency more specifically.

29. Hugh Grady, *Shakespeare, Machiavelli, and Montaigne: Power and Subjectivity from Richard II to Hamlet* (Oxford: Oxford University Press, 2002), asks an inverted version of this question: "Any attentive reader or viewer of *1 Henry IV* can work up a long list of ethically dubious actions by Falstaff.... How, then, does he come away with readers' and views' good feelings?" (153).

30. Anonymous, *A Looking Glasse for Drunkards; or, The Hunting of Drunkennesse* (London: [By M. Flesher] for F. C[oules], 1627), A4r.

31. This Maynwaring text appears in J. H., *Two Broad-sides against Tobacco* (London: Printed for John Hancock, 1672), 21–22, 24, 26. See original Everard Maynwaring, *A Treatise of the Scurvy* (London: Printed by R. D. for T. Basset under S. Dunstans Church in Fleetstreet, 1665).

32. William Fulbecke, *A Booke of Christian Ethicks or Moral Philosophie* (London: Richard Jones, 1587), 23.

33. In his encomium, Falstaff argues that sack causes "inflammation," fighting the weakness and weariness attendant on a malady like melancholy. His use of the term "inflammation" is innovative — Shakespeare's play is one of the first texts to deploy it to describe a mental state, such as a passion, or an excited condition. Richard Hooker enlists the term in the same year, in his *Lawes of Ecclesiastical Polity*, to signal the ardor of keen devotion. Even as Shakespeare and Hooker might use the term innovatively to signal ardor or excitement, inflammation more generally signals a pathological condition in medical literature: "a morbid process affecting some organ or part of the body, characterized by excessive heat, swelling,

pain, and redness." Precisely at the moment he defends sack, then, Falstaff deploys a term that also evokes drinking's deleterious effects. See *OED Online*, 2nd ed., s.v. "inflammation," def. 3, http://www.oed.com .libproxy.usc.edu/view/Entry/95466 (accessed May 31, 2012).

34. Samuel Ward, *Woe to Drunkards* (London: A. Math for John Marriott, 1622), 2, 3, 10.

35. As Derek Peat's analysis in "Falstaff Gets the Sack," *Shakespeare Quarterly* (Fall 2002): 379–85, reveals, the scene might be played for laughs, as in a production at the University of Sidney where Falstaff caught the bottle Hal threw at him, and drank out of it.

36. See Philip Stubbes, *The Anatomie of Abuses* (London: Richard Jones, 1583): "The Drunkard in his drunkenness killeth his freend, revileth his lover, discloseth secrets and regardeth no man:... so that I will not feare to call drunkerds beasts, and no men, and much wurse then beasts, for beasts never exceed in such kind of excesse, or superfluitie" (ivr–v).

37. "Classical Latin *addīctus* assigned by decree, made over, bound, devoted, past participle of *addīcere* to assign, to make over by sale or auction, to award, to appoint, to ascribe, to hand over, surrender, to enslave, to devote, to sentence, condemn, from ad-dicere, to say, speak. *OED Online*, 3rd ed., s.v. "addict," v., November 2010; online version June 2012. http://www.oed.com.libproxy.usc.edu/view/Entry/2176 (accessed June 28, 2012). An entry for this word was first included in *New English Dictionary*, 1884.

38. Thomas Cooper, *Thesaurus linguae Romanae & Britannicae*, 4th ed. (London, 1584); John Florio, *A Worlde of Wordes; or, Most copious, and exact Dictionarie in Italian and English* (London, 1598). Cooper also deploys "addict" more festively, in the definition for *Geniales dies luuen*, which he lists as "a day addict to iocunduesse and pleasure." Cited in the database *Lexicons of Early Modern English* (http://leme.library .utoronto.ca).

39. John Downame, *Foure Treatises tending to diswade all Christians from Foure no lesse hainous than Common Sinnes, namely the abuses of swearing, drunkenesse, whoredome, and briberie* (London, 1609), 79. For another argument against habitual, daily drunkenness, offered the same year as Downame's, see Thomas Thompson, *A Diet for a Drunkard* (London: Richard Backworth, 1612), 10. See also Junius Florilegus, *The Odious, Despicable, and Dreadfull Condition of a Drunkard* (London: R. Cotes, 1649), 6.

40. John Milton, *Paradise Lost* 4.392–94: "So spake the Fiend, and with necessity / The Tyrant's plea, excus'd his devilish deeds."

41. R. Junius [Richard Young of Roxwell in Essex], *The Drunkard's Character; or, A True Drunkard with such sinnes as raigne in him* (London, 1638), 233–34.

42. Florilegus, *Condition of a Drunkard*, 6.

43. Ward, *Woe to Drunkards*, 10.

44. E. G., Gent and Practicioner in Physicke, *The Trial of Tabacco* (London: H. L. for Mathew Lownes, 1610), 16v–17r.

45. Downame, *Foure Treatises*, 93.

46. The Galenic formula, for example, was invoked by medical pioneer Thomas Trotter in the first official study of addiction in 1800. Thomas Trotter, *An essay, medical, philosophical, and chemical, on drunkenness, and its effects on the human body*, 4th ed. (London: Longman, Hurst, Kees, and Orme, 1810).

47. Florilegus, *Condition of a Drunkard*, 6. Downame, *Foure Treatises*, 93.

48. Thompson, *Diet for a Drunkard*, 14.

49. Everett, "Fatness of Falstaff," 127.

50. Falstaff does, however, hope to dine at one point in the play, when he asks, "Master Gower, shall I entreat you with me to dinner?" (*2H4*, 2.1.159–60), "Will you sup with me, Master Gower?" (165). Unable to recruit this dinner companion, and indeed ridiculed by the lord chief justice for his request, Falstaff appears more and more isolated, his habitual drinking leading to solitary necessity.

51. Indeed, Shakespeare's play demands, as Richard Strier argues, Falstaff's rejection: "It is impossible not to know that [Hal] is doing the right thing in rejecting Falstaff." Shakespeare "was pre-committed to the rejection of the comic character" of Falstaff. Richard Strier, "Shakespeare against Morality," in *Reading Renaissance Ethics*, ed. Marshall Grossman (New York: Routledge, 2007), 211.

52. Joseph R. Roach, *The Player's Passion: Studies in the Science of Acting* (Newark: University of Delaware Press, 1985), 42.

53. Thomas Heywood quoted in ibid., 41–42; with thanks to Barbara Mello for drawing my attention to this point.

54. Strier, "Shakespeare against Morality," 212.

Notes to Chapter 7 / Lanier

1. The latter (but not the former) detail is included in the redaction of Plutarch in the twenty-eighth novel of William Painter's *Palace of Pleasure* (1566), entitled "Of the straunge and beastlie nature of Timon of Athens."

2. Robert S. Miola, "Timon in Shakespeare's Athens," *Shakespeare Quarterly* 31, no. 1 (Spring 1980): 30.

3. James Bulman, "The Date and Production of *Timon* Reconsidered," *Shakespeare Survey* 26 (1974): 111–27. Bulman dates *Timon* to 1601–02.

4. The term "banqueting ideology" is taken from Dennis E. Smith, *From Symposium to Eucharist: The Banquet in the Early Christian World* (Minneapolis: Fortress Press, 2003), 1–12. The issue of food and eating

imagery, often linked to the trope of cannibalism, has been widely addressed in criticism on *Timon of Athens*. See, for example, Ruth Morse, "Unfit for Human Consumption: Shakespeare's Unnatural Food," *Shakespeare Jahrbuch—West* 119 (1983): 125–49; Daniel W. Ross, "'What a Number of Men Eats Timon': Consumption in *Timon of Athens*," *Iowa State Journal of Research* 59, no. 3 (1985): 273–84; Michael Chorost, "Biological Finance in Shakespeare's *Timon of Athens*," *English Literary Renaissance* 21 (1991): 349–70; and Jody Greene, "'You Must Eat Men': The Sodomitical Economy of Renaissance Patronage," *GLQ: A Journal of Lesbian and Gay Studies* 1 (1994): 163–97. With the exception of Morse, the tendency among these scholars has been to see eating in the play as a metaphor for something else (for finance, consumption, homosocial relations, or the like), rather than addressing feasting itself as a social practice.

5. See Coppélia Kahn, "'Magic of Bounty': *Timon of Athens*, Jacobean Patronage, and Maternal Power," *Shakespeare Quarterly* 38, no. 1 (Spring 1987): 34–57; David Bevington and David L. Smith, "James I and *Timon of Athens*," *Comparative Drama* 33, no. 1 (Spring 1999): 56–87; and Andrew Hadfield, "*Timon of Athens* and Jacobean Politics," *Shakespeare Survey* 56 (2003): 215–26. A full discussion of the relationship between banqueting and gift-giving may be found in Patricia Fumerton's "Consuming the Void: Jacobean Banquets and Masques," in her *Cultural Aesthetics: Renaissance Literature and the Practice of Social Ornament* (Chicago: University of Chicago Press, 1991).

6. Thomas More, *Utopia*, trans. Ralph Robinson (1566), in *Three Early Modern Utopias: "Utopia," "New Atlantis," and "The Isle of Pines,"* ed. Susan Bruce (Oxford: Oxford University Press, 1999), 144–45. All quotations from More's *Utopia* are taken from this edition and are noted parenthetically in the text. The role of the syphogrant corresponds roughly to the traditional role of the symposiarch, the temporary ruler of the *symposium* who regulated the evening's alcohol intake and dictated the tone of the gathering. More's description of this feast also maintains a gender hierarchy, with nurses and children (and the domestic realm they stand for) segregated in a separate dining room specially fitted for them. More mentions women in the dining room only in terms of the wives of the syphogrant and priest, who are allowed to sit with their husbands at high table. This arrangement not only indicates that More's gendered imagining of dining arrangements has its source in monastic practices—indeed, a label in this section comments that "today scarcely the monks observe this custom" (*id hodie uix monachi obseruant* [144–45])—and so retains some of monastic antifeminism, but also how from More's perspective the intellectual purpose of banqueting demands its separation from the material realities of domestic production.

7. For a full discussion of the humanist ideal of the banquet, see Michel Jeanneret, *A Feast of Words: Banquets and Table Talk in the Renaissance,*

trans. Jeremy Whiteley and Emma Hughes (Chicago: University of Chicago Press, 1991).

8. In his discussion of Greek banqueting practices in *Food and Society in Classical Antiquity* (Cambridge: Cambridge University Press, 1999), 129–30, Peter Garnsey notes that though the *symposium* originally indicated a bout of drinking after eating was completed, increasingly the *symposium* invaded the dinner proper so that the two could not always be distinguished. This "bleed" between meal and after-meal is also reflected in the ambiguity surrounding the word "banquet," which originally indicated an after-meal of sweets and drink. See Julia Lupton's essay, chapter 10 in this volume, for more on banqueting and its role in the meal's architecture. The standard account of the classical *sympotic* tradition remains Josef Martin, *Symposion, die Geschichte einer literarischen Form* (Paderborn: Ferdinand Schöningh Verlag, 1931); Fiona Hobden's *The Symposion in Ancient Greek Society and Thought* (Cambridge: Cambridge University Press, 2013), takes a more anthropological approach. See also *Sympotica: A Symposium on the Symposion*, ed. Oswyn Murray (Oxford: Oxford University Press, 1990); *Dining in a Classical Context*, ed. William Slater (Ann Arbor: University of Michigan Press, 1991); Garnsey, "You Are with Whom You Eat," in *Food and Society*, 128–39; and Smith, *From Symposium to Eucharist*, 13–65.

9. In a letter to Paetus (*Epistolae ad familiares*, 9.24), Cicero ventures a noteworthy distinction between Greek *symposia* and Latin *convivia*, suggesting that *symposium* means "drinking together" or "dining together" ("compotationes aut concenationes"), whereas the Latin word *convivia* means "living together," suggesting a more profound form of social bond.

10. The link between the convivial and the eucharistic is made abundantly clear in the practice of placing paintings of the Last Supper in refectories (as in, to take the most famous example, Leonardo da Vinci's *Last Supper* in the refectory of the convent of Santa Maria della Grazie, Milan), so that those sharing a meal in the space might be encouraged to contemplate the divine model for their own communal dining.

11. This is not to say that humanist disillusionment about banqueting escalated in some smooth fashion throughout the sixteenth century. Henry VIII and James I were very visibly invested in lavish court entertainments as instruments of their rule and so tended to be especially troublesome for humanist idealists. Edward VI and Elizabeth I, by contrast, were far more restrained. Elizabeth's signature court entertainment was the progress, not the court masque, though such progresses did involve feasting. At court, Elizabeth often preferred to dine modestly with only a few attendants. A German visitor notes that there was much ceremony surrounding the announcement of the queen's meal—fanfares, ceremonial tasting for poison—but the meal itself was private. Alison Sim, *Food and Feast in Tudor England* (Stroud, U.K.: Sutton Publishing, 1997), 111–12.

Nonetheless, in many ways Elizabeth's relative restraint, both in dining and in patronage, led to greater pressure for feasts and favor being placed on the aristocratic class, particularly on courtiers. Though different monarchial styles of court entertainment prompted different forms and intensities of humanist response, the overarching trend throughout the sixteenth century was of increasing disillusionment regarding the convivial ideal, particularly as it was manifested at court and in aristocratic circles.

12. Bruce Thomas Boehrer, *The Fury of Men's Gullets: Ben Jonson and the Digestive Canal* (Philadelphia: University of Pennsylvania Press, 1997), 47–54, notes that the tension between commensality and clientage is part of banqueting discourse from at least as far back as Martial, a tension that informs Jonson's discussion of the private banquet.

13. Kahn, "'Magic of Bounty,'" 34–57.

14. For evidence of the interplay between culinary and political developments in the Jacobean masque, see Fumerton, "Consuming the Void," 111–67.

15. William J. Bouwsma, *The Waning of the Renaissance, 1550–1640* (New Haven, Conn.: Yale University Press, 2000), esp. 112–28.

16. This anticonvivial tradition, in which banquets were portrayed as occasions for sensual indulgence or political intrigue, is exemplified by dining scenes in Homer's *Odyssey*, Seneca's *Thyestes*, Petronius's *Satyricon*, and, most importantly, Ovid's *Metamorphoses*. These provided the counterpoint to humanist ideals, and it was this tradition that proved more attractive to English playwrights, particularly in the early seventeenth century. Noteworthy too is Garnsey's observation that though the convivial ideal was still often articulated in Latin literature, the reality was that such meals were far more typically occasions for creating or consolidating political alliances—that is, an extension of, rather than freedom from, the realm of *negotium* (*Food and Society*, 138–39).

17. The authorship and date of *The Bloody Banquet* remain a matter of debate; the title page lists only "T. D." as the author, and the 1639 quarto text is that of a play clearly written much earlier. Scholars generally agree that the play dates from some time in the first decade of the seventeenth century, and that the likeliest authorship is a collaboration between Middleton and Dekker. For more on the controversy, see Julia Gasper's discussion of the play in her introduction to the edition of *The Bloody Banquet* in *Thomas Middleton and Early Modern Textual Culture*, ed. Gary Taylor and John Lavagnino (Oxford: Oxford University Press, 2007), 364–68.

18. Thomas Middleton, *A Chaste Maid in Cheapside*, in *Thomas Middleton: The Collected Works*, ed. Gary Taylor and John Lavagnino (Cambridge: Cambridge University Press, 2007), 957.

19. The phrase appears with this meaning in Shakespeare's *Henry VIII, or All Is True*, 1.4.61.

20. Though *Timon of Athens* is certainly a collaboration between Shakespeare and Middleton, I will be contextualizing the play within the Shakespeare canon. I do not have space to address in detail the nature of Shakespeare and Middleton's collaboration, which is covered in John Jowett's Oxford edition of the play (Oxford: Oxford University Press, 2004), 120–53, and Anthony Dawson and Gretchen Minton's Arden edition (London: Cengage, 2009), 4–10 and 401–07. All citations from *Timon of Athens* are taken from Jowett's Oxford edition and are cited by scene and line number. The reader is reminded that Jowett's edition is divided into scenes, not acts and scenes.

21. In his Oxford edition of *Timon of Athens*, Jowett assigns the two banquet scenes firmly to Middleton, and Timon's scenes of exile almost exclusively to Shakespeare. As do many other critics, Jowett emphasizes the disjunction in the crucial first two scenes in how they initially present Timon. The Timon of the first scene, Jowett observes, is "quietly benevolent" and "consistent with noble liberality," whereas the Timon of the second scene (the banquet scene) is "a prodigal who parts with wealth needlessly," the object of satire in the spirit of the "new bitter comedy" (151). In the Arden edition, Dawson and Minton substantially agree with Jowett on the authorial assignment of the first two scenes, but they differ with him on the assignment of the mock banquet scene, which, they assert, is "certainly Shakespeare's" (406). I tend to concur with Dawson and Minton's assignment of the mock banquet scene to Shakespeare.

22. For an overview of Cynicism as a philosophy, see I. G. Kidd, "Cynicism," in *The Concise Encyclopedia of Western Philosophy*, ed. Jonathan Rée and J. O. Urmson (London: Routledge, 2005).

23. See, for example, Fumerton, "Consuming the Void," 162–67, who links potlatch, cannibalistic consumerism, and the political ideology of Jacobean feasting.

24. On early modern vegetarianism, see Michel Jeanneret, "'Ma salade et ma muse': On Renaissance Vegetarianism," in *At the Table: Metaphorical and Material Cultures of Food in Medieval and Early Modern Europe*, ed. Timothy J. Tomasik and Jilann M. Vitullo (Turnhout, Belgium: Brepols, 2007), 211–20; and Tristram Stuart, *The Bloodless Revolution* (New York: Norton, 2007). Stuart notes the Cynical tradition among the biblical and classic philosophical contexts for Renaissance vegetarianism.

25. According to the *OED*, the word "meat" was in transition during the early modern period, moving from a general word for "food" (as opposed to "drink") or a meal to the more specialized meanings of "flesh used as food" or "animals raised or killed for food." Though the former meaning is dominant in *Timon of Athens*, the latter is also often in play, particularly in the context of Apemantus's (and, later, Timon's) preference for roots. *Oxford English Dictionary*, 3rd ed. (Nov. 2010), s.v. "meat," http://www.oed.com.libproxy.usc.edu/view/Entry/2176 (accessed June 28, 2012).

26. This formulation is indebted to Daniel W. Ross's discussion of "consumption" in the play in all its forms in "'What a number of men eats Timon': Consumption in *Timon of Athens*," *Iowa State Journal of Research* 59, no. 3 (1985): 273–84.

27. The First Stranger uses the same allusion in condemning Ventidius's ingratitude toward Timon: "Who can call him his friend / That dips in the same dish?" (*Tim.*, 6.62–63). So, too, does the stranger pointedly conflate the consumption of Timon's largesse with that of Timon himself: "For mine own part, I never tasted Timon in my life" (6.73–74).

28. Seneca, *Epistulae morales ad Lucilium*, letter 47; Cicero, *Pro Rege Deiotaro*; and the life of Vitellius in Suetonius, *De vita Caesarum*, chap. 13. The image cluster of food, poison, and purging is developed later by Flaminius, expressing his rage at Lucullus's crabbed response to Timon's request for help:

> This slave
> Unto this hour has my lord's meat in him.
> Why should it thrive and turn to nutriment,
> When he is turned to poison?
> O, may diseases only work upon't;
> And when he's sick to death, let not that part of nature
> Which my lord paid for be of any power
> To expel sickness, but prolong his hour.   (*Tim.*, 5.55–62)

This is one of several false hints that the second banquet scene might involve poison and revenge.

29. Marc Shell's discussion of *The Merchant of Venice* in *The Economy of Literature* (Baltimore: Johns Hopkins University Press, 1978), 111, notes that in early modern English drama heartless capitalism was often metaphorically linked to cannibalism. See also the rich discussion in Jerry Phillips, "Cannibalism qua Capitalism: The Metaphorics of Accumulation in Marx, Conrad, Shakespeare, and Marlowe," in *Cannibalism and the Colonial World*, ed. Francis Barker, Peter Hulme, and Margaret Iversen (Cambridge: Cambridge University Press, 1998), 183–203.

30. For "typhos," see Luis E. Navia, *Classical Cynicism: A Critical Study* (Westport, Conn.: Greenwood Press, 1996), 115, 130–32; and William Desmond, *Cynics* (Stocksfield: Acumen, 2008). Shakespeare and Middleton might have encountered the metaphor of "smoke" in Horace or Lucian.

31. The origin of *asperges* is ultimately the Jewish ritual of cleansing before offering a sacrifice, a detail that links "sprinkling" both to baptism and the Passover meal.

32. If not a kind of wild root regarded as inedible by most men, the likely candidates are radish, carrot, turnip, parsnip, beet, or navews. The

potato, widely regarded as an aphrodisiac, was introduced to Britain only in the 1590s.

33. See Joan Thirsk, *Food in Early Modern England: Phases, Fads, Fashions, 1500–1700* (London: Hambledon Continuum, 2007), 40–41. This connotation, however, is not as monolithic as it might seem. Beets were not unknown as banquet fare because they were available in various colors and could be cut easily into intricate shapes even after they were cooked.

34. The discussion in this paragraph is deeply indebted to Malcolm Thick, "Root Crops and the Feeding of London's Poor in the Late Sixteenth and Early Seventeenth Centuries," in *English Rural Society, 1500–1800*, ed. John Chartres and David Hey (Cambridge: Cambridge University Press, 1990), 279–90. See also Thirsk, *Food in Early Modern England*, 34–41.

35. See, for example, Thomas Elyot's short discussion of root vegetables in book 2, chapter 9, of his much reprinted *The Castell of Helth* (first published 1536). Elyot grudgingly concedes that some roots—turnips, parsnips, and carrots—can be nourishing if cooked for a long time or eaten in small amounts, but he focuses primarily on their ill effects, especially on one's "winds."

36. Richard Gardiner, *Profitable Instructions for the Manuring, Sowing and Planting of Kitchin Gardens* (London: Printed by Edward Allde for Edward White, 1603). Thick ("Root Crops") cites this manual.

37. William Harrison *The Description of England* (1587), ed. George Edelen (Washington, D.C.: Folger Shakespeare Library, 1968; repr., New York: Dover Publications, 1994), 265. Harrison's list of garden vegetables is dominated by root varieties—"melons, pompions, gourds, cucumbers, radishes, skirrets, parsnips, carrots, cabbages, navews, turnips, and all kinds of salad herbs" (265).

38. In Lucian's *Timon, or the Misanthrope*, an indifferent Jove loses track of Timon after he spends up his fortune and descends into poverty. When Timon calls upon aid from the gods, Jove rather arbitrarily sends him gold in the form of the character Riches. (In Lucian's version, Timon has become a poor servant-farmer, not an exile, and through that occupation he is repeatedly associated with digging.) The absence of any clear metaphysical realm in *Timon of Athens* makes Timon's discovery of gold all the more perverse, an utterly capricious twist of fate. Jove explicitly leaves the issue of punishing the ingratitude of Timon's so-called friends to another time.

NOTES TO CHAPTER 8 / DÖRING

1. Thomas Nashe, *The Works of Thomas Nashe*, ed. Ronald B. McKerrow and F. P. Wilson (Oxford: Basil Blackwell, 1958), 145.

2. Ibid., 208, 209, 210.

3. Robert Appelbaum, *Aguecheek's Beef, Belch's Hiccup, and Other Gastronomic Interjections: Literature, Culture, and Food among the Early Moderns* (Chicago: University of Chicago Press, 2006), 201–18, 211.

4. All citations to Shakespeare's plays are from *The Norton Shakespeare*, ed. Stephen Greenblatt et al. (New York: Norton, 2015), hereafter cited in the text.

5. Alan Davidson, *The Oxford Companion of Food* (Oxford: Oxford University Press, 1999), 379.

6. Ibid., 308.

7. *The good Huswifes Handmaide for the Kitchin* (London: Richard Jones, 1594), 36a, f28r, digital text and notes by Sam Wallace, http://www.uni-giessen.de/gloning/ghhk (accessed Sept. 1, 2012); Thomas Dawson, *The good huswifes Iewell* (London: Edward White, 1596), 28.

8. Claude Lévi-Strauss, "The Culinary Triangle" (1966), trans. Peter Brook, in *Food and Culture: A Reader*, ed. Carole Counihan and Penny van Esterik (London: Routledge, 1997), 29.

9. Christopher Marlowe, *Doctor Faustus*, ed. David Scott Kastan, Norton Critical Edition (New York: Norton, 2005), B-text, 3.2, 91.

10. David Cressy and Lori Anne Ferrell, eds., *Religion and Society in Early Modern England: A Sourcebook* (London: Routledge, 1996), 65.

11. John Willis, *Mnemonica; or, The Art of Memory* (London, 1661), 52; originally published in Latin in 1618. Frances Yates, *The Art of Memory* (London: Routledge and Kegan Paul, 1966), 336–38.

12. Appelbaum, *Aguecheek's Beef*, 212.

13. Francis Meres, *Palladis Tamia* (London, 1598), fol. 286ᵛ; see William Shakespeare, *Twelfth Night*, ed. Keir Elam, The Arden Shakespeare, 3rd ser. (London: Cengage, 2008), 192.

14. Marlowe, *Doctor Faustus*, 32.

15. Andrew Dalby and Maureen Dalby, *The Shakespeare Cookbook* (London: British Museum Press, 2012); Joan Fitzpatrick, "Apricots, Butter and Capons: An Early Modern Lexicon of Food," *Shakespeare-Jahrbuch* 145 (2009): 74–90.

16. Alison Sim, *Pleasures and Pastimes of Tudor England* (Stroud, U.K.: Sutton, 1999), 86.

17. Roger Warren and Stanley Wells, eds., *Twelfth Night*, The Oxford Shakespeare (Oxford: Clarendon, 1994), 123.

18. Thomas Middleton, *The Collected Works*, ed. Gary Taylor and John Lavagnimo (Oxford: Clarendon, 2007), 1165.

19. Chris Meads, *Banquets Set Forth: Banqueting in English Renaissance Drama* (Manchester: Manchester University Press, 2001), and chapter 7 in this volume.

20. Ben Jonson, *The Complete Masques*, ed. Stephen Orgel (New Haven, Conn.: Yale University Press, 1969), 411.

21. Only the head and master cooks of royal households enjoyed prominence and social status; see Kate Colquhoun, *Taste: The Story of Britain through Its Cooking* (London: Bloomsbury, 2007), 47–48, 89.

22. Plato, *Gorgias*, trans. W. R. M. Lamb, Loeb Classical Library (Cambridge, Mass.: Harvard University Press, 1967), 464.

23. Michel Jeanneret, *A Feast of Words: Banquets and Table Talk in the Renaissance*, trans. Jeremy Whitley and Emma Hughes (Chicago: University of Chicago Press, 1991), 81.

24. Drinking and gluttony rank high on Stubbes's list of abuses, all prompted by the playhouse:

> if you will learne falsehood, if you will learn cozenage: if you will learn to deciue: if you will learn to play the Hippocrit: to cogge, lye and falsifie: if you will learn to iest, laugh and fleer, to grin, to nod, and mow, if you will learn to play the vice, to swear, teare, and blaspheme, both Heauen and Earth: If you will learn to become a bawde, vncleane, and to deuerginat Mayds, to deflour honst Wyues: if you will learn to rebel against Princes, to commit treasons, to consume treasurs, to practise ydlenes, to sing and talke of bawdie loue and venery: if you will lerne to deride, scoffe, mock and flowt, to falter and smooth: If you will learn to play the whore-maister, the glutton, Drunkard, or incestuous person: if you learn to become proude, hawtie and arrogant: and finally, if you will learne to contemne GOD and al his laws.

Phillip Stubbes, *The Anatomie of Abuses* (London: Richard Iones, 1583; facs. repr., Amsterdam: Da Capo Press, 1972), n.p.

25. See Helmut Castrop, "Die elisabethanischen Theater," in *Shakespeare-Handbuch*, ed. Ina Schabert (Stuttgart: Kröner, 2000), 80.

26. Elizabeth Freund, "*Twelfth Night* and the Tyranny of Interpretation," *English Literary History* 53 (1986): 476.

27. Michael Bristol, *Carnival and Theatre: Plebeian Culture and the Structure of Authority in Renaissance England* (London: Routledge, 1989).

28. Mikhail M. Bakhtin, *Rabelais and His World*, trans. Hélène Iswolsky (Bloomington: Indiana University Press, 1984), 316.

29. For instance, Stephen Greenblatt, *Hamlet in Purgatory* (Princeton, N.J.: Princeton University Press, 2001), or François Laroque, *Shakespeare's Festive World: Elizabethan Seasonal Entertainment and the Professional Stage*, trans. Janet Lloyd (Cambridge: Cambridge University Press, 1991).

30. Ibid., 81.

31. Paul Dean, "'Nothing that is so is so': *Twelfth Night* and Transubstantiation," *Literature and Theology* 17, (2003): 281–97.

32. Ken Albala, *Eating Right in the Renaissance* (Berkeley: University of California Press, 2002), 230.

33. I would like to thank Gilly Lehmann for great help in clarifying this important point.

34. Peter Clark, *The English Alehouse: A Social History, 1200–1830* (London: Longman, 1983), 32.

35. Mary Anne Caton, ed., *Fooles and Fricassees: Food in Shakespeare's England* (Seattle: University of Washington Press, 1999), 49.

36. Hans-Dieter Metzger, "'Küchlein und Bier': Shakespeare und der englische Kirchweihstreit im ausgehenden 16. und frühen 17. Jahrhundert," *Historische Anthropologie* 4, no. 1 (1996): 34–56.

37. Colquhoun, *Taste*, 92.

38. Sheila Sweetinburgh, "Remembering the Dead at Dinner-Time," in *Everyday Objects: Medieval and Early Modern Material Culture and Its Meanings*, ed. Tara Hamling and Catherine Richardson (Farnham, U.K.: Ashgate, 2010), 263.

39. Greenblatt, *Hamlet in Purgatory*, 240.

40. Thomas Becon, *The Sicke Mans Salue* (1560; repr., London: John Daye, 1582), 114.

41. Elam, *Twelfth Night*, 319.

42. Tobias Döring, *Performances of Mourning in Shakespearean Theatre and Early Modern Culture* (London: Palgrave, 2006).

43. Sibylle Krämer, "Das Vergessen nicht vergessen! Oder: ist das Vergessen ein defizienter Modus von Erinnerung?" *Paragrana* 9, no. 2 (2000): 251–75.

44. Umberto Eco, "An Ars Oblivionalis? Forget It!," *PMLA* 103 (1988): 254–61.

45. Willis, *Mnemonica*, 30–31.

46. Niccolò Machiavelli, *Discorsi: Gedanken über Politik und Staatsführung*, übers Rudolf Zorn (Stuttgart: Kröner, 1977), 183.

47. Willis, *Mnemonica*, 138, 139, 140.

48. Garret A. Sullivan Jr., *Memory and Forgetting in English Renaissance Drama: Shakespeare, Marlowe, Webster* (Oxford: Oxford University Press), 30.

49. Willem Schrickx, "'Pickleherring' and English Actors in Germany," *Shakespeare Survey* 36 (1983): 135–47.

50. Ralf Haekel, *Die englischen Komödianten in Deutschland: Eine Einführung in die Ursprünge des deutschen Berufsschauspiels* (Heidelberg: Winter, 2004), 236; Manfred Pfister, *A History of English Laughter: Laughter from Beowulf to Beckett and Beyond* (Amsterdam: Rodopi, 2002).

51. *Good Huswifes Handmaide*, A2a. Brawn is meat from the head of pig, cooked and pressed into a block.

52. Richard Wilson, *Secret Shakespeare: Studies in Theater, Religion and Resistance* (Manchester: Manchester University Press, 2004), 279.

53. Sullivan, *Memory and Forgetting*, 20; Isabel Karremann, "'Drinking the wyne of forgetfulnesse': The Ambivalent Blessings of Oblivion and the Early Modern Stage," *Wissenschaftliches Seminar Online* 6 (2008), www.shakespeare-gesellschaft.de/publikationen/seminar/ausgabe 2008/ Karremann.html (accessed Sept. 1, 2012).

54. For discussions of Falstaff and his cultural functions, see the various other contributions in this volume, especially chapter 6.

55. *Il piacevole viaggio di Cuccagna*, see Piero Camporesi, *Land of Hunger*, trans. Tania Croft-Murray, Claire Foley, and Shayne Mitchell (Cambridge: Polity Press, 1996), 160–63.

Notes to Chapter 9 / Yates

1. Donna Haraway, *When Species Meet* (Minneapolis: University of Minnesota Press, 2008), 17. See also Donna Haraway, *The Companion Species Manifesto: Dogs, People, and Significant Otherness* (Chicago: Prickly Paradigm Press, 2003), and "A Cyborg Manifesto: Science, Technology, and Socialist-Feminism in the Late Twentieth Century," in her *Simians, Cyborgs and Women: The Reinvention of Nature* (New York: Routledge, 1991), 149–82.

2. On the naming of domestic animals in early modern England, see Keith Thomas, *Man and the Natural World: Changing Attitudes in England, 1500–1800* (London: Penguin Books, 1983), 113–15.

3. On "culinary desolation," see Eugene Thacker, "Spiritual Meat: Resurrection and Religious Horror in Bataille," *Collapse* 7 (2011): 437–97.

4. I derive the figure of a "general ecology" from Bataille's "general economy"; see Georges Bataille, *The Accursed Share*, vol. 1, *Consumption*, trans. Robert Hurley (New York: Zone Books, 1991).

5. William Shakespeare, *Hamlet*, ed. Ann Thompson and Neil Taylor, The Arden Shakespeare, 3rd ser. (London: Thomson Learning, 2006), 3.6.16–24; hereafter cited parenthetically in the text by act, scene, and line number.

6. *Oxford English Dictionary Online*, s.v. "kitchen," v.; Oxford University Press, http://www.oed.com/view/Entry/103731?rskey=PLBWE o&result=2 (accessed Jan. 30, 2013).

7. See Marcel Mauss, *The Gift*, trans. W. D. Halls (New York: W. W. Norton, 1950); Claude Lévi-Strauss, *The Raw and the Cooked: Mythologiques*, vol. 1 (1969; repr., Chicago: University of Chicago Press, 1983); and Mary Douglas, "Deciphering a Meal," *Daedalus* 101, no. 1 (Winter 1972): 61–77.

8. The signal figure that designates this purely neutral, proximal relation is Michel Serres's model of the parasite, which carries with it no guarantees as to symbiosis or well-being and which he assumes will

turn lethal. Symbiosis remains a desired but fragile condition, a niche or eddy of negentropy, amid a flux. See Michel Serres, *The Parasite*, trans. Lawrence R. Schehr (Minneapolis: University of Minnesota Press, 2007).

9. Haraway, *When Species Meet*, 16.

10. Stephen Greenblatt, *Hamlet in Purgatory* (Princeton, N.J.: Princeton University Press, 2002), 241.

11. On the zoological quotient of Hamlet's invocation of vermiculation, see Ian MacInnes, "The Politic Worm: Invertebrate Life in the Early Modern English Body," in *The Indistinct Human in Renaissance Literature*, ed. Jean E. Feerick and Vin Nardizzi (New York: Palgrave Macmillan, 2012), 253–73.

12. See Haraway, *Companion Species Manifesto*, 55–62, and *When Species Meet*, 205–46.

13. Throughout *Companion Species Manifesto* and *When Species Meet* there are nods to what remains of the Catholicism of Haraway's childhood. In one instance, she writes, "I grew up in the bosom of two major institutions that counter the modernist belief in the no-fault divorce, based on irreconcilable differences, of story and fact. Both of these institutions—the Church and the Press [her father was a sports reporter].... Sign and flesh, story and fact. In my natal house, the generative partners could not separate.... No wonder culture and nature imploded for me as an adult" (*Companion Species Manifesto*, 18). In another, Haraway writes, "raised a Roman Catholic, I grew up knowing that the Real Presence was present under both 'species,' the visible form of the bread and the wine. Sign and flesh, sight and food, never came apart for me again after seeing and eating that hearty meal" (*When Species Meet*, 18).

14. Haraway, *When Species Meet*, 4.

15. On asociality and the structure of socially inconsequential sexual exchange in early modern England, see Daniel Juan Gil, *Before Intimacy: Asocial Sexuality in Early Modern England* (Minneapolis: University of Minnesota Press, 2006).

16. Such a condition corresponds, perhaps, to what Julia Reinhard Lupton describes as the potentiality installed or conserved in the figure of the creature, which, as she writes, "at various points in the theological imagination of the West.... has served to localize a moment of passionate passivity of an abjected thing-like (non)being, a being of subjected becoming, that precipitates out of the divine Logos as its material remnant." Julia Reinhard Lupton, "Creature Caliban," *Shakespeare Quarterly* 51, no. 1 (Spring 2000): 2.

17. On the potential of the figure of the multitude as keyed to a non-mystified democracy, see, among other works, Michael Hardt and Antonio Negri, *Multitude: War and Democracy in the Age of Empires* (London: Penguin Books, 2005).

18. On the witches as the true heroes of Macbeth, see Terry Eagleton's still wonderful reading, *William Shakespeare* (Oxford: Basil Blackwell, 1991), 1–8.

19. All references will be to William Shakespeare, *The Comedy of Errors*, ed. T. S. Dorsch (Cambridge: Cambridge University Press, 2004).

20. On the efficacy of the table/feast as marking an ending, see Francis Teague, *Shakespeare's Speaking Properties* (Canterbury, N.J.: Associated University Presses, 1991).

21. On the violence of decision as cutting or the creation of an edge, see, in different registers, Michel Serres, *The Natural Contract*, trans. Elizabeth MacArthur and William Paulson (Ann Arbor: University of Michigan Press, 1995), 55; and Jacques Derrida, *The Gift of Death*, trans. David Wills (Chicago: University of Chicago Press, 1992), 53–82.

22. William Shakespeare, *The Tempest*, rev. ed., ed. Virginia Mason Vaughan and Alden T. Vaughan, The Arden Shakespeare, 3rd ser. (London: Bloomsbury, 2011), 1.2.1–2; hereafter cited in the text.

23. On the play's affiliation with the key trope of philosophical inquiry, that of the disinterested spectator observing a shipwreck, see Hans Blumenberg, *Shipwreck with Spectator: Paradigm for a Metaphor of Existence*, trans. Steven Rendall (Cambridge, Mass.: MIT Press, 1997); and Steve Mentz, *At the Bottom of Shakespeare's Ocean* (London: Continuum Books, 2009), 21. For the key passage in Lucretius's designating the trope of gazing out to sea, see *De rerum natura*, trans. W. H. D. Rouse; revised by Martin F. Smith (Cambridge, Mass.: Harvard University Press, 1992), 2.1–2.

24. For a treatment of such feeding in *Timon of Athens*, see Ruth Morse, "Unfit for Human Consumption: Shakespeare's Unnatural Food," *Shakespeare Jahrbuch* 119 (1983): 125–49.

25. On the allegation of rape as ideological lure, see Jonathan Goldberg, *Tempest in the Caribbean* (Minneapolis: University of Minnesota Press, 2004), 20. Goldberg draws on Richard Halpern, "'The Picture of Nobody': White Cannibalism in *The Tempest*," in *The Production of Renaissance Culture*, ed. David Lee Miller, Sharon O'Dair, and Harold Weber (Ithaca, N.Y.: Cornell University Press, 1994), 262–92.

26. On Caliban's diet, see Joan Fitzpatrick, "'I Must Eat My Dinner': Shakespeare's Foods from Apples to Walrus," in *Renaissance Food from Rabelais to Shakespeare*, ed. Joan Fitzpatrick (Farnham, U.K.: Ashgate, 2010), 137–44.

27. Anthony B. Dawson and Paul Yachnin, *The Culture of Playgoing in Shakespeare's England: A Collaborative Debate* (Cambridge: Cambridge University Press, 2001), 157. See also chapter 4 in this volume in which Karen Raber reads Caliban's enjoyment of sack and inducement to drunkenness in terms of a false sacramentality that resonates with a wider topical set of discourses about Roman Catholicism and Spanishness in the period.

28. On Caliban's minority/majority as tied to a putative set of possibilities in the play for democratic futures, see Julia Reinhard Lupton, *Thinking with Shakespeare: Essays on Politics and Life* (Chicago: University of Chicago Press, 2011), 187–218. On Caliban's imagined afterlives, see Richard Burt and Julian Yates, *What's the Worst Thing You Can Do to Shakespeare* (London: Palgrave Macmillan, 2013), esp. chap. 4, "Drown before Reading: Prospero's Missing...Books," 75–110.

NOTES TO CHAPTER 10 / LUPTON

I would like to thank audiences at the University of Utah and the School for Criticism and Theory as well as University Synagogue, Irvine, and Congregation B'nai Israel, Tustin, for their responses to this work.

1. Blake Gopnik, "Rarely One for Sugarcoating: Kara Walker Creates a Confection at the Domino Refinery," *New York Times*, Apr. 25, 2014, http://www.nytimes.com/2014/04/27/arts/design/kara-walker-creates-a-confection-at-the-domino-refinery.html?_r=0 (accessed July 17, 2015).

2. Jean-Louis Flandrin, *Arranging the Meal: A History of Table Service in France*, trans. Julie E. Johnson with Sylvie and Antonio Roder (Berkeley: University of California Press, 2007), 104. On banqueting in and as Renaissance theater, see Chris Meads, *Banquets Set Forth: Banqueting in English Renaissance Drama* (Manchester, U.K.: Manchester University Press, 2001).

3. On dwelling, see especially Martin Heidegger, "Building Dwelling Thinking," in *Poetry, Language, Thought*, trans. Albert Hofstadter (New York: Harper and Row, 1971), 143–59; Emmanuel Levinas, "The Dwelling," in *Totality and Infinity*, trans. Alphonso Lingis (Pittsburgh: Duquesne University Press, 1969), 152–74; and Christian Norberg-Schulz, *The Concept of Dwelling* (New York: Rizzoli, 1985).

4. Platina, *On Right Pleasure and Good Health*, ed. and trans. Mary Ella Milham (Tempe, Ariz.: Medieval and Renaissance Texts and Studies, 1998), 105. The editor suggests as a source for this passage Pietro de' Crescenzi's "On Choosing a Place to Live" (52–53). On Cresenzi, see Lois Olson, "Pietro de Crescenczi: The Founder of Modern Agronomy," *Agricultural History* 18, no. 1 (1944): 35–40. Some scholars have argued that Platina's recipe for eels, bread, and apricots is depicted in Leonardo's *Last Supper*; see John Varriano, "At Supper with Leonardo," *Gastronomica* 8, no. 1 (Winter 2008): 75–79.

5. Heidegger, "Building Dwelling Thinking," 148–49.

6. Platina, *On Right Pleasure*, 463.

7. See Douglas Lanier's discussion of roots as food in chapter 7 of this volume.

8. On cosmic cooking processes (the chemistry-cuisine-creation continuum), see Ian Grant, "The Chemical Paradigm," *Collapse VII* (2011):

39–82. On sugar, gender, and the slave trade in the early modern period, see Kim F. Hall, "Culinary Spaces, Colonial Spaces: The Gendering of Sugar in the Seventeenth Century," in *Feminist Readings of Early Modern Culture: Emerging Subjects*, ed. Valerie Traub, M. Lindsay Kaplan, and Dympna Callaghan (Cambridge: Cambridge University Press, 1996), 168–90. The classic study of sugar remains Sidney W. Mintz, *Sweetness and Power: The Place of Sugar in Modern History* (New York: Viking Penguin, 1986).

9. Michael Krondl, *Sweet Invention: A History of Dessert* (Chicago: Chicago Review Press, 2011), 15–18; see also Ken Albala, *Cooking in Europe, 1250–1750* (Westport, Conn.: Greenwood Press, 2006), 1–3.

10. On preservation and the Renaissance kitchen, see Wendy Wall on "canning and the uncanny," *Staging Domesticity: Household Work and English Identity in Early Modern Drama* (Cambridge: Cambridge University Press, 2006), 18–42; and Hilary Spurling, *Elinor Fettiplace's Receipt Book: English Country House Cooking* (London: Faber and Faber, 2011).

11. Bartolomeo Scappi, *Opera: L'arte et prudenza d'un maestro Cuoco*, trans. Terence Scully (Toronto: University of Toronto Press, 2008), 99.

12. On the taskscape as a congeries of affordances, see Tim Ingold, "The Temporality of the Landscape," *World Archaeology* 25, no. 2 (Oct. 1993): 152–74.

13. The term "affordance" was coined by environmental psychologist James J. Gibson, *The Ecological Approach to Visual Perception* (New York: Taylor and Francis, 1986). On affordances and the aesthetics of landscape, see Harry Heft, "Affordances and the Perception of Landscape: An Inquiry into Environmental Perception and Aesthetics," in *Innovative Approaches to Researching Landscape and Health*, ed. Catherine Ward Thompson (London: Taylor and Francis, 2010), 9–24. On affordances and Shakespearean theater, see Evelyn Tribble, *Cognition at the Globe: Attention and Memory in Shakespeare's Theater* (New York: Palgrave Macmillan, 2011); W. B. Worthen, *Drama between Poetry and Performance* (Malden, Mass.: Wiley and Blackwell, 2012); and Julia Reinhard Lupton, "Making Room, Affording Hospitality: Environments of Entertainment in *Romeo and Juliet*," *Journal of Medieval and Early Modern Studies* 43, no. 1 (Winter 2013): 145–72.

14. Scappi, *Opera*, 381.

15. See, e.g., ibid., 408.

16. Ibid., 385–86, 396.

17. Patricia Fumerton, *Cultural Aesthetics: Renaissance Literature and the Practice of Social Ornament* (Chicago: University of Chicago Press, 1993), 112. See also C. Anne Wilson, ed., *Banquetting Stuffe: The Fare and Social Background of the Tudor and Stuart Banquet* (Edinburgh: Edinburgh University Press, 1991); and Mead, *Banquets Set Forth*, 2, 12, 55.

18. Fumerton, *Cultural Aesthetics*, 114.

19. Anonymous, *A Book of Fruits and Flowers, Shewing the Nature and Use of them, either for Meat or Medicine. As Also: To Preserve, Conserve, Candy, and in Wedges, or Dry Them* (London: Thomas Jenner, 1653).

20. *OED Online*, s.v. "leach," n^2, 1390: "a dish consisting of sliced meat, eggs, fruits, and spices in jelly or some other coagulating material"; *OED Online*, "leach," n. 1, Oxford University Press, Dec. 2015 (accessed Dec. 25, 2015).

21. "Cut in Wedges before it be through cold, gild it, and so you may box it, and keep it all the year. It is a fine sort of Banquetting stuffe" (*Book of Fruits and Flowers*, 27). Here "banquetting" refers to the dessert course or dessert party.

22. Robert May, *The Accomplisht Cook* (London: Nathaniel Brooke, 1660), n.p.

23. Ibid., preface. "In the contrivance of these my Labours, I have so managed them for the general good, that those whose Purses cannot reach to the cost of rich Dishes, I have descended to their meaner Expences, that they may give, though upon a sudden Treatment, to their Kindred, Friends, Allies, and Acquaintance, a handsome and relishing entertainment n all Seasons of the year, though at some distance from Towns or Villages" (ibid.).

24. Robert May, *The Accomplisht Cook* (London: Nathaniel Brooke, 1660). Quince pie with *fleur de lis* crust (225); marchpane garnished with "pretty conceits" (253).

25. Hannah Woolley, *The Queen-Like Closet or Rich Cabinet*, 4th ed. (London: R. Chisewel, 1681), 341–43. On the writings and career of Hannah Woolley, see David Goldstein, "Woolley's Mouse: Early Modern Recipe Books and the Uses of Nature," in *Ecofeminist Approaches to Early Modernity*, ed. Jennifer Munroe and Rebecca Laroche (London: Palgrave Macmillan, 2011), and "Recipes for Living: Martha Stewart and the New American Subject," in *Ordinary Lifestyles: Popular Media, Consumption and Taste Cultures*, ed. David Bell and Joanne Hollows (London: Open University Press, 2005), 47–62. On Woolley's instructions for letter writing, see Jennifer Summit, "Hannah Wolley, the Oxinden Letters, and Household Epistolary Practice," in *Women, Property, and the Letters of the Law in Early Modern England*, ed. Margaret W. Ferguson, A. R. Buck, and Nancy Wright (Toronto: University of Toronto Press, 2004). I write about Woolley in "Thinking with Things: From Hannah Woolley to Hannah Arendt," *postmedieval* 3 (2012): 1–17.

26. Woolley, *The Queen-Like Closet*, 328; emphasis added.

27. On thrift, see Jessica Rosenberg, "'Leave Husbandry Sleeping: The Other Time of Hospitality in Thomas Tusser's *Hundredth Good Pointes of Husbandry*" (paper presented at Shakespeare Association of America seminar on "Shakespeare and Hospitality," Mar. 29, 2013.

28. On building, dwelling, and the genius loci, see Christian Norberg-Schulz, *Genius Loci: Towards a Phenomenology of Architecture* (New York: Rizzoli, 1991).

29. Giorgio Agamben, *The Time that Remains: A Commentary on the Letter to the Romans* (Stanford, Calif.: Stanford University Press, 2005).

30. William Shakespeare, *The Taming of the Shrew: Texts and Contexts*, ed. Frances E. Dolan (Boston: Bedford/St. Martins, 1996), 5.2.8–11. Dolan notes that "banquet," which appears in both the stage direction and in Lucentio's speech, means "dessert."

31. Ibid., 5.2, s.d. Dolan glosses "banquet" as "dessert."

32. Platina, *On Right Pleasure*, 463.

33. Michel Jeanneret, *A Feast of Words: Banquets and Table Talk in the Renaissance* (Chicago: University of Chicago Press, 1991).

34. See Julia Reinhard Lupton, *Thinking with Shakespeare: Essays on Politics and Life* (Chicago: University of Chicago Press, 2011), for a version of this argument.

35. On decorated trenchers and their role in after-dinner conversation, see Jennifer Stead, "Bowers of Bliss: The Banqueting Setting," in Wilson, *Banquetting Stuffe*, 135–37.

36. William Shakespeare, *Romeo and Juliet*, ed. Jill Levenson, The Oxford Shakespeare (Oxford: Oxford University Press, 2000). Quotations from the play are from this edition, hereafter cited in the text.

37. See Hugh Platt, "To make an excellent Marchpane Paste to printe of in Moulds for Banqueting Dishes," in *Delights for Ladies, to Adorn Their Persons, Tables, Closets, and Distillatories* (London: R. W., 1654), 4.

38. I provide an extended reading of this little exchange in "Making Room, Affording Hospitality," 154–58.

39. Levenson, *Romeo and Juliet*, 199n. See also *Oxford English Dictionary*, s.v. "wine," sb.[1] 3.

40. On Romeo as torchbearer, see Lupton, "Making Room, Affording Hospitality," 163–66. On sweetness and queer address, see Jeffrey Masten, "Toward a Queer Address: The Taste of Letters and Early Modern Male Friendship," *GLQ: A Journal of Gay and Lesbian Studies* 10, no. 3 (2004): 367–84. He writes of Meres's characterization of Shakespeare's sweetness: "it is a trope for circulation or fungibility, not just among bodies but also across senses" (377).

41. William Shakespeare, *Romeo and Juliet*, ed. René Weis, The Arden Shakespeare, 3rd ser. (London: Bloomsbury, 2012), 302n.

42. On tragedy, carnival, and *Romeo and Juliet*, see Naomi Conn Liebler, *Shakespeare's Festive Tragedy: The Ritual Foundations of Genre* (New York: Routledge, 1995), 149–52.

43. Stead ("Bowers of Bliss," 121–23) documents the location of banqueting rooms in turrets topped with lanterns in a number of six-teenth century structures, including Nonesuch and the banqueting

turrets at Longleat in 1568, the first documented work by architect Robert Smythson. He completed a similar "roofscape" at Worksop Manor in the 1580s. These may have been the first cupolas in English architecture.

44. William Shakespeare, *The Tempest*, ed. Stephen Orgel, The Oxford Shakespeare (Oxford: Oxford University Press, 1987), 3.3.19, s.d.; hereafter cited in the text.

45. See Masten, "Toward a Queer Address," on the many senses of sweet.

46. "Desert" stems from *deserere*, to sever connection with, leave, abandon (*OED*); although its etymology is distinct from "dessert," a word with which it is often confused, both have a privative origin. *OED Online*, "desert," n. 2, Oxford University Press, Dec. 2015 (accessed Dec. 25, 2015).

47. William Shakespeare, *The Winter's Tale*, ed. Stephen Orgel, The Oxford Shakespeare (Oxford: Oxford University Press, 1996), 4.3.35–49; hereafter cited in the text.

48. Joan Fitzpatrick, *Food in Shakespeare: Early Modern Dietaries and the Plays* (Aldershot, U.K.: Ashgate, 2007), 77.

49. The Christian Pentecost is based on the Jewish Shavuot, a feast traditionally celebrated by eating sweet dairy foods.

50. In Platt, "To make an excellent Marchpane," see, for example, "Spirit of Hony" (13), "Spirit of Herbs and Flowers (17), and "Wine tasting of Wormwood, made speedily" (33). A similar image appears in *Pericles:* "It hath been sung at festivals, / On ember eves and holy ales / And lords and ladies in their lives / Have read it for restoratives" (Gower's chorus, 1.0.5–8). William Shakespeare, *Pericles, Prince of Tyre*, ed. Roger Warren, The Oxford Shakespeare (Oxford: Oxford University Press, 2003).

51. Rue counts among the kitchen herbs offered by Perdita to the disguised Polixenes and Leontes, "For you there's rosemary and rue: these keep / Seeming and savor all the winter long. / Grace and remembrance to you both, / And welcome to our shearing" (4.4.74–77). Various culinary and medicinal affordances and associations mix and mingle in Perdita's messianic posy.

52. Gillian Woods, *Shakespeare's Unreformed Fictions* (Oxford: Oxford University Press, 2013), 191. Compare the aromatic embalming spices that Pericles packs into Thaisa's bitumened coffin (*Per.* 11.64).

53. *Book of Fruits and Flowers*, frontispiece.

54. On vegetarianism in *The Winter's Tale*, see Fitzpatrick, *Food in Shakespeare*, 67–68.

55. See, for example, Helle Porsdamn, *Civil to Human Rights: Dialogues on Law and Humanities in the United States* (Cheltenham, U.K.: Edward Elgar , 2009), citing Dick Stanley in a study for the Council of Europe: "'So are the arts and humanities only auxiliary functions, icing on the cake, nice to have but not essential to the nutritional needs of society?" (138). My thanks to Ian Baucom for pointing me to the dessert/humanities metaphor.

About the Contributors

Tobias Döring is professor of English and chair of the English department at Ludwig-Maximilians-Universität-München. Specializing in early modern and postcolonial literature and culture, he is the author of four books, including *Performances of Mourning in Shakespearean Theatre and Early Modern Culture*; eight essay collections, including *Eating Culture: The Poetics and Politics of Food*, edited with Susanne Mühleisen and Markus Heide; and numerous articles.

Ernst Gerhardt is associate professor of English at Laurentian University. He has published articles in *Reformation, Early Theatre,* and *Renaissance Quarterly*. His current research project investigates the relationship between material food practices and English drama in the late fifteenth and sixteenth centuries, examining how those practices made sensible the limits of various collective communities.

David B. Goldstein is associate professor of English at York University in Toronto. He is the author of *Eating and Ethics in Shakespeare's England*, which shared the Shakespeare's Globe Book Award for a first book. His scholarly work on Shakespeare, modern poetry, and food studies has appeared in numerous journals, including *Studies in English Literature, Shakespeare Studies,* and *Gastronomica,* and in several essay collections. He has also written a book of poetry, *Laws of Rest*.

Peter Kanelos is professor of literature and humanities and dean of Christ College, Valparaiso University. Kanelos's scholarly work focuses primarily on early modern drama, specifically Shakespeare. His publications include *Thunder at a Playhouse: Essaying Shakespeare and the Early Modern Stage; The New Kittredge Much Ado about Nothing; The New Variorum Twelfth Night;* and *A History of the*

Theater. He has also published articles, reviews, and entries in numerous journals and collections.

Douglas M. Lanier is professor of English and the director of the London Program at the University of New Hampshire. He has published on Shakespeare, Jonson, Marston, Milton, and the Jacobean masque, in addition to the appropriation of Shakespeare in mass media. His book, *Shakespeare and Modern Popular Culture,* was published in 2002, and he contributed a bibliography of nearly 900 films for *Shakespeares after Shakespeare,* edited by Richard Burt. His work also has appeared in many journals and collections.

Rebecca Lemon is associate professor of English at the University of Southern California. She is the author of *Treason by Words: Literature, Law, and Rebellion in Early Modern England;* coeditor of *The Blackwell Companion to the Bible in English Literature;* and associate editor of the three-volume *Blackwell Encyclopedia of English Renaissance Literature.* Her work on literature, law, and political theory has appeared in numerous journals and edited collections. She is currently completing a monograph on early modern concepts of addiction.

Julia Reinhard Lupton is professor of English and comparative literature at the University of California, Irvine, where she has taught since 1989. Lupton is the author or coauthor of four books on Shakespeare, including *Thinking with Shakespeare: Essays on Politics and Life,* and is the coeditor with Graham Hammill of *Political Theology and Early Modernity.* She also writes about design and everyday life with her sister, designer and design educator Ellen Lupton.

Peter Parolin is associate professor of English at the University of Wyoming. Together with Pamela Allen Brown, he coedited *Women Players in England 1500–1660: Beyond the All Male Stage.* In 2012 he edited and contributed to an issue of *Early Theatre Journal.* Parolin has published on representations of Italy in early modern drama and on the changing place of Shakespeare at the Stratford Shakespeare

Festival of Canada. He has appeared in productions of *Love's Labour's Lost, Much Ado about Nothing,* and *The Duchess of Malfi.*

Karen Raber is professor of English at the University of Mississippi. She is the author of *Animal Bodies, Renaissance Culture,* several edited books, and many articles on early modern women writers and gender, ecostudies, and animal studies. She is also coeditor with Treva J. Tucker of *The Culture of the Horse: Status, Discipline and Identity in the Early Modern World,* and coeditor with Tom Hallock and Ivo Kamps of *Early Modern Ecostudies: From the Florentine Codex to Shakespeare.*

Barbara Sebek is professor of English at Colorado State University. She has published essays in *Shakespeare Studies; Teaching Medieval and Early Modern Cross-Cultural Encounters,* edited by Karina Attar and Lynn Shutters; *Emissaries in Early Modern Literature,* edited by Brinda Charry and Gitanjali Shahani; and in *A Companion to the Global Renaissance,* edited by Jyotsna Singh. She is coeditor with Stephen Deng of *Global Traffic: Discourses and Practices of Trade in Early Modern Literature and Culture from 1550 to 1700.*

Amy L. Tigner is associate professor of English at the University of Texas, Arlington, and the author of *Literature and the Renaissance Garden from Elizabeth I to Charles II: England's Paradise.* She has published articles in *Modern Drama, English Literary Renaissance, Drama Criticism, Milton Quarterly, Gastronomica,* and *Early Theatre Journal* and in the collections *Global Traffic: Discourses and Practices of Trade in English Literature and Culture from 1550 to 1700,* edited by Barbara Sebek and Stephen Deng, and *Ecofeminist Approaches to Early Modernity,* edited by Jennifer Munroe and Rebecca Laroche.

Wendy Wall is professor of English and director of the Alice Kaplan Institute for the Humanities at Northwestern University. She is author of *The Imprint of Gender: Authorship and Publication in the English Renaissance* and *Staging Domesticity: Household Work and English Identity in Early Modern Drama.* She has published articles on topics as wide-ranging as editorial theory, gender, poetry, national identity, the history of authorship, food studies, domesticity, theatrical practice, and Jell-O.

Julian Yates is professor of English at the University of Delaware, where he teaches courses on medieval and Renaissance British literature, literary theory, and material culture studies. He is the author of *Error, Misuse, Failure: Object Lessons from the English Renaissance,* a finalist for the MLA Best First Book Prize in 2003; *What's the Worst Thing You Can Do to Shakespeare?* coauthored with Richard Burt; and *The Multispecies Impression.*

Index

CPSIA information can be obtained
at www.ICGtesting.com
Printed in the USA
BVHW080056211121
622010BV00001B/51